IMAGES
of America

St. Mary Parish

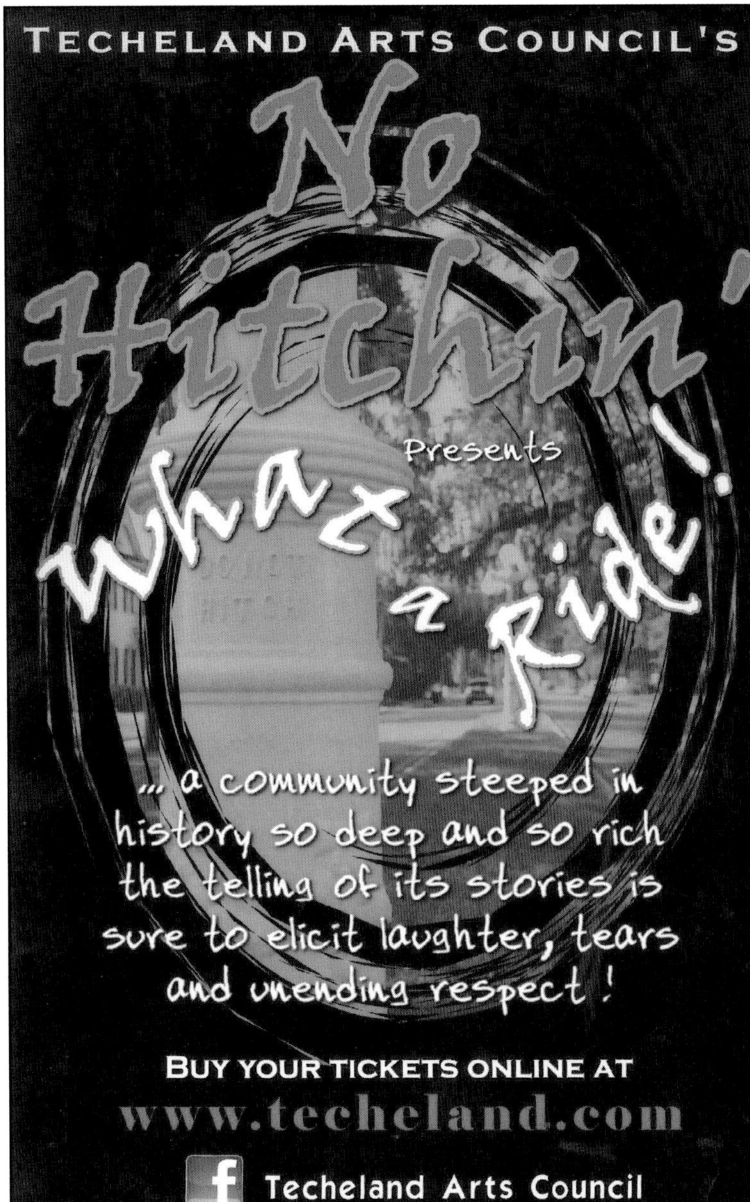

In the early 1900s, the city of Franklin installed distinctive, ornate lamps along the boulevard of Main Street in what would become, decades later, the city's historic district. As horses and cattle were common on Main Street, the "Do Not Hitch" sign in the background of this program for the local history series *No Hitchin'* was meant to keep horses or that prized bull from being tied to the shiny new lampposts, which in those days were painted black.

On The Cover: Charenton Beach was a destination back in its heyday and included a dancehall and bathhouse for men and women. This photograph was taken in the 1930s and shows Walter A. O'Niell (with hat, sitting on the right of log), Laura O'Niell Himel (second from right), and June H. O'Niell (fourth from right). Sheila O'Niell Lobdell is swimming just outside of the photograph to the right. (Courtesy of Ory Miguez.)

IMAGES
of America

St. Mary Parish

Julana M. Senette

ARCADIA
PUBLISHING

ISBN 978-0-7385-9397-5

Published by Arcadia Publishing
Charleston, South Carolina

Printed in the United States of America

Library of Congress Control Number: 2012938240

For all general information, please contact Arcadia Publishing:
Telephone 843-853-2070
Fax 843-853-0044
E-mail sales@arcadiapublishing.com
For customer service and orders:
Toll-Free 1-888-313-2665

Visit us on the Internet at www.arcadiapublishing.com

This book is dedicated to Ann Lobdell Connors, "Aunt Ann." Through your loving heart, warm smile, and Southern grace, you are forever in our hearts.

Contents

Acknowledgments

First and foremost, my undying gratitude to Joey and Jay Bergeron, Mike Viguerie, and the staff of Cashway, for without their understanding and support, my wild endeavors would have never seen the light of day

To Leonard Battaglia, the founder and keeper of the St. Mary Landmarks Society archives, and Malisa Mayon, of the Morgan City Archives. Thanks to Jackie, Frank, and Deborah Price of the Frame Shop in Morgan City.

To the late Fay G. Brown, Stephen Stirling, Tony Scelfo, Craig Landry, and especially Perry Lowery, the keepers of our history. Our communities' amazing past will live on through your efforts. Thank You. Your photographic history of St. Mary Parish and your knowledge of events is a credit to your determination that the past not be forgotten.

In grateful appreciation to Ken Miguez of Miguez Photography Studio for use of the cover photograph of Charenton Beach by his father, Ory Miguez.

My heartfelt thanks to Kim Walden of the Chitimacha tribe of Louisiana for opening doors into a culture that was all but forgotten. My deepest appreciation to Shane Bernard, with the McIhenny Archives on Avery Island, for sharing his historical knowledge.

To the Techeland Arts Council, which preserves our past through stories presented to the public in the form of folklore, my congratulations on a great first season. Not only have barriers been knocked down, but a new sense of awareness for the need to archive and document the life of our community members for future generations has been achieved.

To my proofreaders, Charley Richard and Peter Nowack, for their suggestions, comments, and technical advice, I am eternally grateful.

Finally, to Judith and Brent Allain, for their unwavering support through countless ups and downs. I could not have accomplished this without you. Judith has taught me so much, listened to my concerns, and guided me through the often-dark waters of the bayou. And I have taught her a few unexpected things: to eat cupcakes on Thursday before lunch, that the world can never have enough rubber chicken jokes, and that laughter can be found in the strangest and most stressful of times. And "Thank You Simone."

INTRODUCTION

All good stories begin with "once upon a time." So, *once upon a time*, there was a small town in the southern part of the great state of Louisiana. The people who lived in this community loved it dearly and knew that there were many special places and people in their area. However, theirs was like many small towns in many states across the country: just barely hanging on and struggling with the economic decline that has left many rural communities dotted with abandoned buildings and overgrown yards. They also lost population, especially young people, as there were few meaningful jobs. Familiar stores that had been there for years closed, and few successful new ones opened up.

Judith Allain, founder of Techeland Arts Council, took her inspiration from Karen Kimbrel and Joy Jinks, the creators of Swamp Gravy, in Colquitt, Georgia. These two passionate women shared a common goal: to revitalize their community. Working through the Colquitt/Miller County Arts Council, Kimbrel and Jinks initially received a $700 grant in 1992 from the Georgia Arts Council to put on a performance with a troupe of all-volunteer actors from within the community. They titled their production *Swamp Gravy*.

Their local arts council and its other programs have grown rapidly since 1992, with the Arts Council's budget expanding from $2,000 in 1992 to $2.2 million in 2006. It now provides 60 full-time or part-time jobs and the economic impact from its *Swamp Gravy* plays alone is estimated to be $2 million a year. With this as a living, working model, the Techeland Arts Council was formed in September 2007.

Through story gathering, we have discovered our own unique history, culture, and traditions, which were hidden inside ordinary, or slightly mundane, local stories. In October 2011, Techeland Arts Council presented its production, *No Hitchin'*, for the first time, to sellout crowds. An encore performance presented in March 2012 was also well received, inspiring us once more to gather, archive, and share our local stories.

St. Mary Parish was formed from the division of the Attakapas district in 1811. It reached as far west as Petite Anse Island (Avery Island), and as far east as Tiger Island/Brashear City (Morgan City), and was bordered by the Atchafalaya Basin and the Gulf of Mexico. This rich landscape has been home to the Native American tribe of the Chitimacha since 500 A.D. The scenic Bayou Teche flows lazily along for 130 miles from Port Barre, fed by Bayou Courtableau, southward to meet the Lower Atchafalaya River near Morgan City. A Chitimacha legend tells of a great battle between their warriors, who fought with arrowheads made from the scale of the garfish, and a great snake, which upon being defeated, surrendered its body to the earth, creating the curving, winding waterway known as Bayou Teche.

One of St. Mary's earliest settlers was Andre Massé, who was known even in those days for wearing fringed leather coats. He lived rustically in a log cabin with his Pawnee wife and slaves. Massé owned land in both St. Mary and what would become Iberia Parish. He settled outside of the present-day township of Baldwin sometime between 1747 and his death in 1774.

Petite Anse Island (Avery Island) was once part of St. Mary Parish and is known today for the Tabasco sauce created by Edmund McIlhenny in the 1860s. In 1868, Avery Island became part of Iberia Parish, but the McIlhenny family continued to play an important role in St. Mary Parish. When the Chitimacha Tribe faced the loss of their lands, Mary Avery McIlhenny Bradford and other members of her family came forward with the financial means to pay the tax liability judgment on the tribe's homeland, which today is part of the Sovereign Nation of the Chitimacha. Mary Bradford, known as "Marigold," believed strongly in the preservation of the intricate baskets made by the Chitimacha.

St. Mary Parish developed into two very distinctive cultures. Although a mainly Protestant area, the Catholic Church played an important role in the everyday life of St. Mary Parish. The west end became the parish seat, with large sugarcane plantations whose beautiful homes were nestled among the magnificent oaks that dotted the landscape. Lumber mills harvested cypress and tupelo. The eastern end of the parish, surrounded by water, encouraged the fishing, trapping, and fur trades to grow and prosper; along with these industries came the development of support businesses along the open dock area of the riverfront.

Fort Star was built during the Civil War to protect the waterways from Union troops. With the coming of the railroad, wooden boxes containing the iced-down catch of the day lined loading docks ready to be shipped to markets in the west. Later, oil and gas developed, along with the associated supply industries. Today, barges pushed by tugs float down the Intracoastal Waterway from Florida to Texas with supplies of oil and gas, sugar and molasses, salt, and other necessities for our modern world.

Over the years, floodwaters have risen and storms with names like Betsy, Camille, and Andrew have ravaged the land, destroying homes and displacing lives. Still, the human spirit lives on. Through our photographs and stories, we invite you to join us as we share our rich heritage. For without knowing our history, how can we grasp the present and fully appreciate the wonders the future may hold?

One hundred percent of the author's proceeds from the sale of this book will go towards the goals of the Techeland Arts Council and its efforts to enhance our communities. We look forward to publishing *St. Mary Parish Revisited* in the near future, as there is so much more of St. Mary's story to be told.

Credits and dates for the photographs and the identification of the people and places in them are based on the most accurate information supplied to the author. If you have any more specific information concerning the photographs in this book or would like to submit photographs for our next book, *St. Mary Parish Revisited*, please contact us at our website at www.techeland.com. Also, if you have personal or family stories and would like to share them, please contact us through our website.

One

Charenton and Avery Island

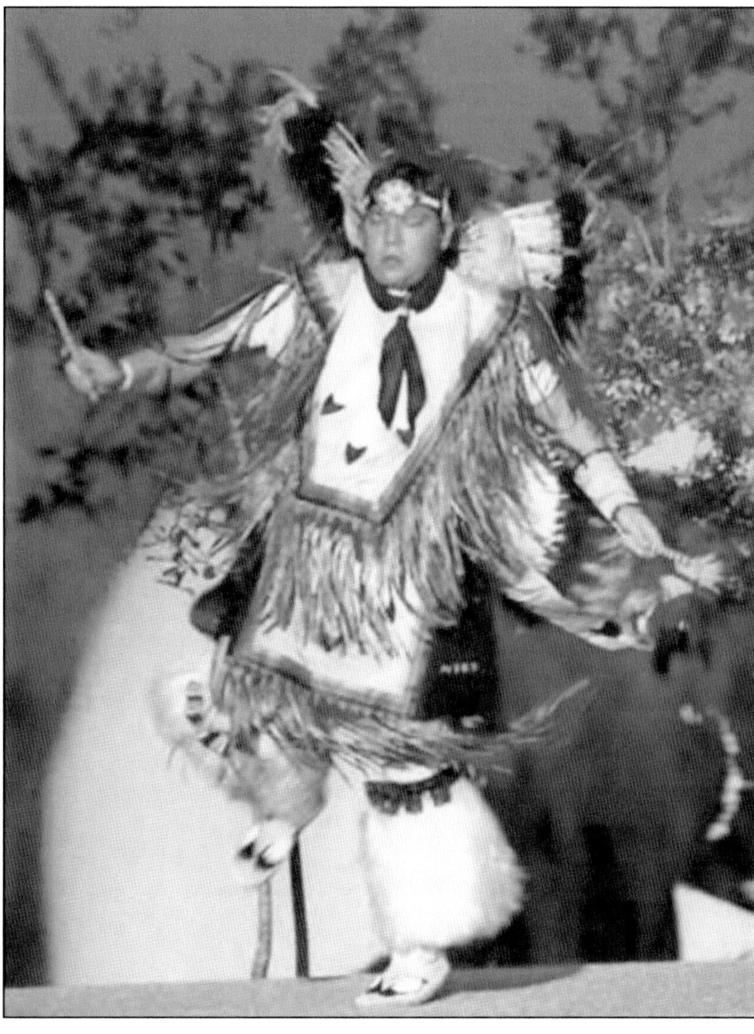

Legend says that Alexandre Frère declared, "Anyone choosing to move to that part of Louisiana belonged in Charenton!" Charenton was the name of a notorious insane asylum outside of Paris. Today, it is recognized as the homeland of the Chitimacha Indian Tribe, who lived along its waterways teeming with wildlife and who walked amidst live oaks draped in Spanish moss during the time of the Romans. (Jules Darden, Courtesy Techeland Arts Council 2012.)

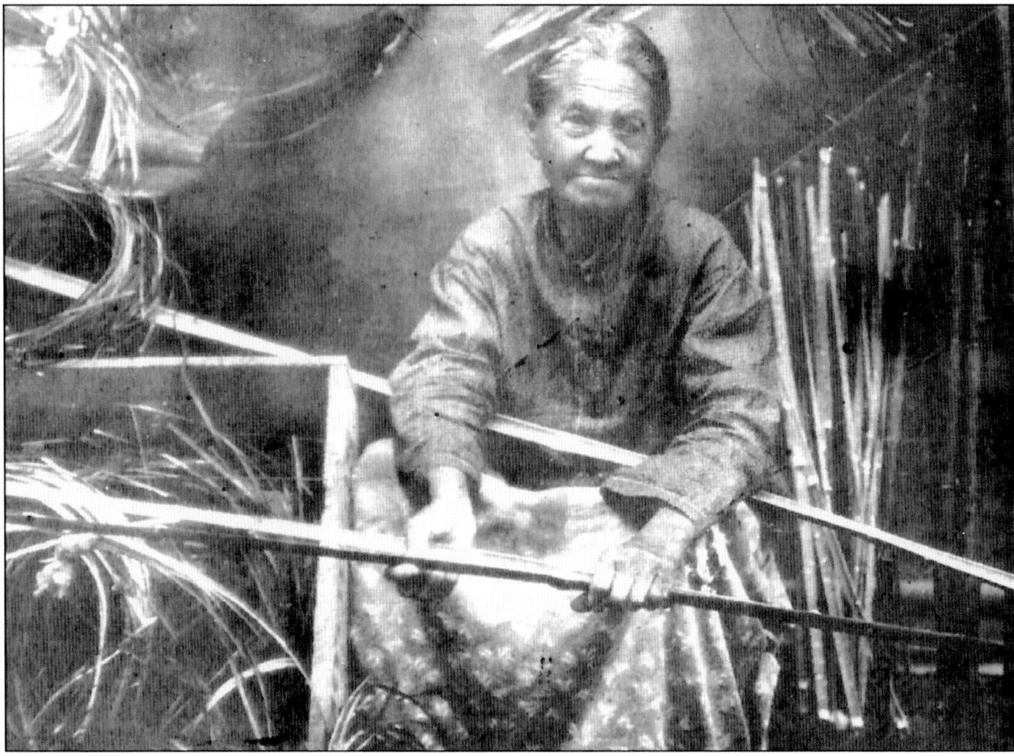

Clara Darden (1829–1910) likely lived her entire life within the boundaries of the Charenton Reservation. She was the sole surviving Chitimacha basket weaver of the intricate double-weave technique, which produces a basket in two continuous layers of river cane, one inside the other. (Courtesy McIlhenny Company Archives.)

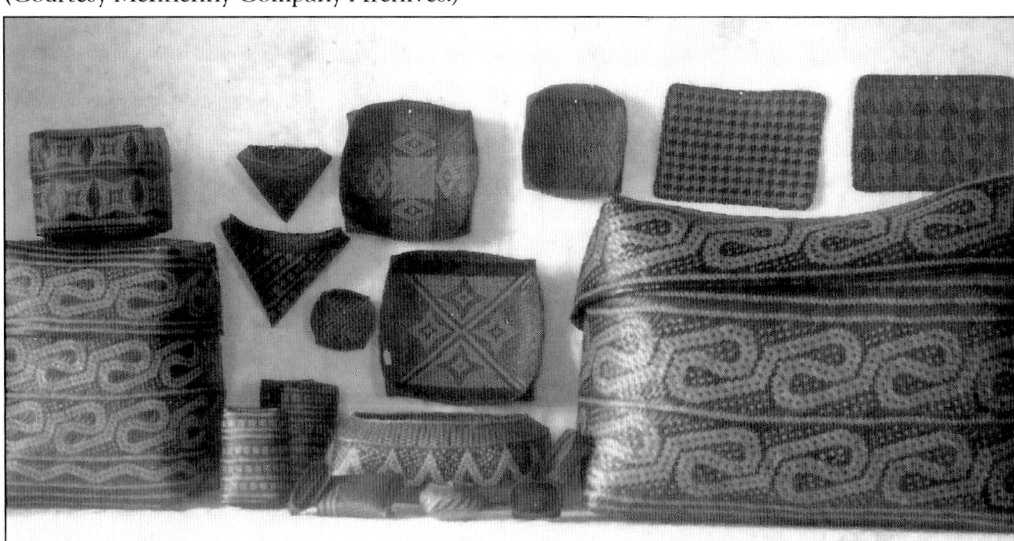

Chitimacha baskets are typically found in red, yellow, black, and plain splints plaited diagonally in single or double weave. Designs like Bull's Eye, Snake, and Rabbits Teeth were committed to the memory of the weaver, who taught by example to the next generation. (Courtesy McIlhenny Company Archives.)

Through a process of cutting, splitting, peeling, drying, and dyeing river cane, weavers like Christine Paul (1874–1946) used only their hands, their teeth, and a knife in the construction of their baskets, some of which took more than a year to complete. This tradition is currently being preserved and passed down within the tribe. (Courtesy McIlhenny Company Archives.)

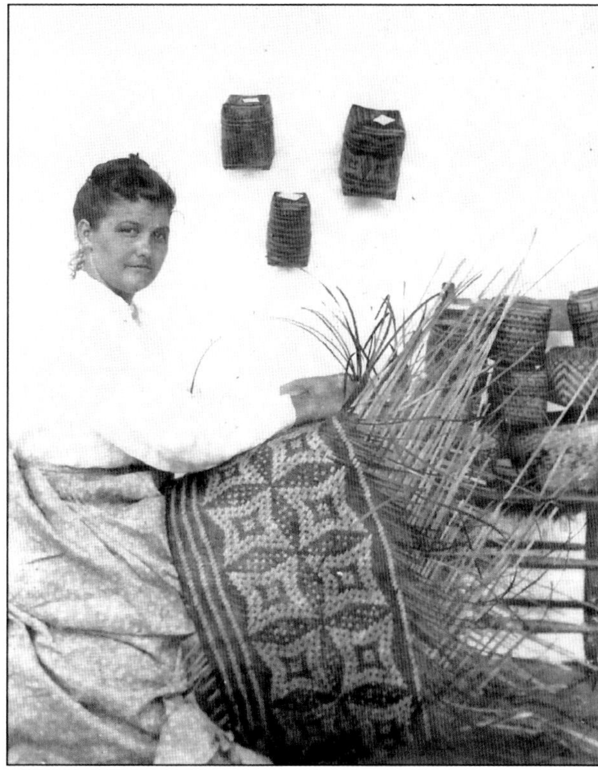

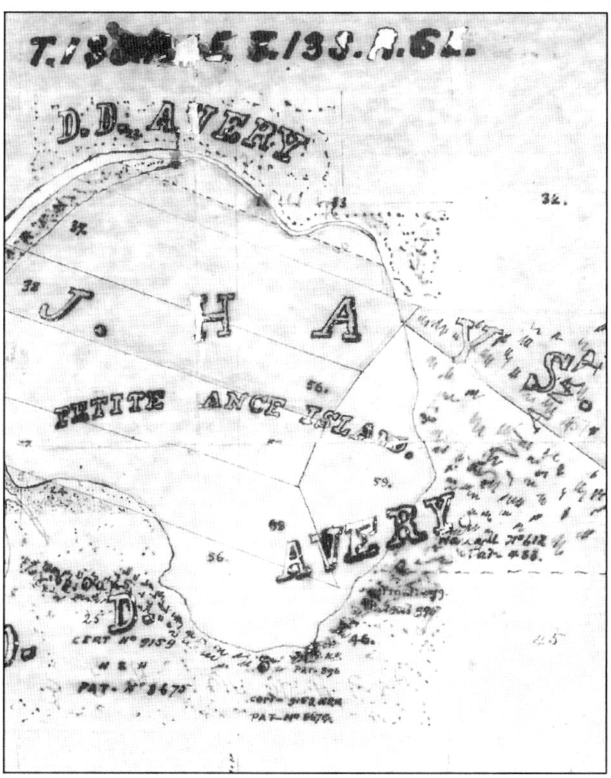

This hand-drawn map shows Petite Anse Island, which was renamed Avery Island in the late 1800s. It was the westernmost part of St. Mary Parish until 1868, when it became part of Iberia Parish. Avery Island has played an important role in the life of the Chitimacha. (Courtesy Avery Island, Inc. Archives.)

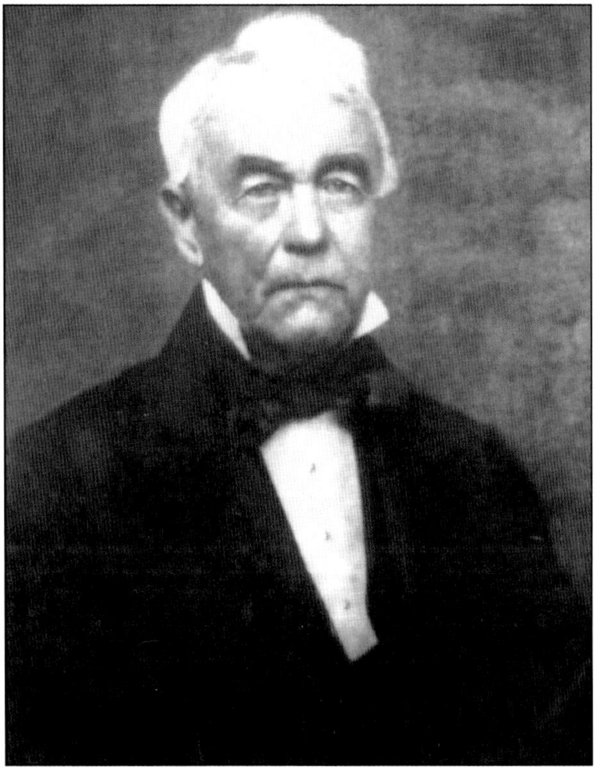

Born in New Jersey, John Craig Marsh came to St. Mary Parish in 1818 to become a sugar planter. He bought part of Petite Anse Island, which is actually an inland salt dome surrounded by coastal marshland, and operated a sugar plantation on the fertile soil. (Courtesy Avery Island, Inc. Archives.)

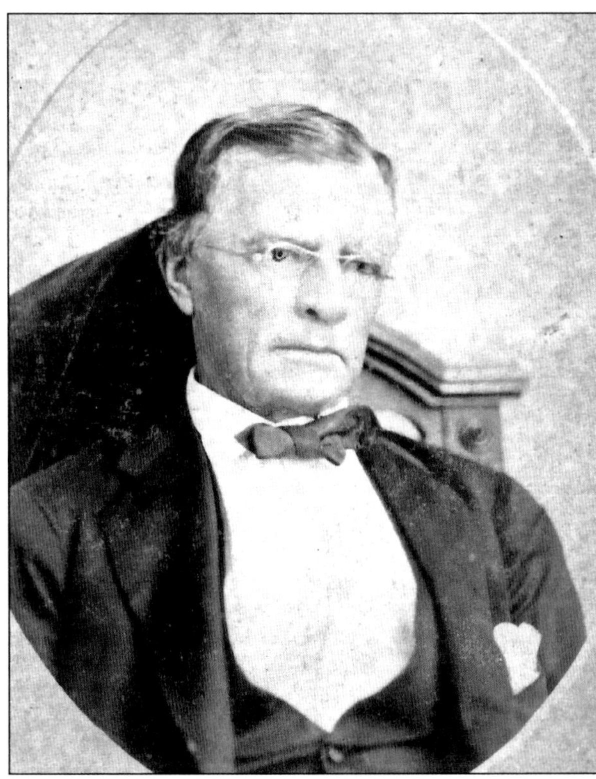

Judge Daniel Dudley Avery, a jurist from Baton Rouge, married Sarah Craig Marsh in 1837, uniting the Marsh and Avery families. Avery became a co-owner of the sugar plantation in 1849, and in 1855, he became the sole owner of Petite Anse Island. (Courtesy Avery Island, Inc. Archives.)

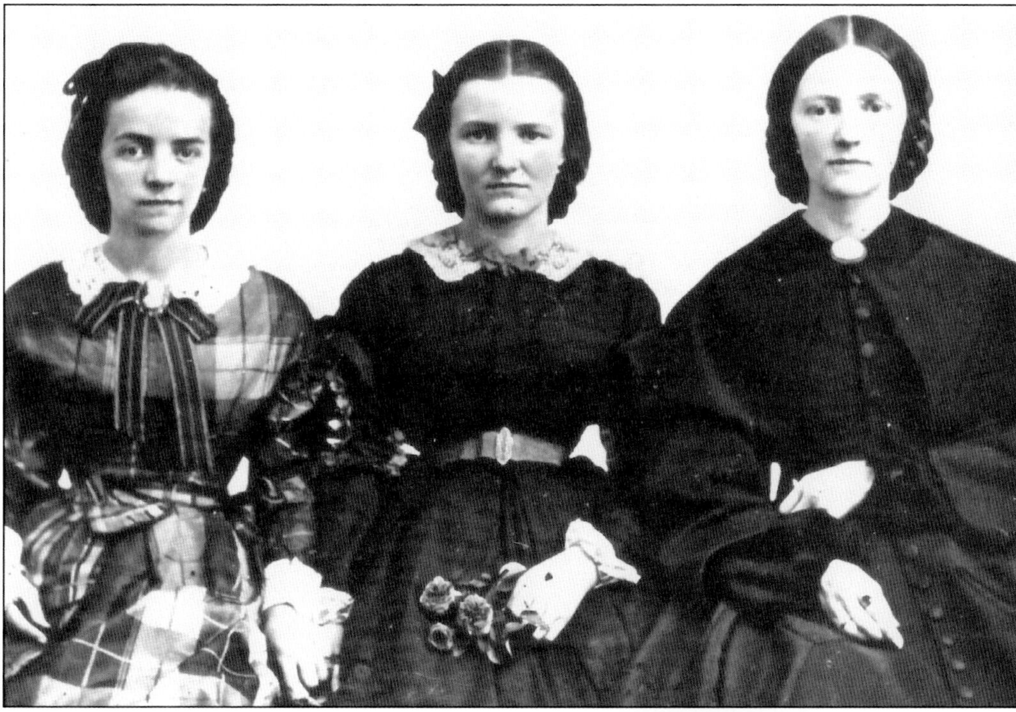

Above are Sarah Craig Marsh (right) and her two daughters, Sarah Avery Leeds (left) and Mary Eliza Avery (center). While spending most of their time in Baton Rouge before the Civil War, the Averys and McIlhennys settled permanently on the island after the war. (Courtesy Avery Island, Inc. Archives.)

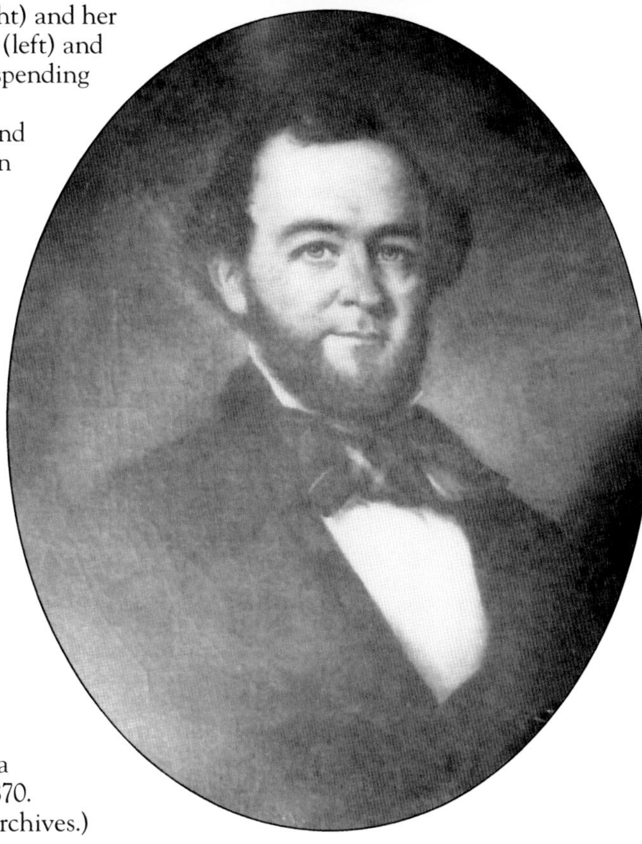

Edmund McIlhenny (right) married Mary Eliza Avery, the daughter of Daniel and Sarah Avery. McIlhenny is the inventor of Tabasco brand pepper sauce, which he perfected in 1868, the same year Petite Anse Island became part of newly formed Iberia Parish. Tabasco was patented in 1870. (Courtesy McIlhenny Company Archives.)

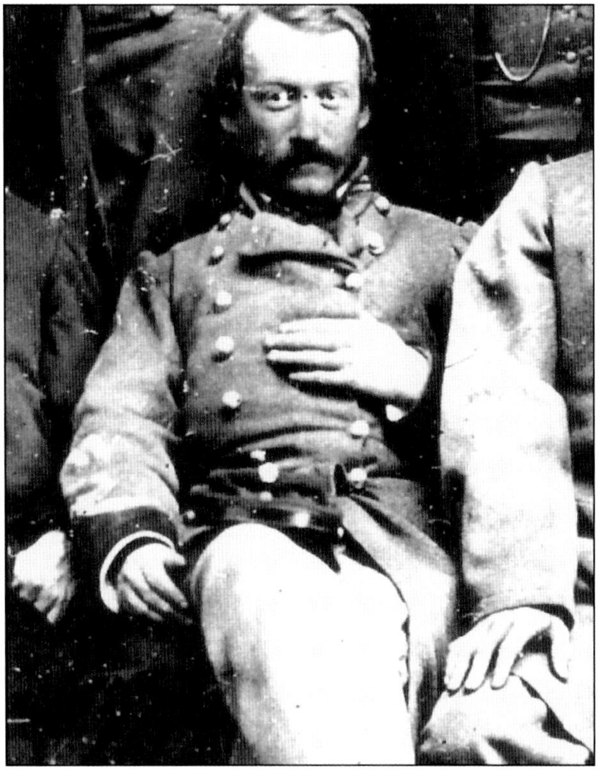

Dudley Avery, the oldest son of Judge Daniel and Sarah Avery, was an officer in the Confederate army. He was shot in both knees at the Battle of Shiloh in 1862, but recovered and returned to the military for the remainder of the war. (Courtesy Avery Island, Inc. Archives.)

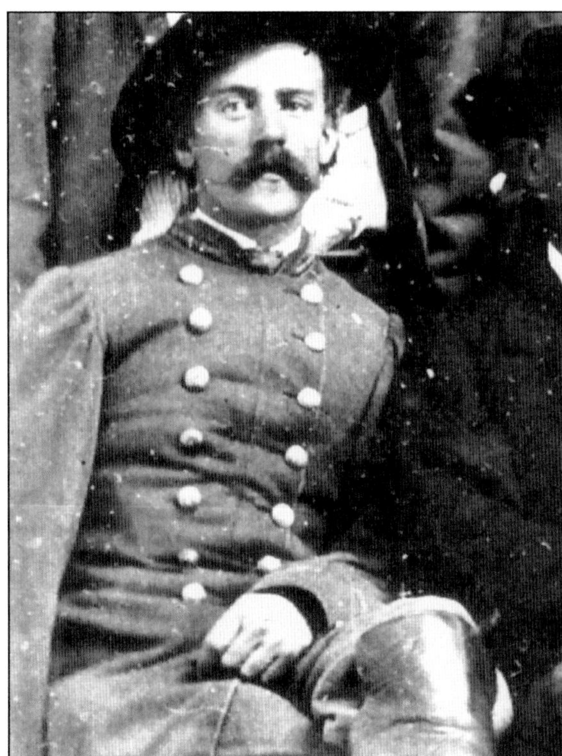

John Marsh Avery, another son of Judge Daniel and Sarah Avery, also served as an officer in the Confederate army and was later elected to the Louisiana state legislature. He is credited with the discovery of a solid mass of rock salt on Avery Island. (Courtesy Avery Island, Inc. Archives.)

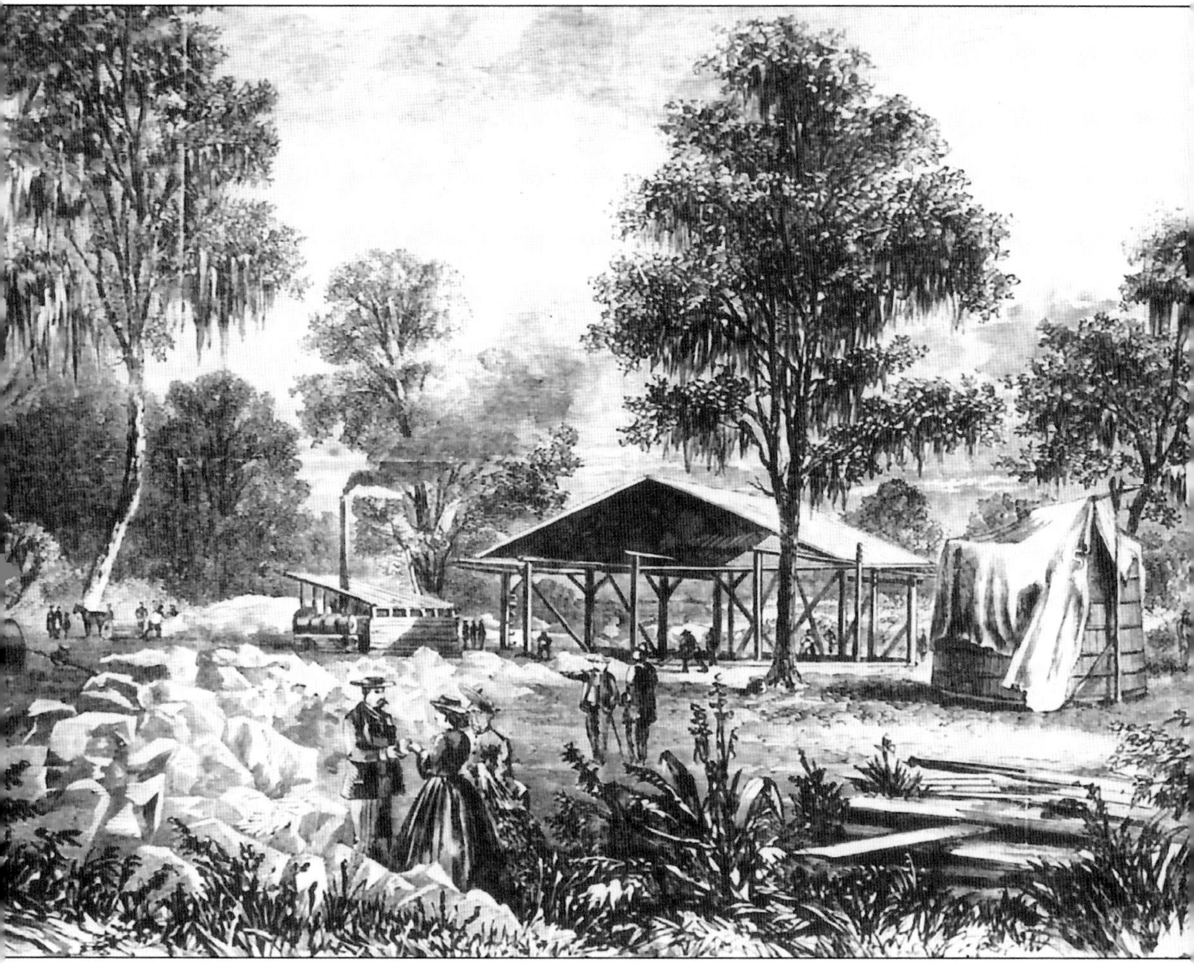

Pure rock salt was discovered in May 1862 and was mined, producing 22 million pounds for use by the Confederacy. The mining was disrupted by Union troops, led by Gen. Nathaniel P. Banks, who marched onto the island, destroying buildings, steam engines, and mining equipment. (Courtesy Avery Island, Inc. Archives.)

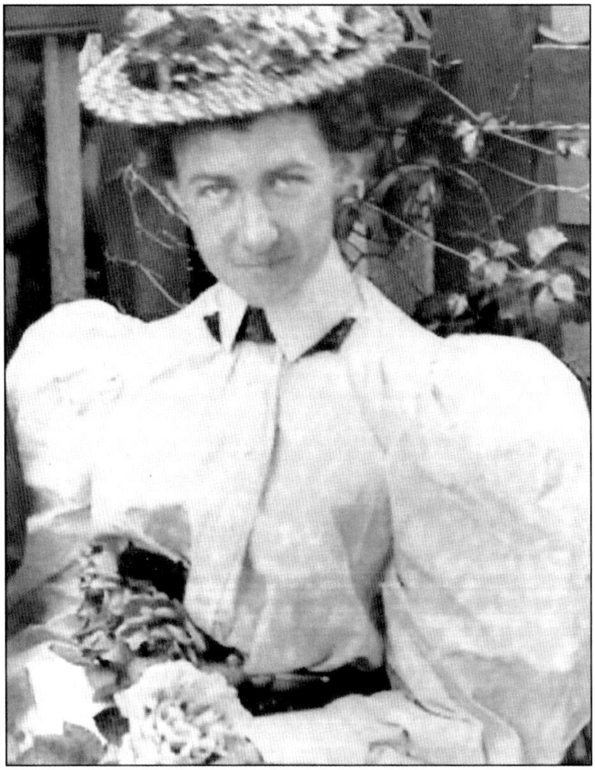

Mary Avery "Marigold" McIlhenny Bradford, the daughter of Edmund McIlhenny and Mary Eliza Avery, is credited with intervening and paying the 1914 tax liability judgment against the Chitimacha Tribe for $1,560 and deeding the property to the federal government so that it could be recognized as a reservation, preventing the loss of the Chitimacha tribal homelands. (Courtesy McIlhenny Company Archives.)

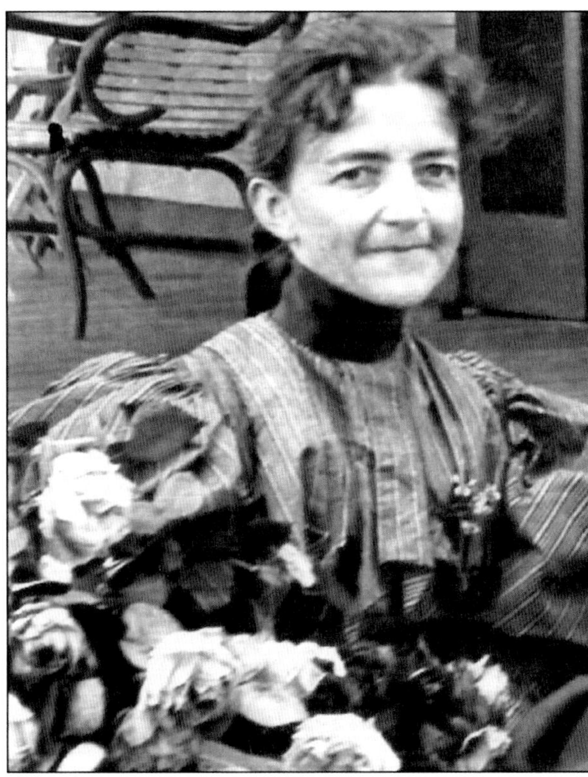

Sara Avery "Sadie" McIlhenny, another daughter of Edmund McIlhenny and Mary Eliza Avery, followed in her sister's footsteps and became very involved with the women of the Chitimacha tribe of Charenton, taking great interest in their handmade baskets. She was also a member of the Christian Women's Exchange. (Courtesy McIlhenny Company Archives.)

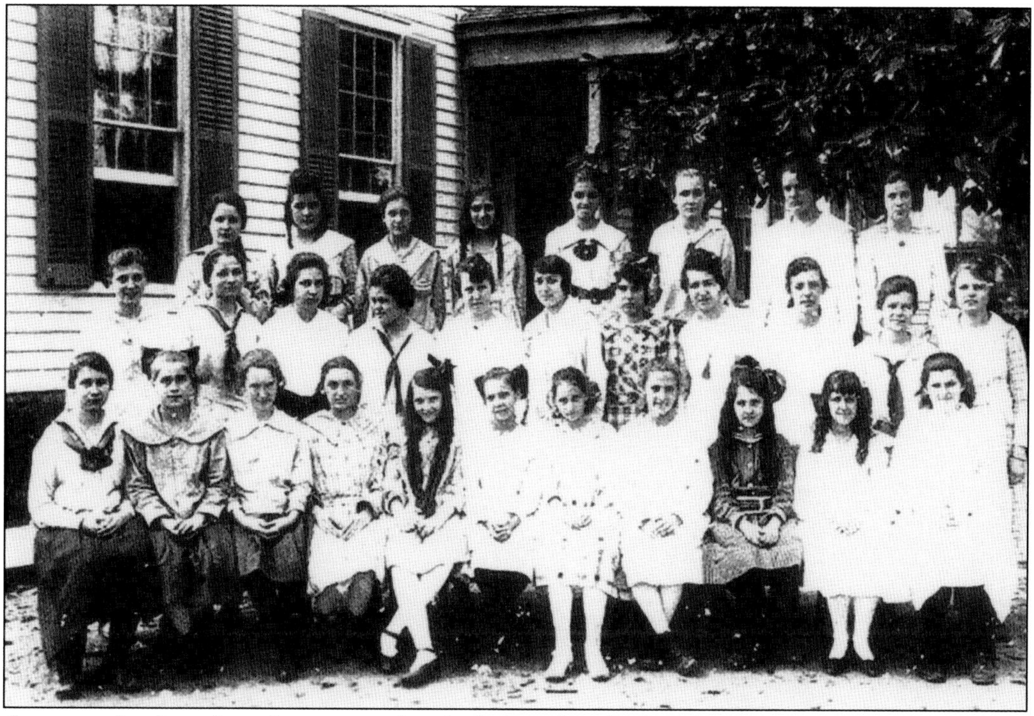

As in much of southern Louisiana, the Catholic Church played an important role in the lives of local citizens. The Sisters of St. Joseph ran the Charenton Convent until it was closed due to hard times in the Great Depression. (Courtesy Perry Lowery.)

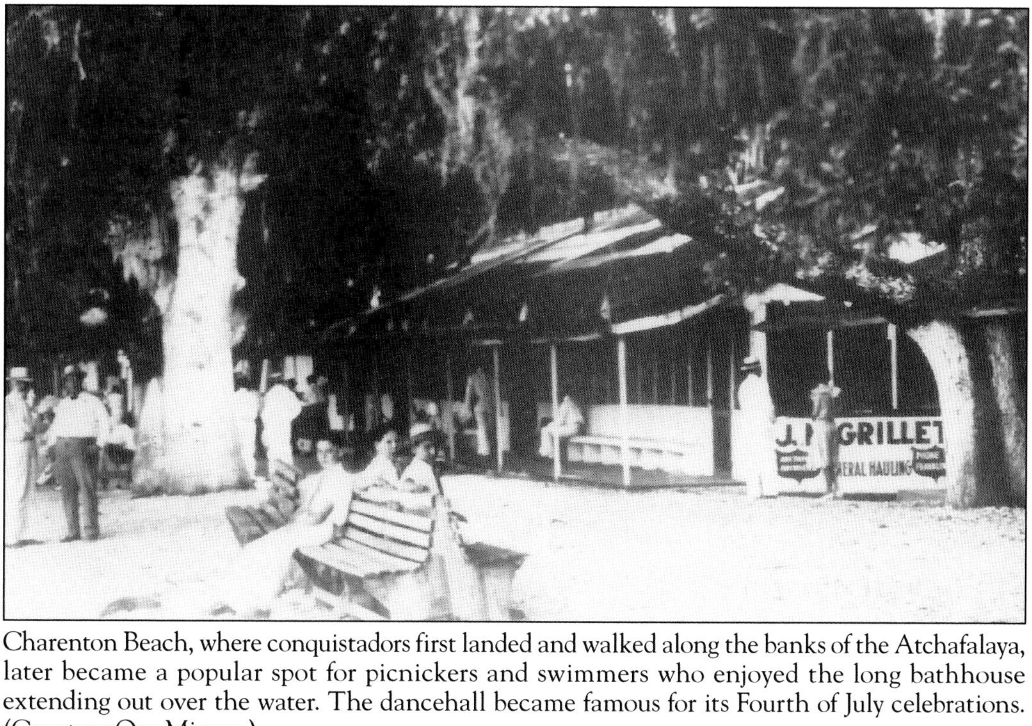

Charenton Beach, where conquistadors first landed and walked along the banks of the Atchafalaya, later became a popular spot for picnickers and swimmers who enjoyed the long bathhouse extending out over the water. The dancehall became famous for its Fourth of July celebrations. (Courtesy Ory Miguez.)

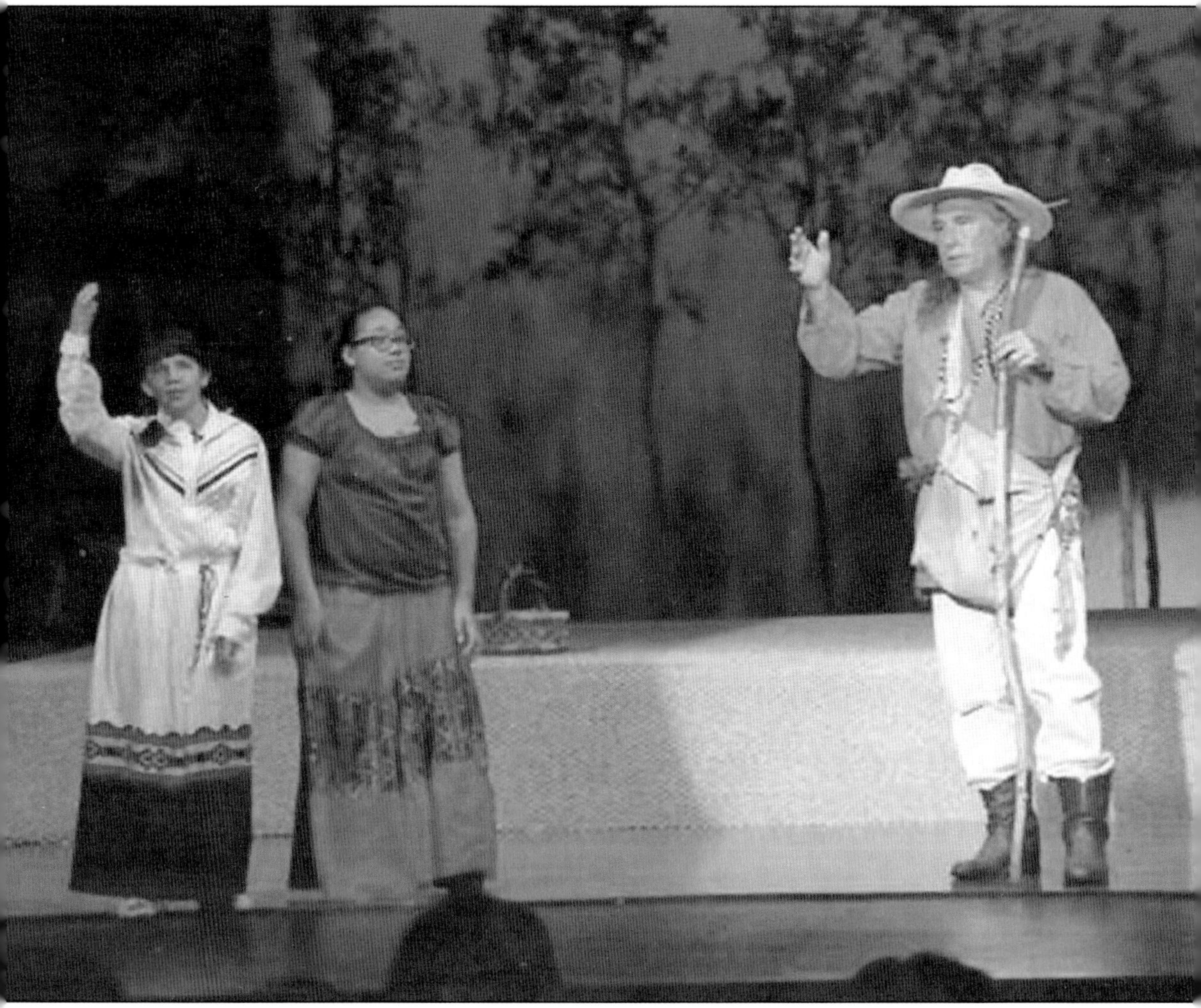

In the opening production of *No Hitchin'*, students from the Chitimacha Tribal School shared the legend of the great snake creator of Bayou Teche while dressed in traditional costumes and speaking their native tongue, which was almost a lost language before members teamed with Rosetta Stone to document and produce a remarkable teaching tool to preserve their native language for future generations. A deep commitment to their heritage is reviving the art of traditional basket making. Theirs is a remarkable story of survival set against the backdrop of the unfathomable natural beauty of the Attakapas. (Courtesy Techeland Arts Council 2012.)

Two
BALDWIN

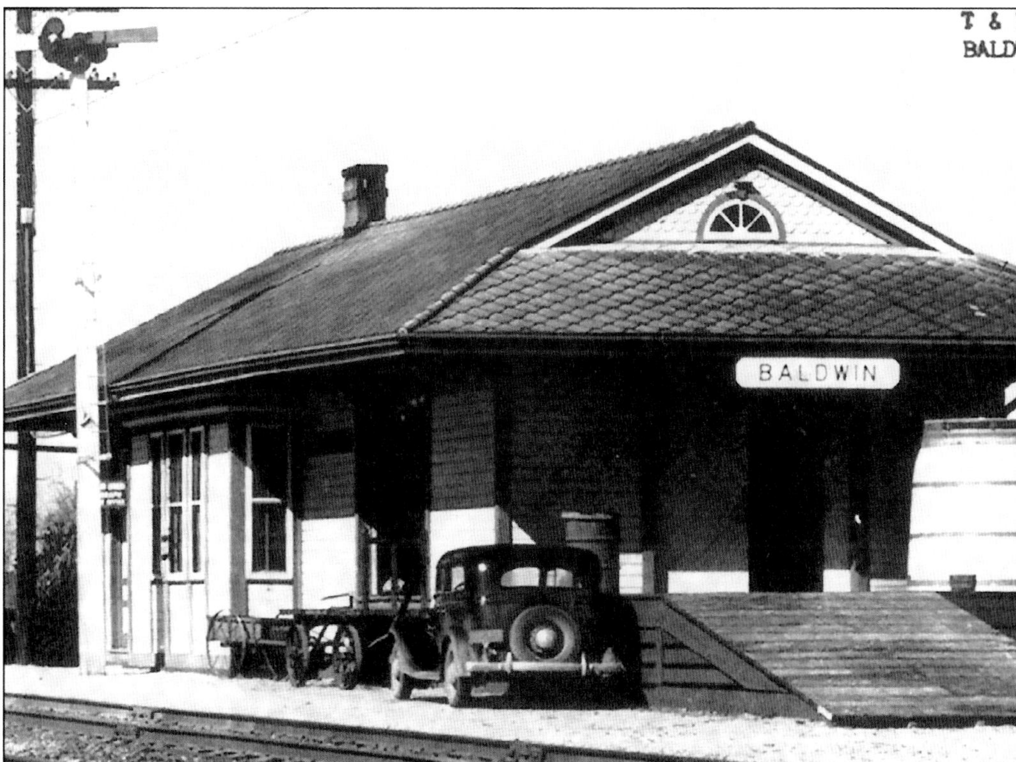

The town of Baldwin's namesake was John Baldwin, who purchased Darby Plantation in 1867. Baldwin, an educator who believed education should not be based on gender or race, founded several institutes of learning during his lifetime. According to J.S. Glass in 1897, "Baldwin is located three miles from Franklin on the Southern Pacific Railroad, it is a great receiving point for supplies for the rich sugar country that lies back of it. Messrs. Charles A Bibbin is the Justice of the Peace and E. Oliveri is constable. Among other things Baldwin boasts of is a high class Dramatic Club who hold entertainments in the town hall." (Courtesy of Perry Lowery.)

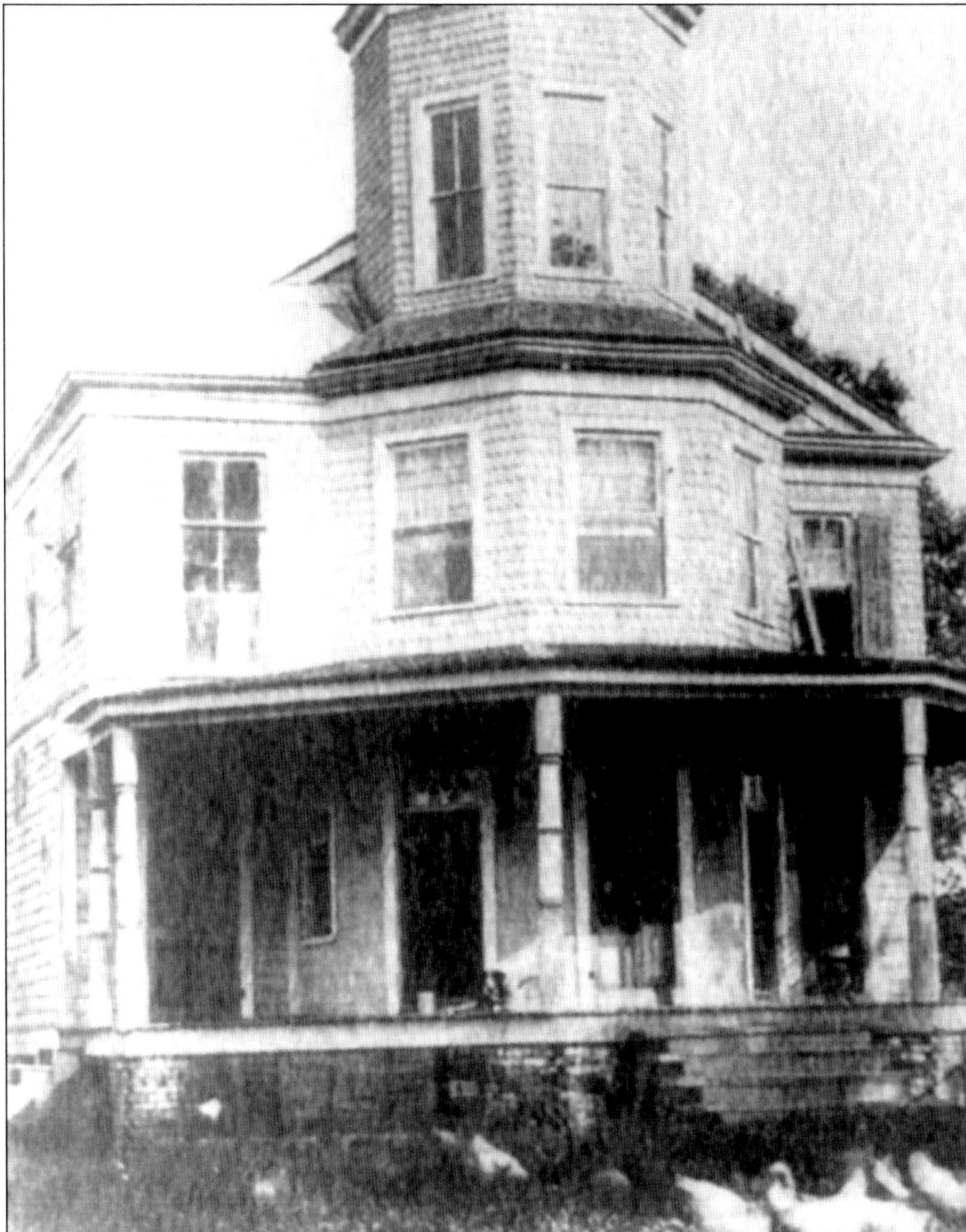

The original Orphan's Home was begun in 1867 by a group of New Orleans women who formed the Orphan's Home Society Corporation. The corporation was a means of raising money to provide a home for African American children who had been orphaned by the Civil War. It was funded primarily by the Freedman's Aid Society, a predecessor to the Black College Fund of the United Methodist Church. (Courtesy Perry Lowery.)

Dr. W.D. Godman (right), with his wife's help, was the director of a school for African Americans in Baldwin, which was built thanks to a large monetary gift from William Gilbert. The institution was originally named the Orphan's Home and contained grades one through eight. Later, it was known as Godman Industrial School. They were also responsible for building a Methodist Church on the property. (Courtesy Perry Lowery.)

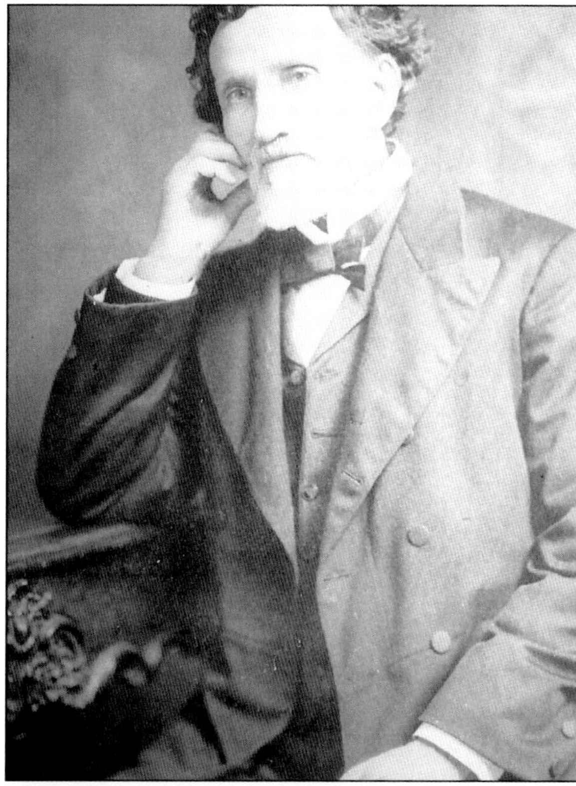

In the early 1900s, the Orphan's Home and Godman Industrial School, attended by the Sager Brown students below, were in dire financial straits. To raise money, Dr. and Mrs. Godman took the student choir, the Jubilee Singers, on a tour of the northeastern United States. Mrs. Sager and Mrs. C.W. Brown purchased the school and gave it to the Women's Home Mission Society. (Courtesy Perry Lowery.)

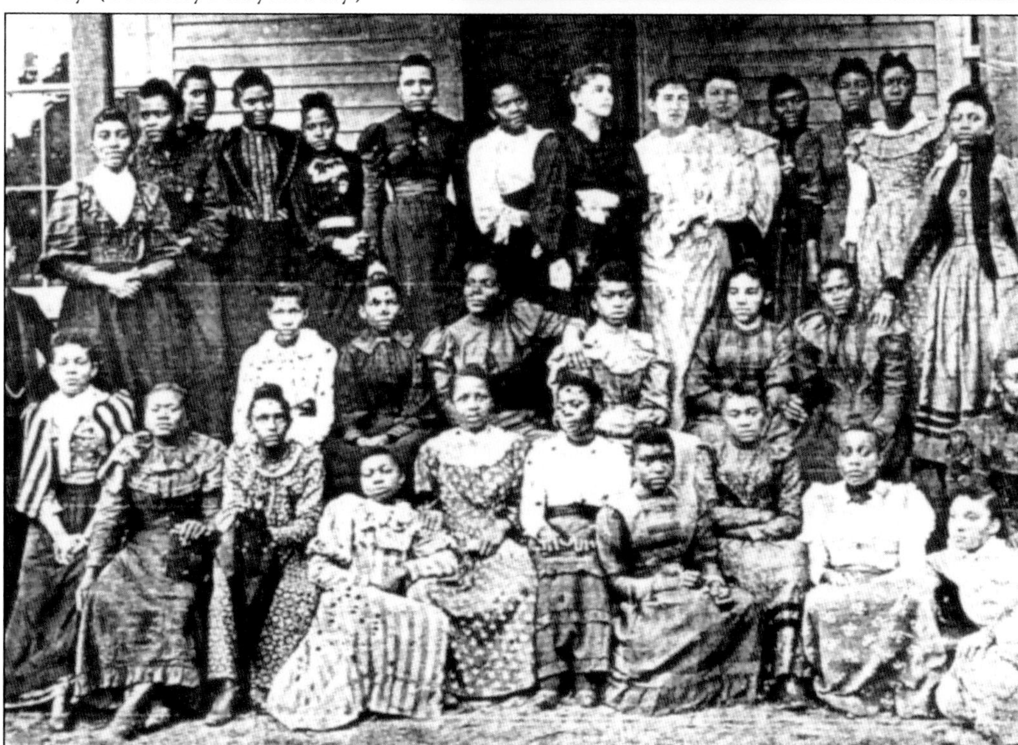

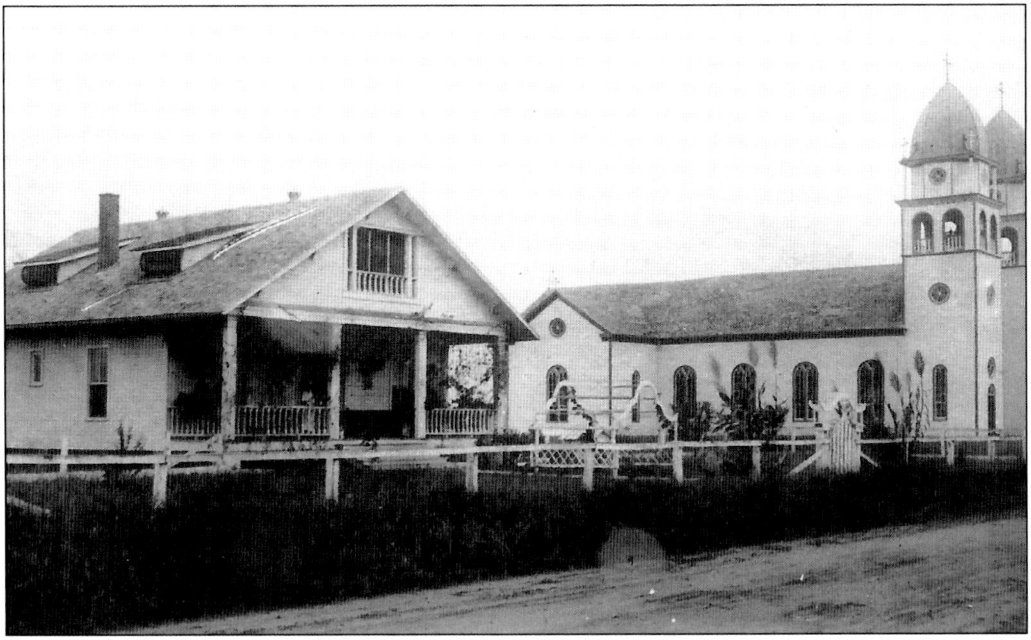

The original Sacred Heart Church in Baldwin was constructed in 1906, with Father J.R. Bollard as its first pastor. The farmers in the Ashton area requested to have the church built because it would make it easier for them to attend mass nearby, instead of having to go to Charenton. The church was made of cypress and was quite large for its day. (Courtesy Perry Lowery.)

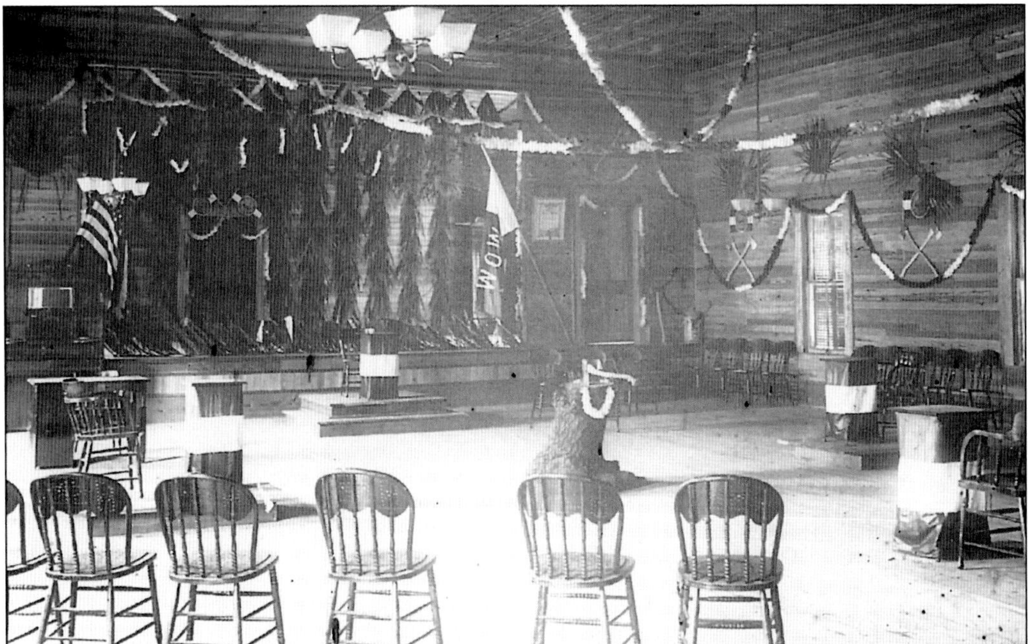

The Woodmen of the World was founded in 1890 in Omaha, Nebraska, as a fraternal organization. Pictured here is Woodmen Hall in Baldwin As one of its benefits, the organization offered a distinctive headstone in the shape of a tree stump until the late 1920s. Many of these can still be found in cemeteries around St. Mary Parish. (Courtesy Perry Lowery.)

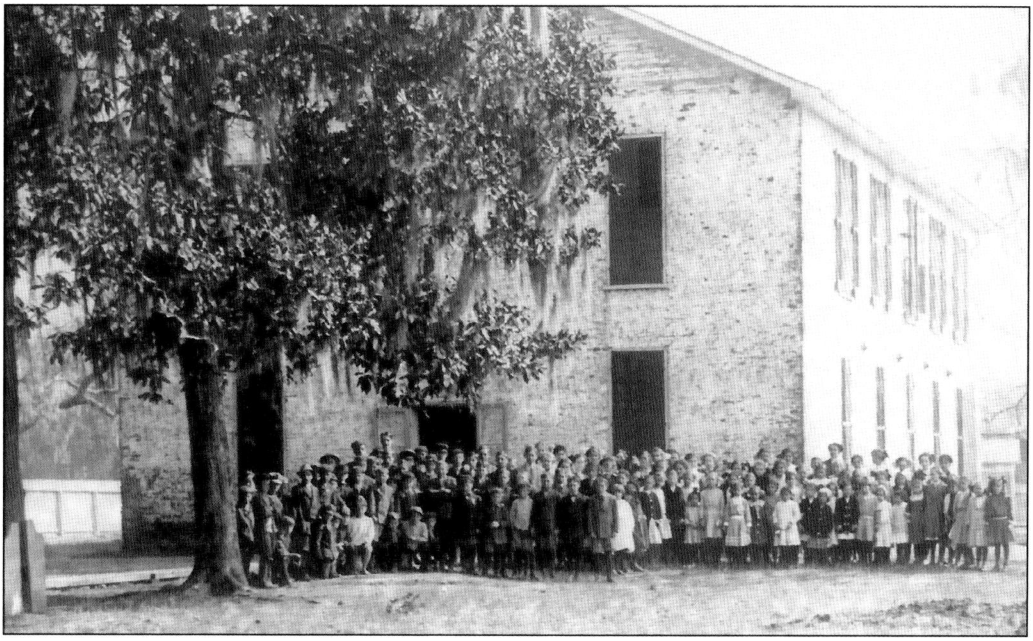

The Old Baldwin Academy was a wonderful example of the town's belief in educating its young citizens; the people of Baldwin matched donations dollar-for-dollar to build it. The two-story brick building was used until 1936, when a new school was built. The second school has since been replaced with a new elementary, secondary, and high school. (Courtesy Perry Lowery.)

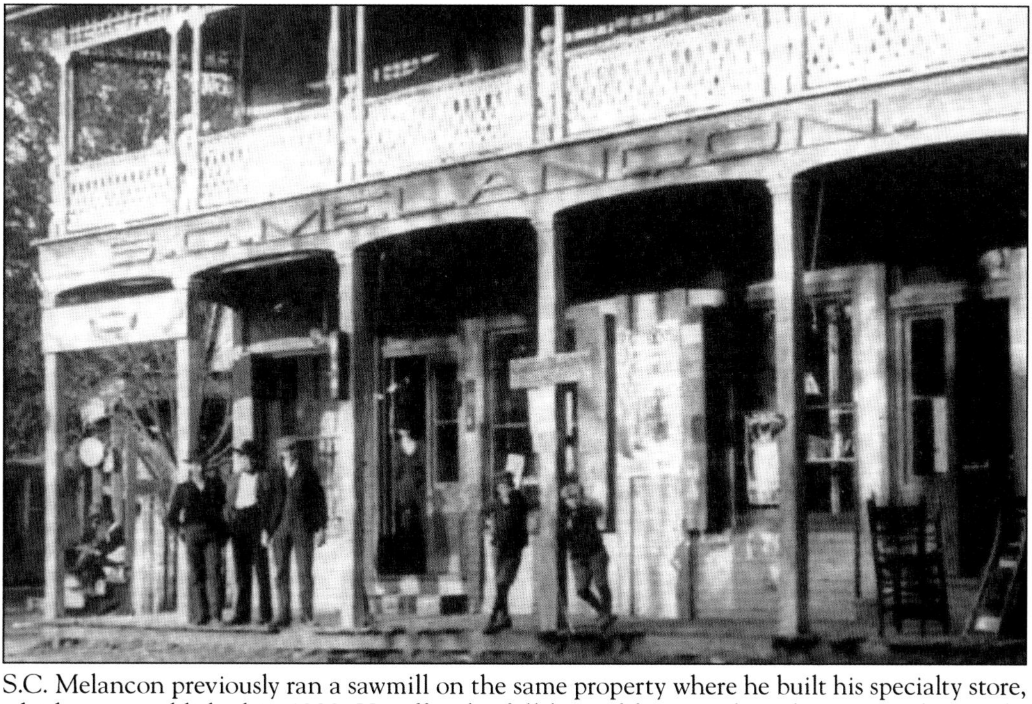

S.C. Melancon previously ran a sawmill on the same property where he built his specialty store, which was established in 1888. He offered a full line of fancy and staple grocery, dry goods, clothing, shoes, hats, and harness supplies. He also offered a complete selection of hardware, crockery, buggies, carts, wagons, and agricultural implements. (Courtesy Perry Lowery.)

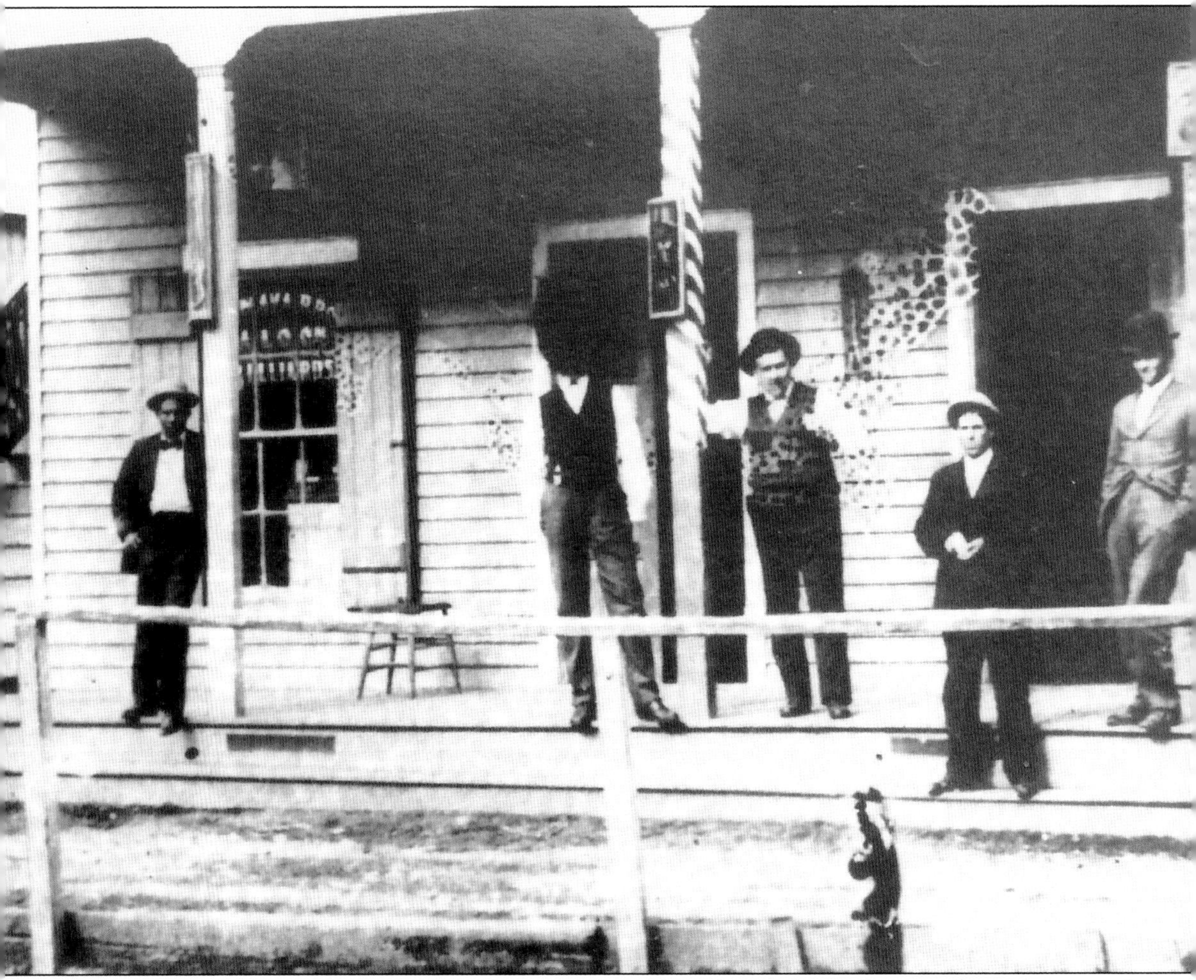

The two-story Navarro Saloon was later purchased by Edgar Achee, who tore down the second floor. The bottom floor was remodeled into Achee Grocery and General Merchandise, whose advertisement offered "staple and fancy groceries, hardware—feed—seeds and Achee delicious boiled hams." (Courtesy Justus Boudreaux.)

Three
FRANKLIN

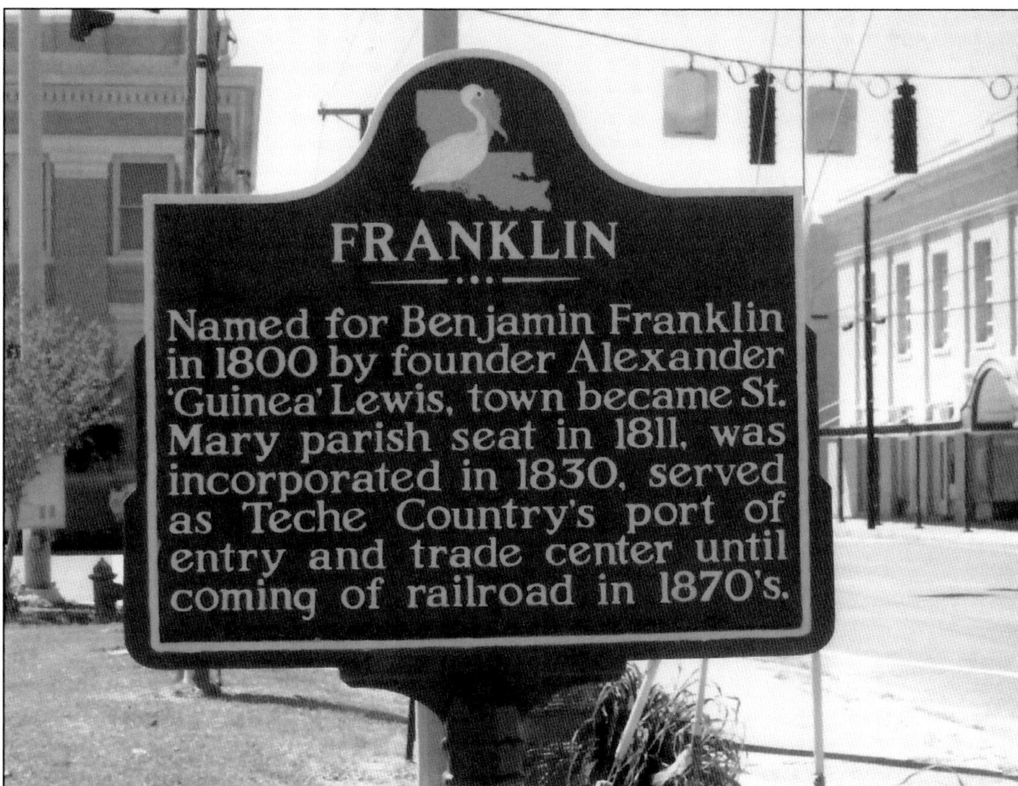

Originally established as Carlin's Settlement in the early 1800s, Franklin was renamed in honor of Benjamin Franklin. Alexander Guinea Lewis donated a tract of land in 1814 for the public square and the courthouse, which is still in use today. Formerly a port of entry for the Teche district, which had a large trading and shipping business, it became the parish seat in 1811. (Courtesy of Techeland Arts Council 2012.)

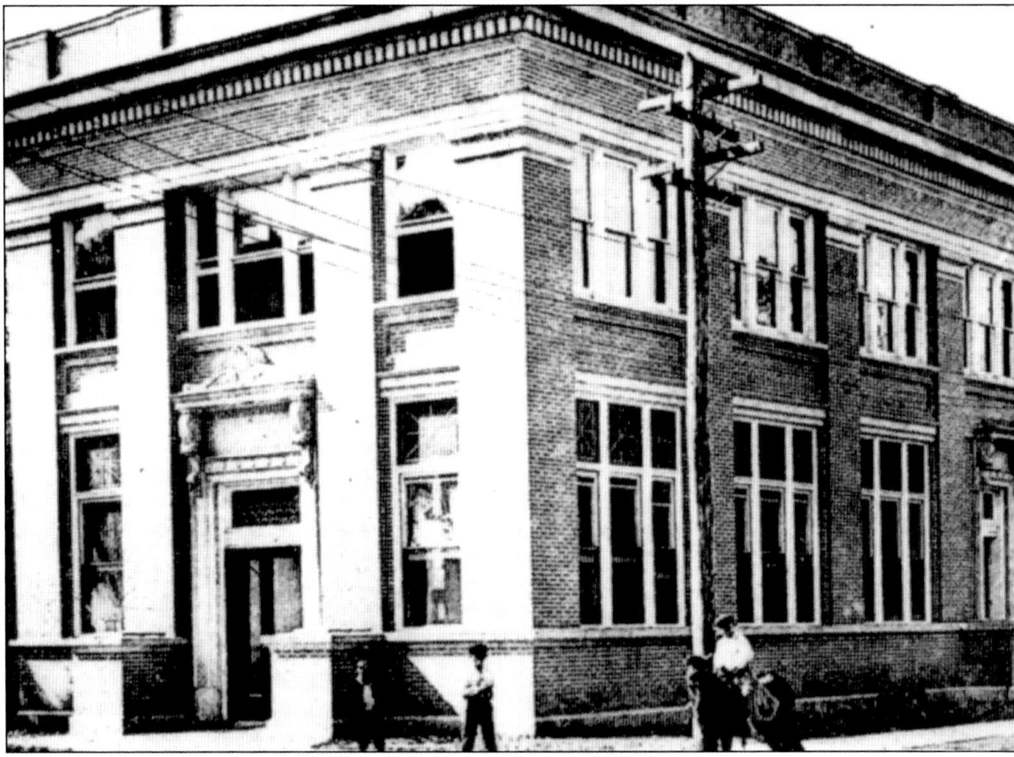

Commercial Bank sits directly across from the courthouse square, with the commercial corridor running between Willow and Adams Streets. Main Street runs parallel to the left bank of Bayou Teche and was also known as the Old Spanish Trail. (Courtesy Perry Lowery.)

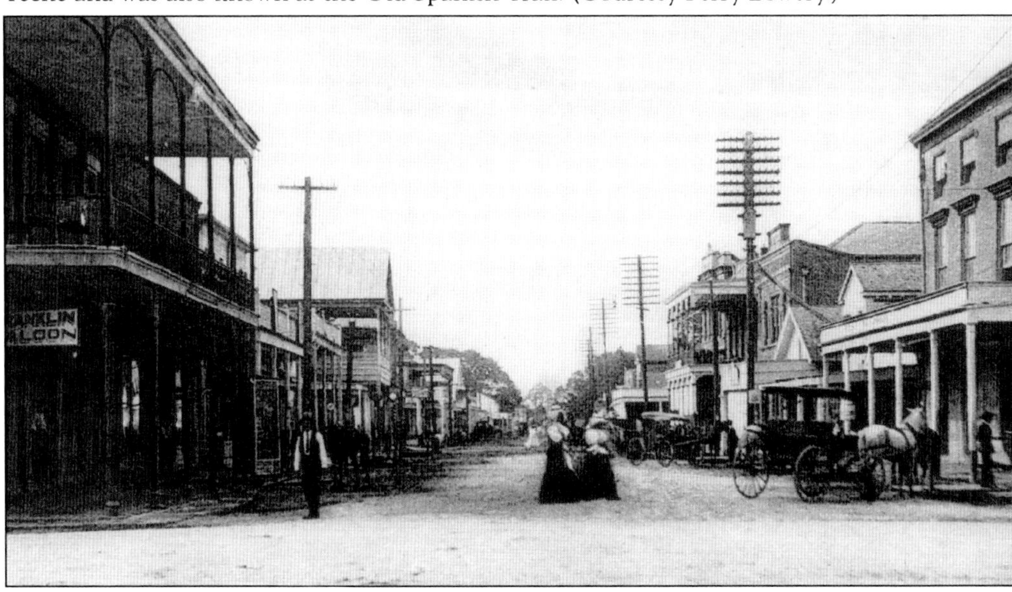

Main Street is seen here in the early 1900s, when the streets were dusty and there was no neutral ground. The building in the foreground on the left was the gathering place of the St. Mary Club. The second floor was used for concerts, theatricals, and balls. The building to the right, on the corner of Willow and Main Streets, was known as Evans Hall. (Courtesy Miss Bernadine O'Connor.)

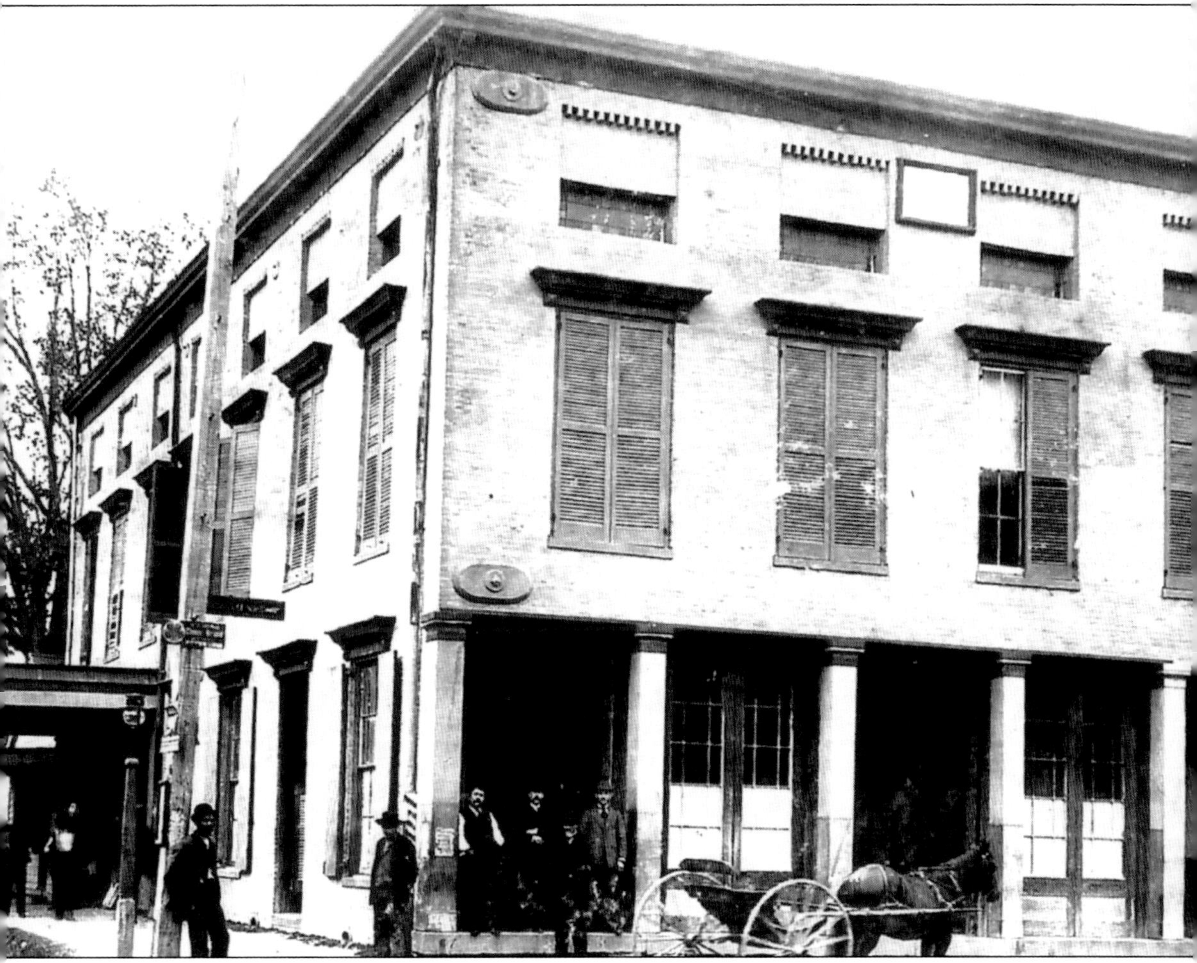

Evans Hall, seen here, had a covered elevated walkway connecting it to the St. Mary Club to keep club members and guests clean and dry. It was the site of many social events but appears to have disappeared during or shortly after the Civil War. (Courtesy Perry Lowery.)

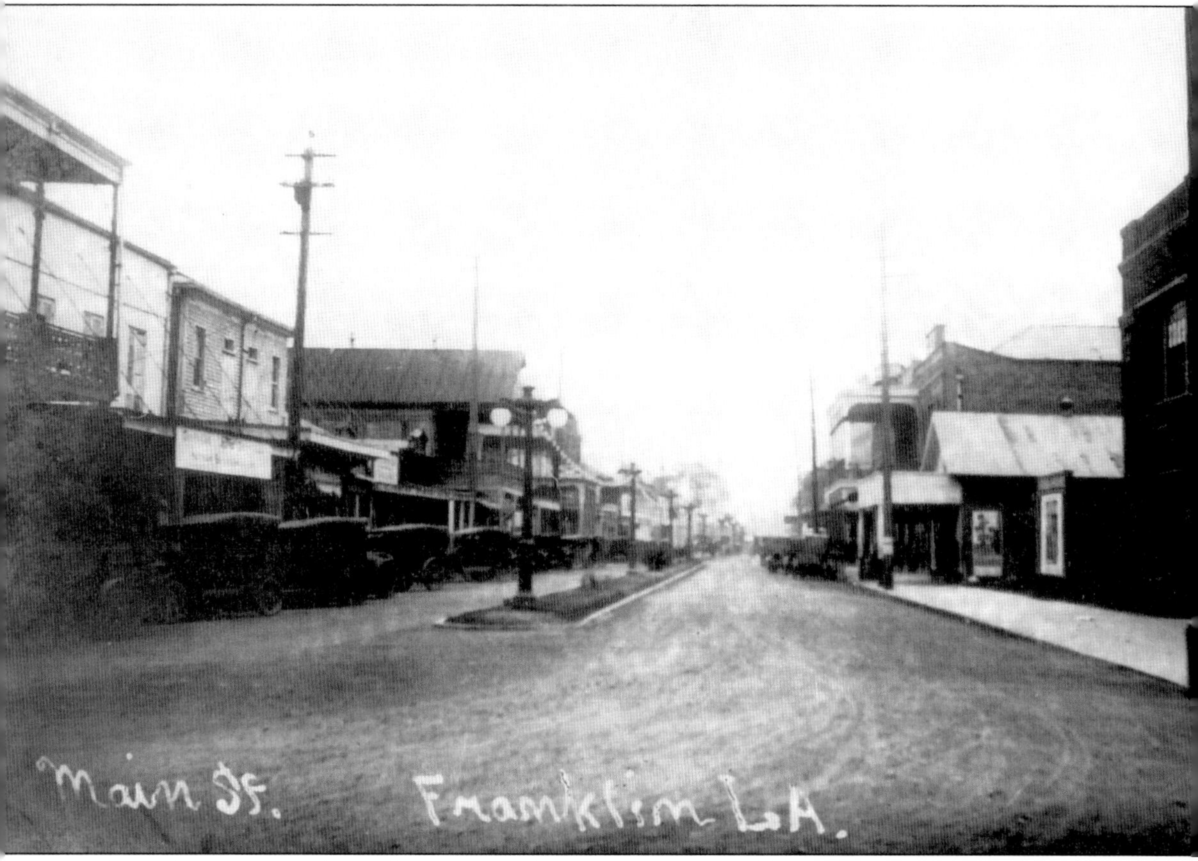

Main Street is seen here after the installation of the original black lampposts with three white globes, the grassy boulevard, and new sidewalks. Although the road was still dirt, at least the pedestrians could avoid the dust and mud. Looking west into a residential area, Evans Hall is on the right. The courthouse square is behind the photographer. (Courtesy Perry Lowery.)

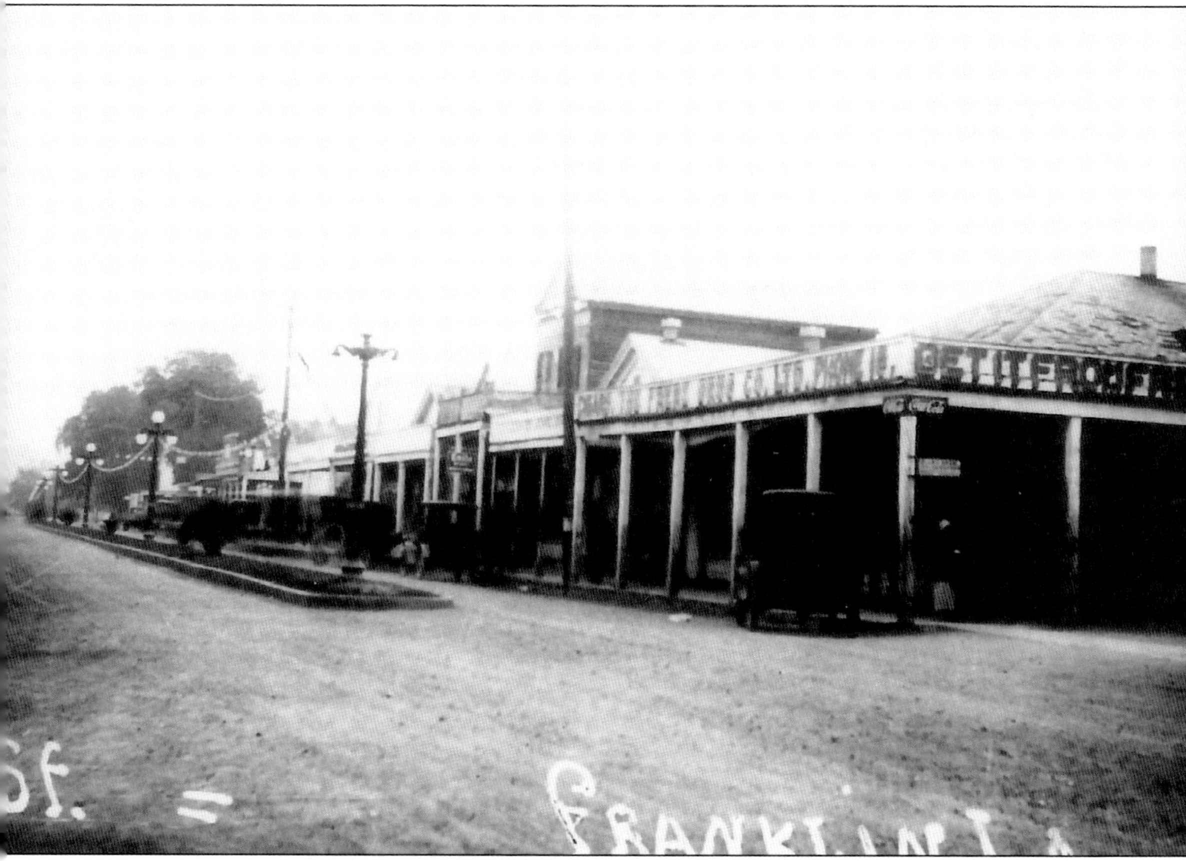

A distinctive black lamppost is seen here along the grassy boulevard of Main Street. Streetlights were installed at a cost of $2 per light by the town of Franklin, which erected a minimum of 40 lights, each with 50 candlepower. There was one provision: "The street lamps shall burn according to the moonlight schedule, which gives the privilege of turning the current off during clear and cloudless moonlight nights." Around 1900, it was law in Franklin that one could not have chickens in town and allow them to peck or scratch on the grassy area of the boulevard. (Courtesy Perry Lowery.)

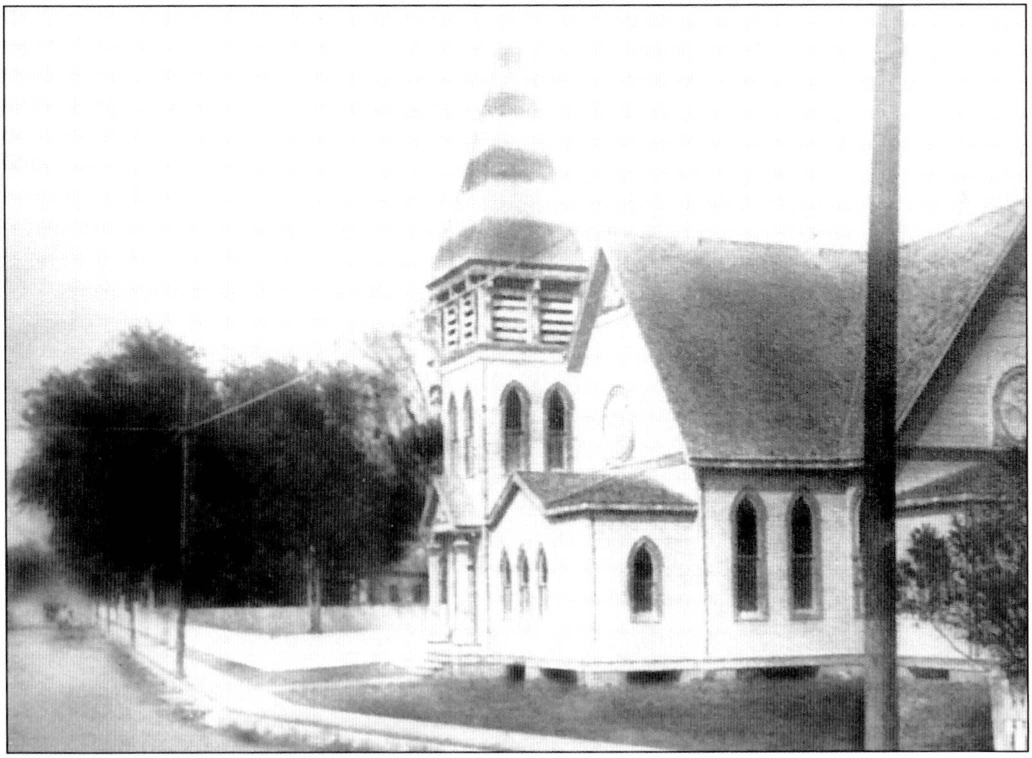

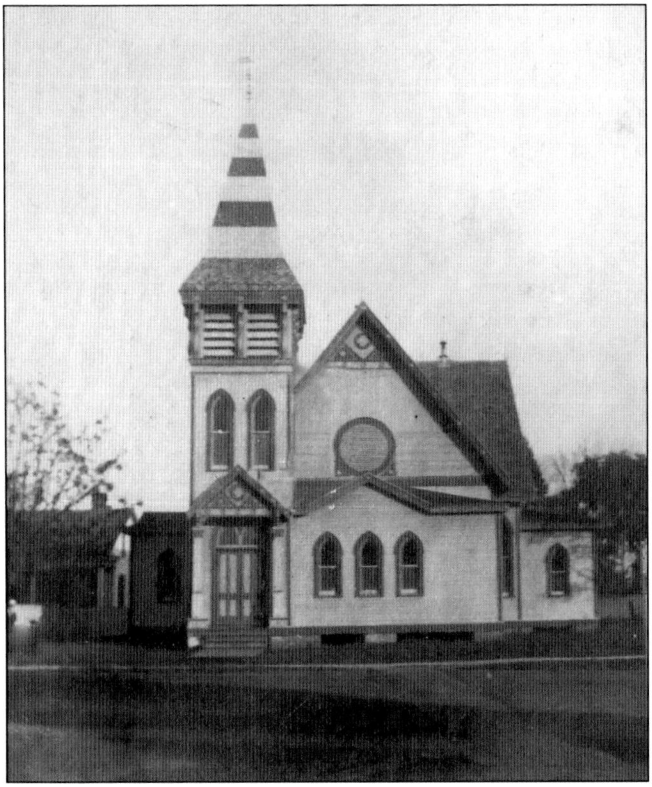

The original First United Methodist Church was at the intersection of Main and Iberia Streets across from the Church of the Assumption. Many of the original founding fathers of St. Mary Parish were buried behind the church and were later moved to the Franklin Cemetery. (Courtesy Perry Lowery.)

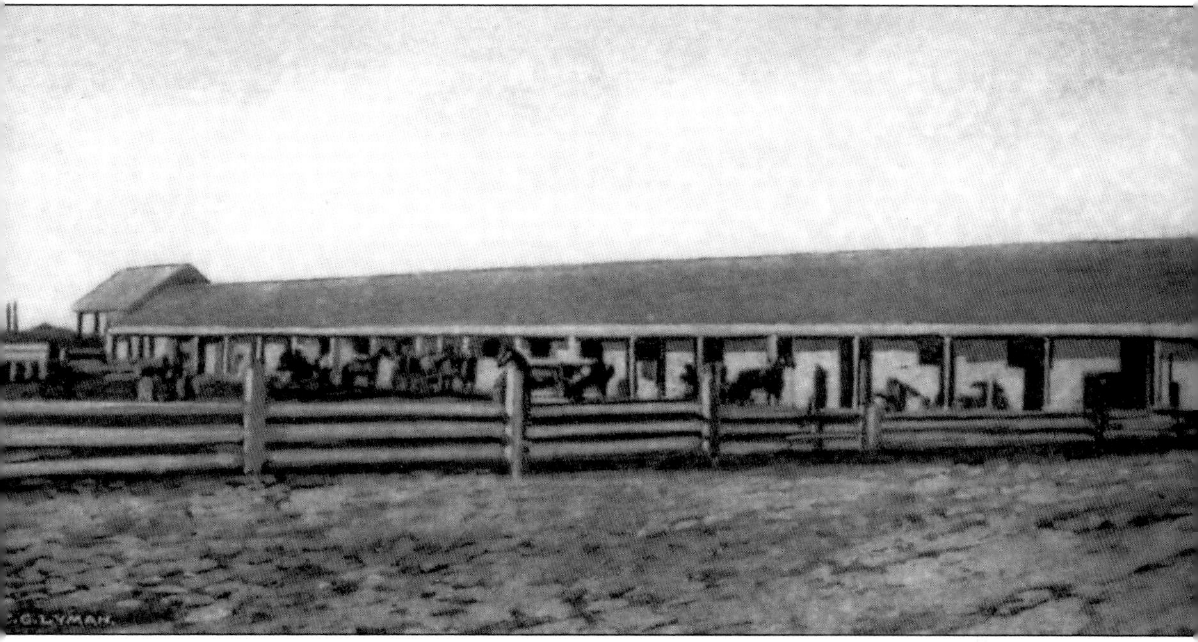

The stables at St. Mary Park were conceived in 1889 by T.J. Shaffer and a group of local citizens who built a half-mile racetrack and procured racehorses. On May 1, 1904, the race track opened with running and trotting races and a baseball game. In 1905, automobile and motorcycle races were held in the park. A bridge crossed the Bayou Teche between Franklin and the St. Mary Park grounds. The oldest building in the area, the Tavern, was built by Barnett Hulick in 1807 directly across the bayou on what is known as the Shawdowlawn estate. The property was previously owned by Simeon Smith of Franklin, who owned the first large vessel in the area, a 31-ton schooner called the *Col. Hanson*. (Courtesy Perry Lowery.)

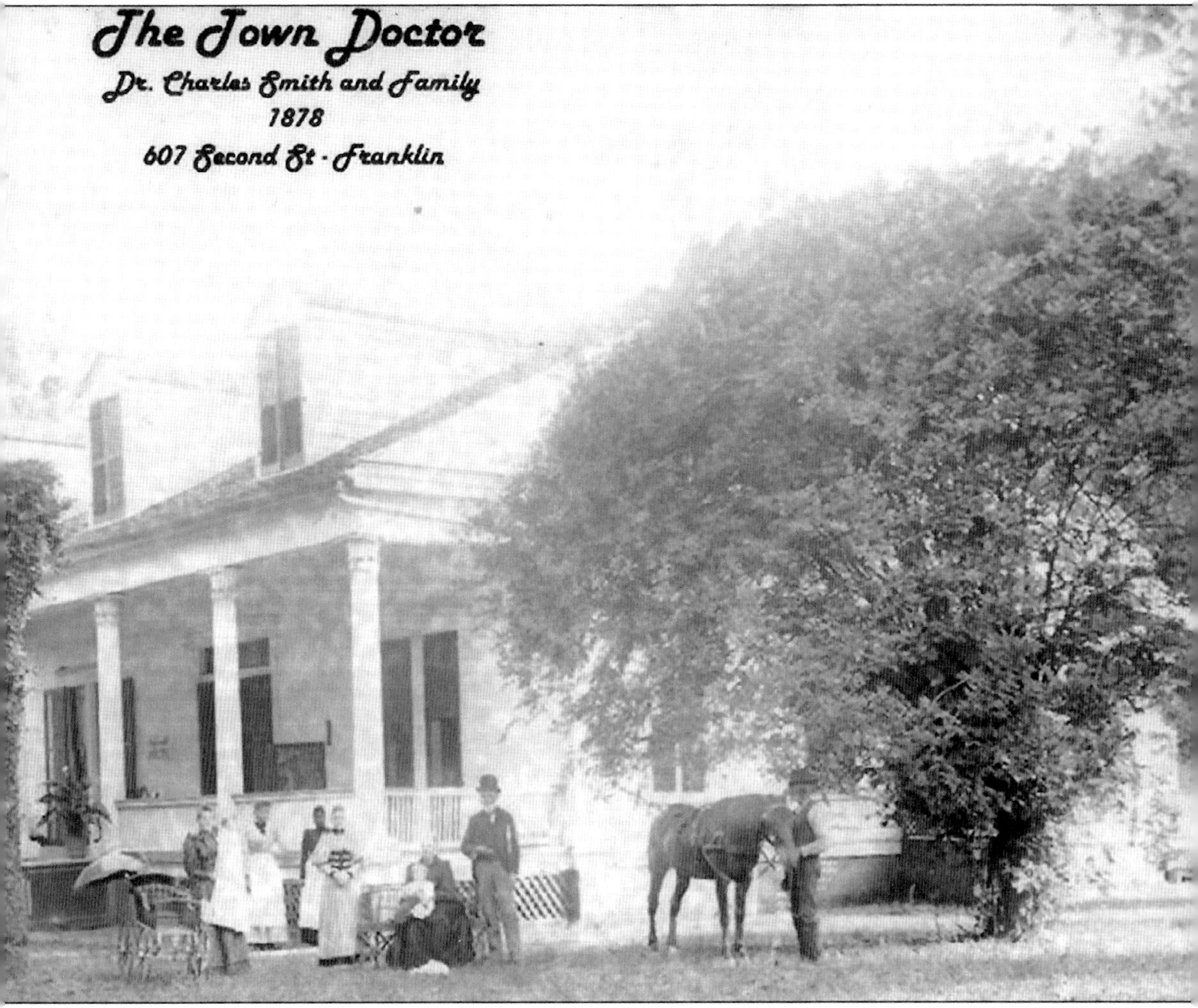

Dr. Charles M. Smith was the health officer for the parish and had an extensive practice in the late 1890s, serving the best class of planters and merchants. He also gave care to those who were unable to pay, often accepting chickens and fresh produce as payment. (Courtesy Perry Lowery.)

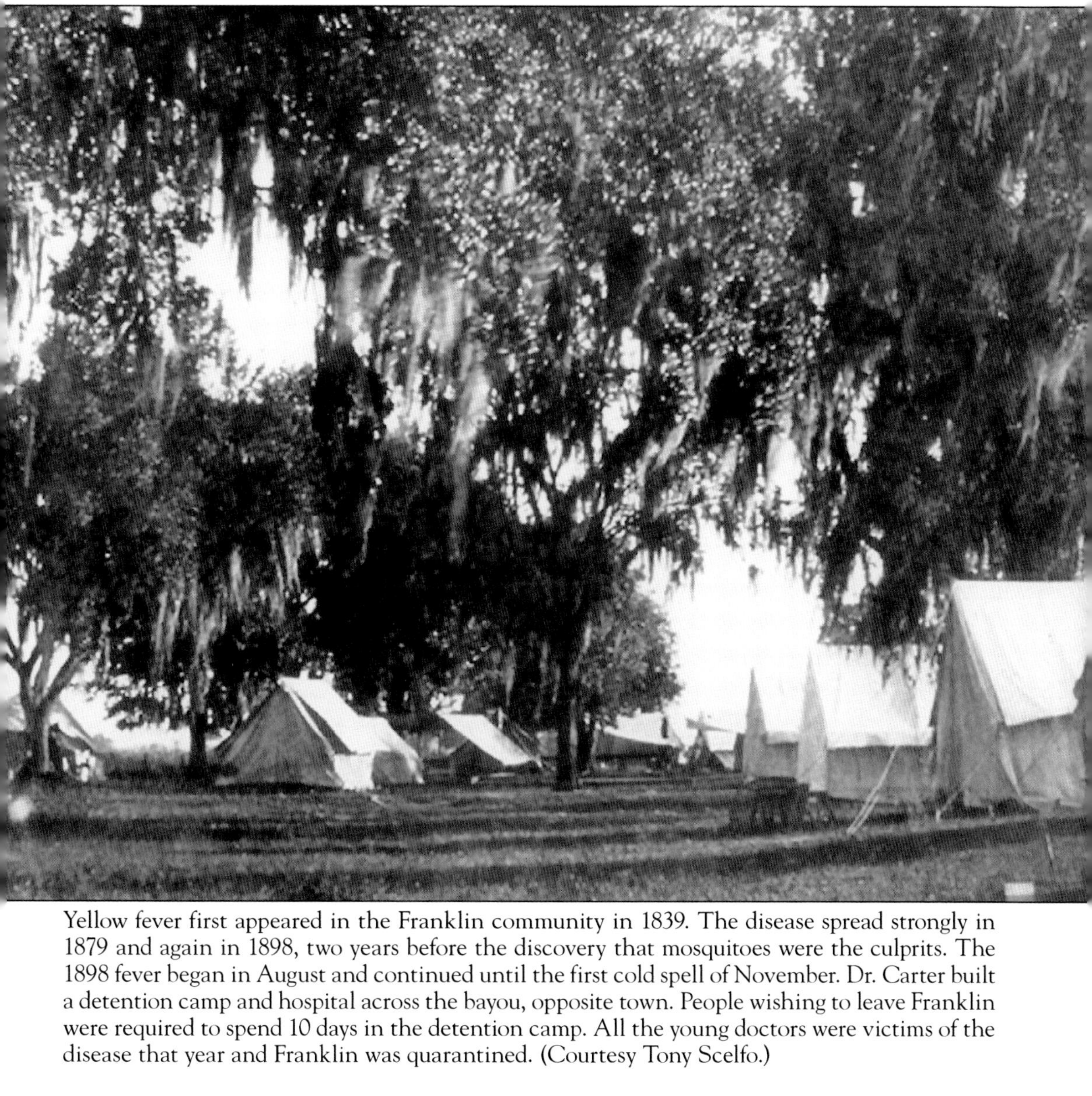

Yellow fever first appeared in the Franklin community in 1839. The disease spread strongly in 1879 and again in 1898, two years before the discovery that mosquitoes were the culprits. The 1898 fever began in August and continued until the first cold spell of November. Dr. Carter built a detention camp and hospital across the bayou, opposite town. People wishing to leave Franklin were required to spend 10 days in the detention camp. All the young doctors were victims of the disease that year and Franklin was quarantined. (Courtesy Tony Scelfo.)

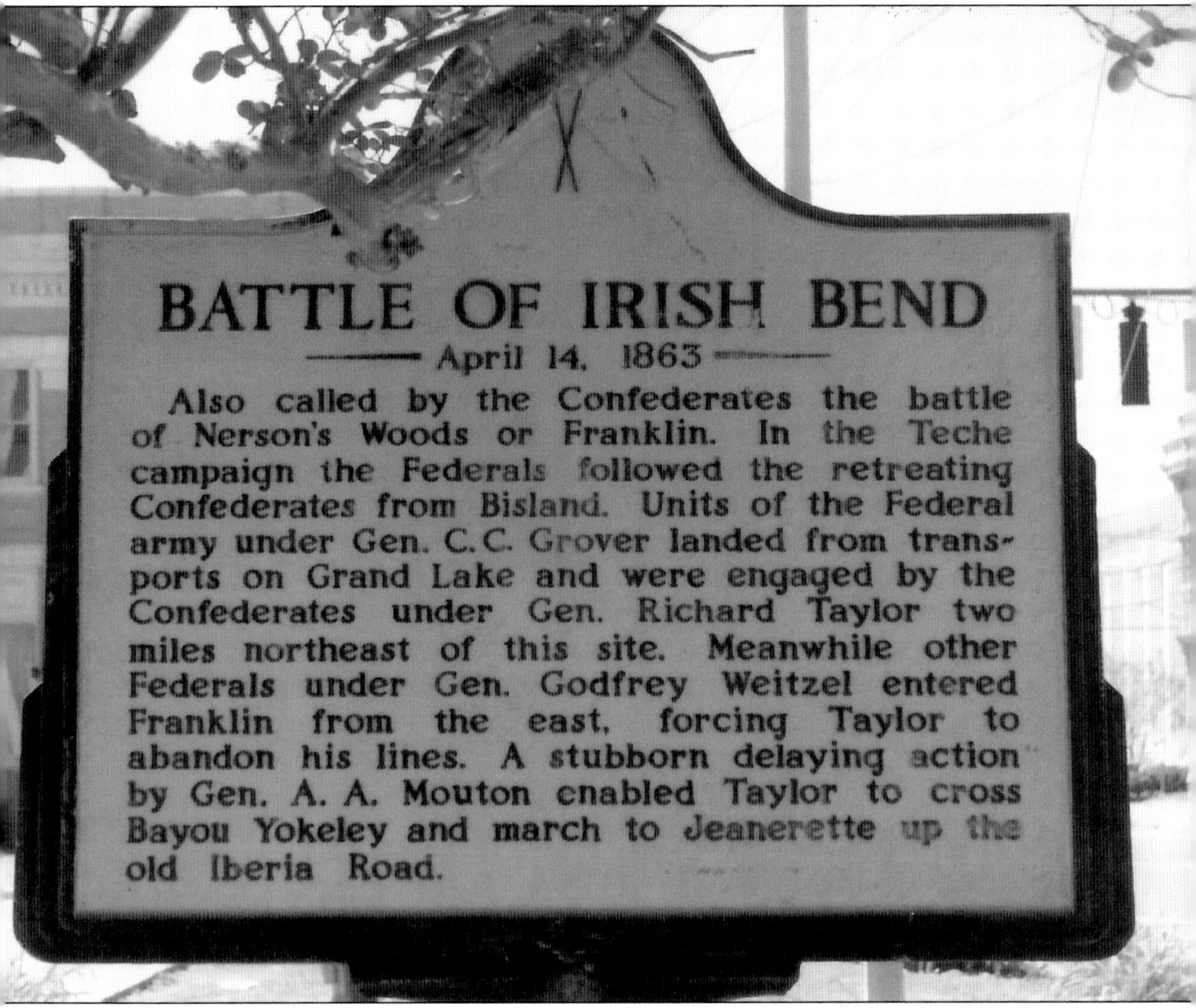

This historical marker is in the courthouse square in Franklin, with the Commercial Bank in the background, Evans Hall to the right, and Bayou Teche about 100 yards away. This intersection played an important role in Franklin's history, with grand homes to the left down Main Street and the business district to the right. (Courtesy Techeland Arts Council 2012.)

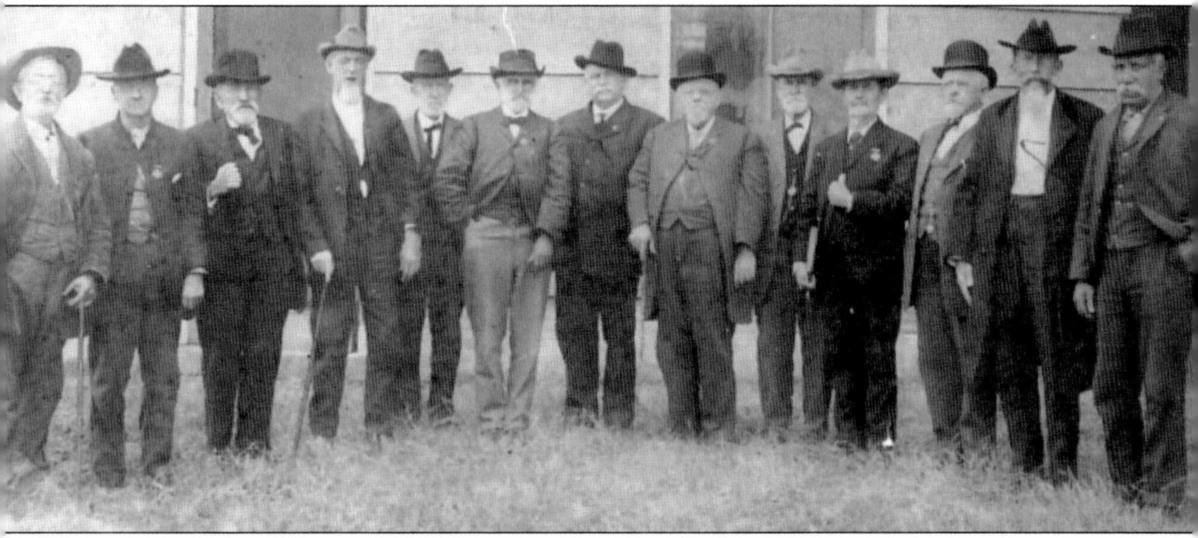

The remaining St. Mary Parish Civil War veterans gathered periodically to celebrate the friendship born from their shared experience. Here, from left to right, are Jessie Baldwin, Alex Todd, Louis Robicheaux, Capt. Edwin Kyle, Henry Kappel, Henri Penn, Tom Schaffer, R.W. Allen, A.A. Delahoussaye, E.J. Trastour, Judge A.C. Allen, Aex Dugas, and Charles Matherne. (Courtesy Nolia Robicheaux.)

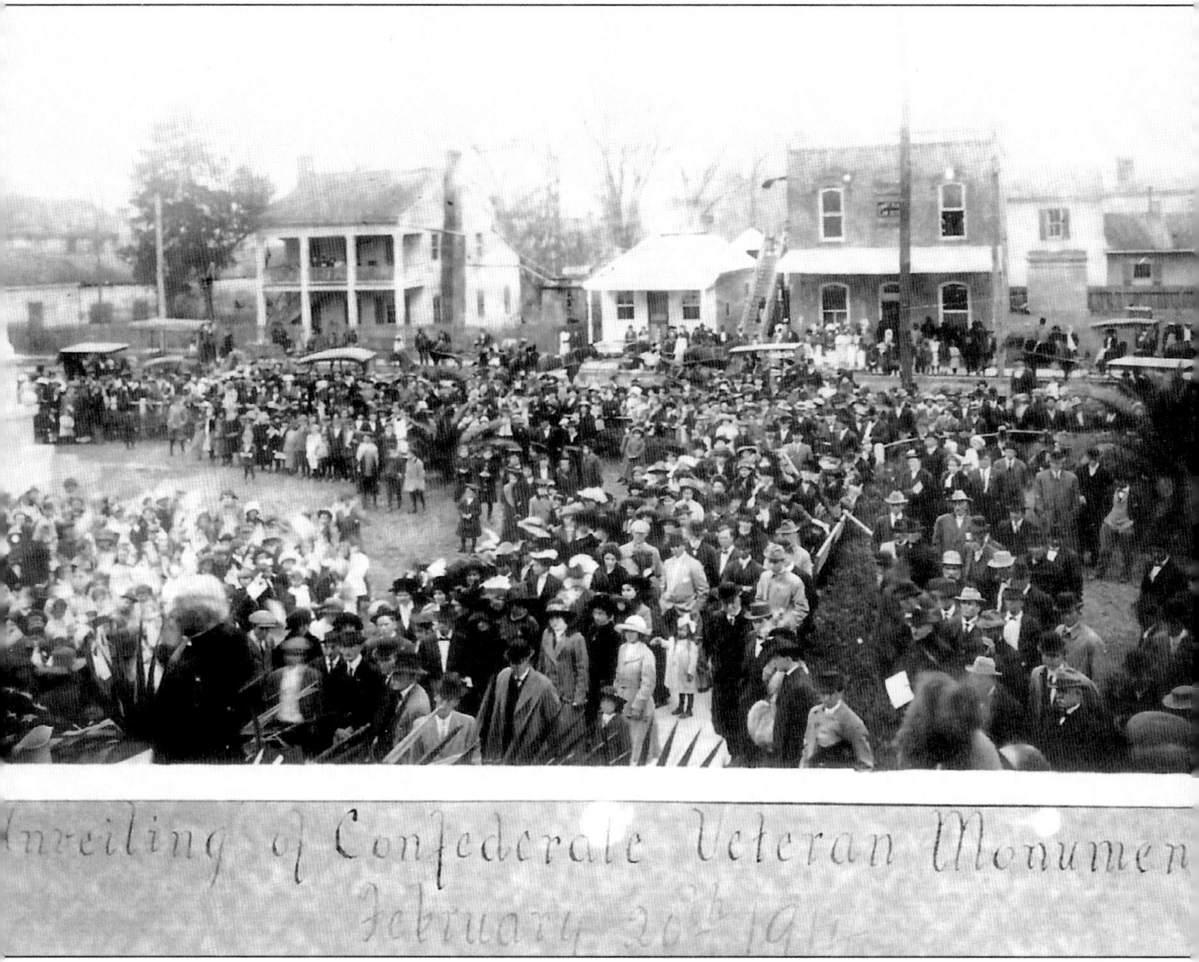

The citizens of St. Mary Parish gathered at the courthouse square for the dedication of the Confederate Veteran Monument, which was engraved with the following words: "To The Confederate Soldiers, St. Mary Parish, Who Fought for the Honor of Their State and Country, This Monument Is Erected. Nobly They Stood the Test, Richly They Earned Their Rest." (Courtesy Perry Lowery.)

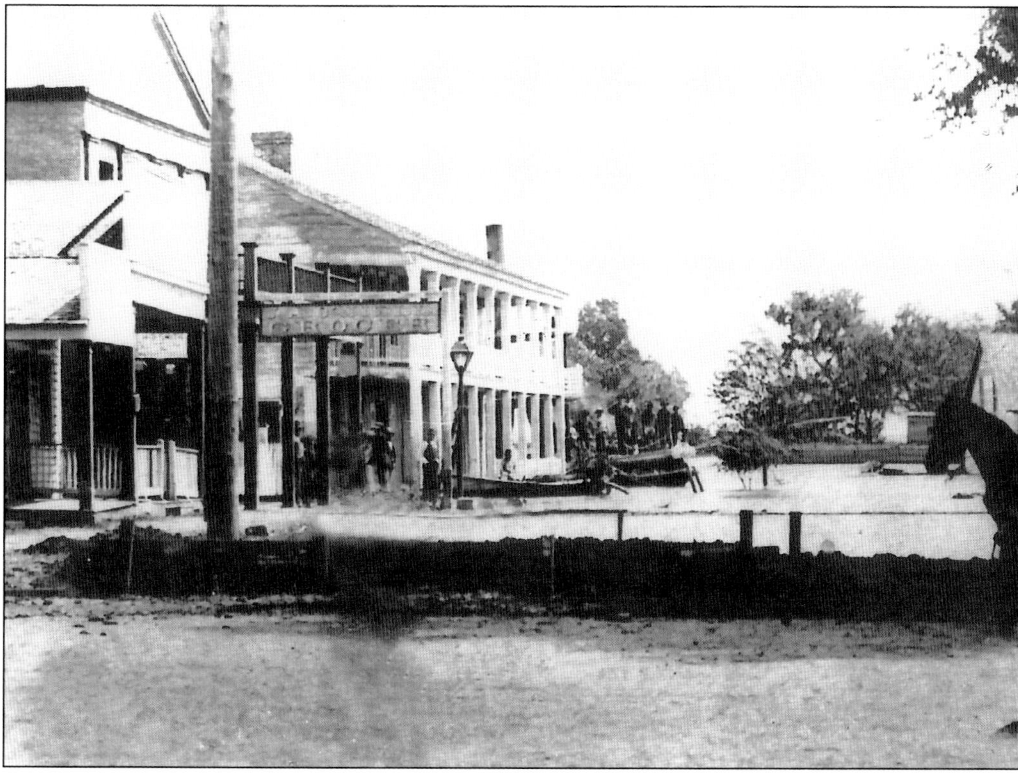

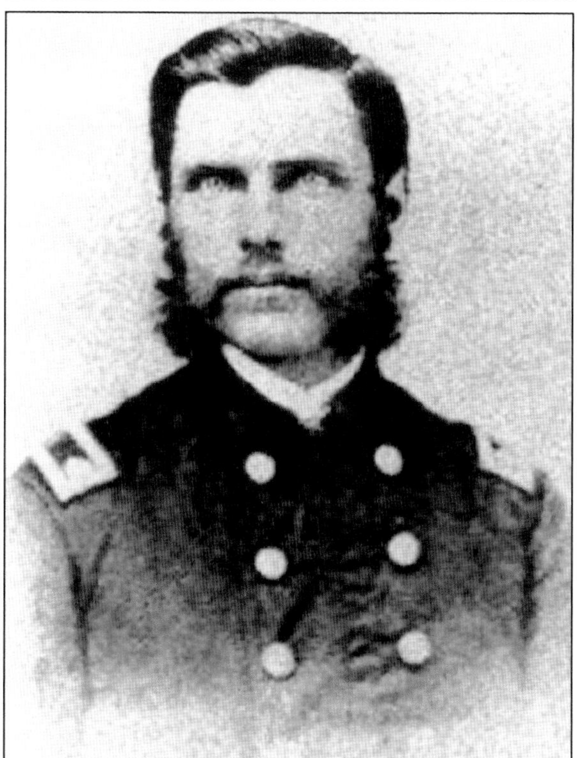

The O'Niell Hotel, on the bayou side of Willow Street, was the scene of the murder of Sheriff Henry H. Pope and Judge Valentine Chase. On the night of October 17, 1868, while the two were in conversation, and with Mrs. Pope present on the gallery, five masked men with guns and knives killed both men. Links between the Ku Klux Klan or the Knights of the White Camelia were never proven. (Courtesy Perry Lowery.)

Lt. Col. Henry Pope was born in Ogdensburg, New York, and was a schoolteacher before enlisting in the Union army in 1861. In 1865, he was promoted to colonel of Company D of the 33rd Illinois Infantry at Vicksburg, Mississippi. After the war, he settled in Franklin. Locals viewed him and Judge Chase as carpetbaggers and scalawags who "organized and stirred up hell in our midst," according to editor Dennett of the *Planters Banner*. (Courtesy Perry Lowery.)

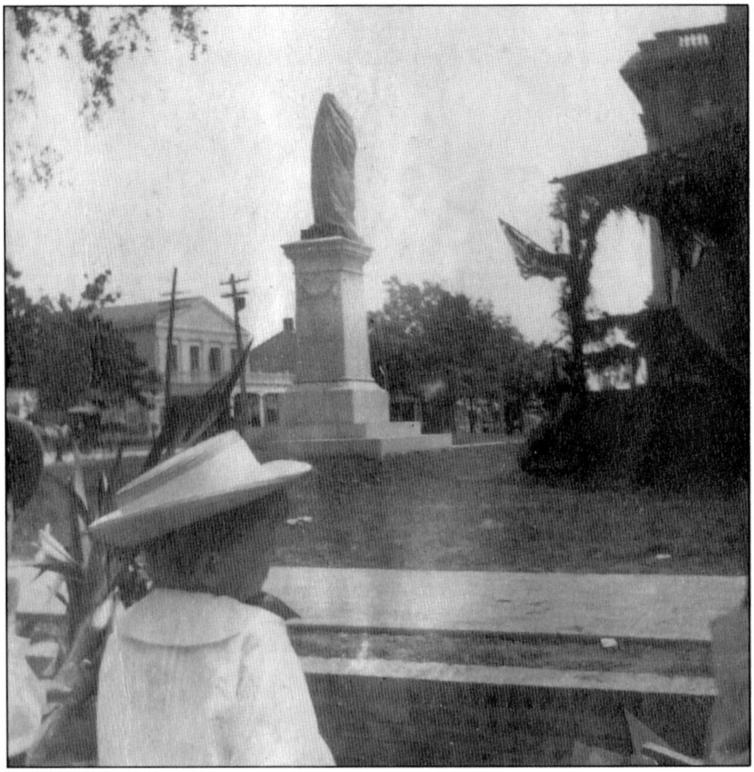

The memorial statue of Sen. Donelson Caffery is unveiled in the courthouse square. Senator Caffery (1835–1906) was born in St. Mary Parish on a sugar plantation near Franklin, and was related to families that were among the first community builders in the parish, arriving in the early 1800s. After completing his studies, he returned to engage in sugar planting on Bayou Cypremort. (Courtesy Stephen Stirling.)

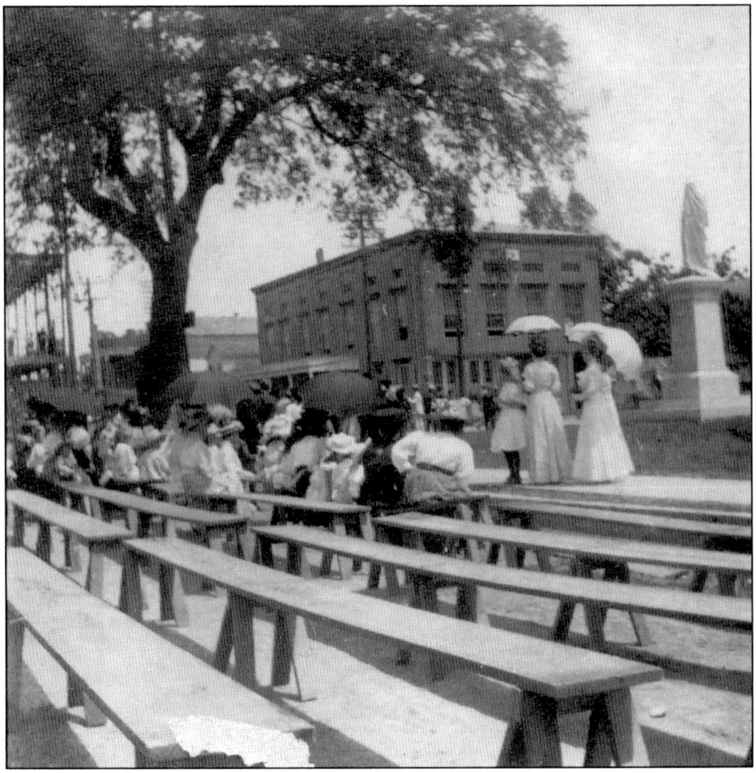

Here, ladies and children gather for the dedication of the memorial statue of Senator Caffery. Once again, one can see the location of the courthouse square, with the Union Hall to the left and Evans Hall (the original Old Opera House) to the right. (Courtesy Stephen Stirling.)

Other citizens await the dedication of Senator Caffery's statue. When Louisiana seceded from the Union, Caffery left his business and plantation in charge of the overseer and joined the Crescent Rifles. Later he was transferred to the Louisiana 13th Regiment and fought in the Battle of Shiloh. He was known for his daring and reckless courage. (Courtesy Stephen Stirling.)

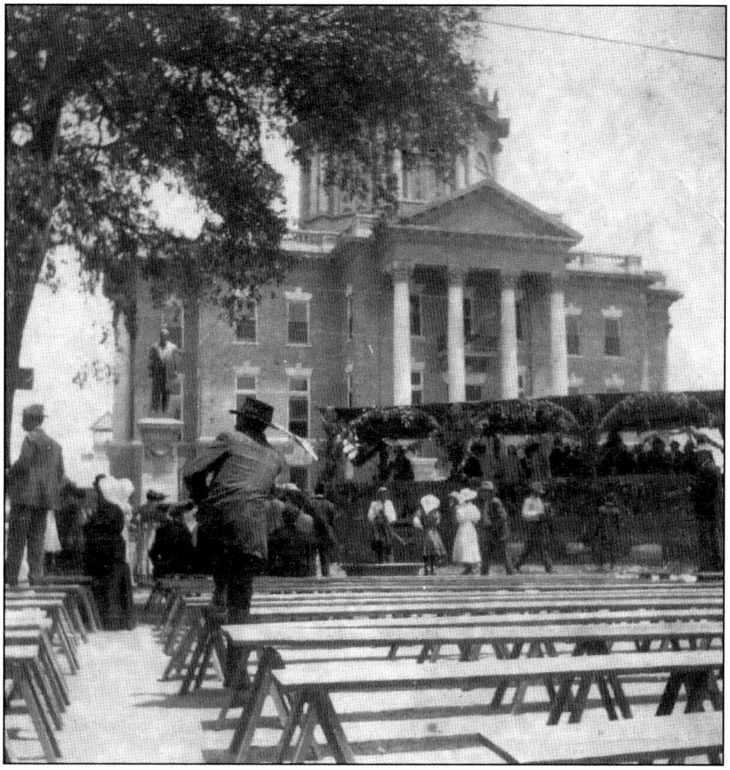

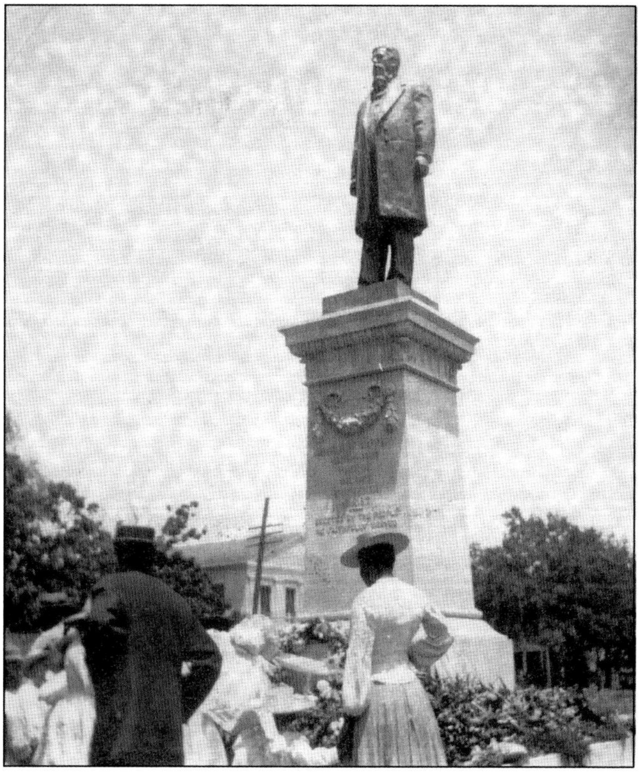

Locals get a closer look at the memorial statue of Senator Caffery. During Reconstruction, Caffery played a major role in ridding Louisiana of carpetbag government. By 1887, two African Americans were serving office in St. Mary Parish: John F. Patty and W.S. Posey, both state representatives. Both Patty and Posey studied at the Gilbert Academy (Sager Brown) in Baldwin. (Courtesy Stephen Stirling.)

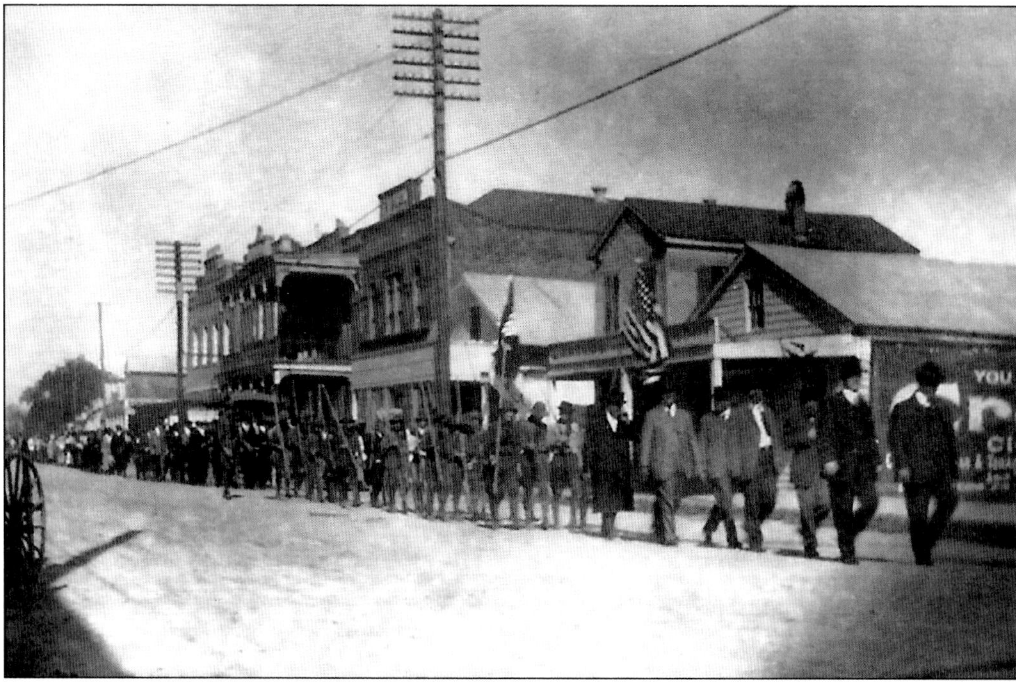

This parade led citizens and schoolchildren from St. Mary Central High School and St. John's Academy to view the Liberty Bell on November 20, 1915, at the Southern Pacific train depot on Anderson Street. First in line were the remaining Civil War veterans, followed by Scoutmaster R.E. Brumby with Boy Scout Troop 1.

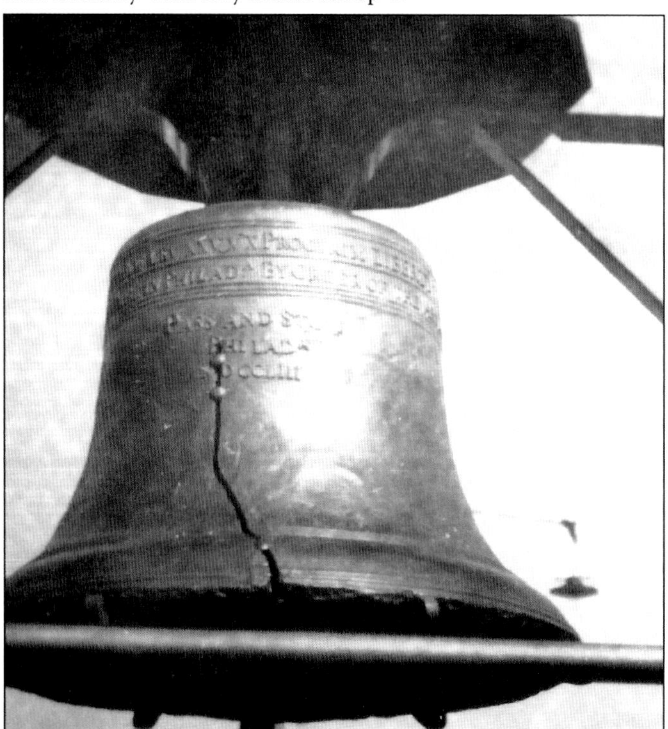

Boy Scout Troop No. 1 petitioned the Philadelphia authorities through their national headquarters in New York in an attempt to bring the Liberty Bell through Franklin. They succeeded and Franklin was placed on the itinerary, even though the original plans had already been finalized. (Courtesy Perry Lowery.)

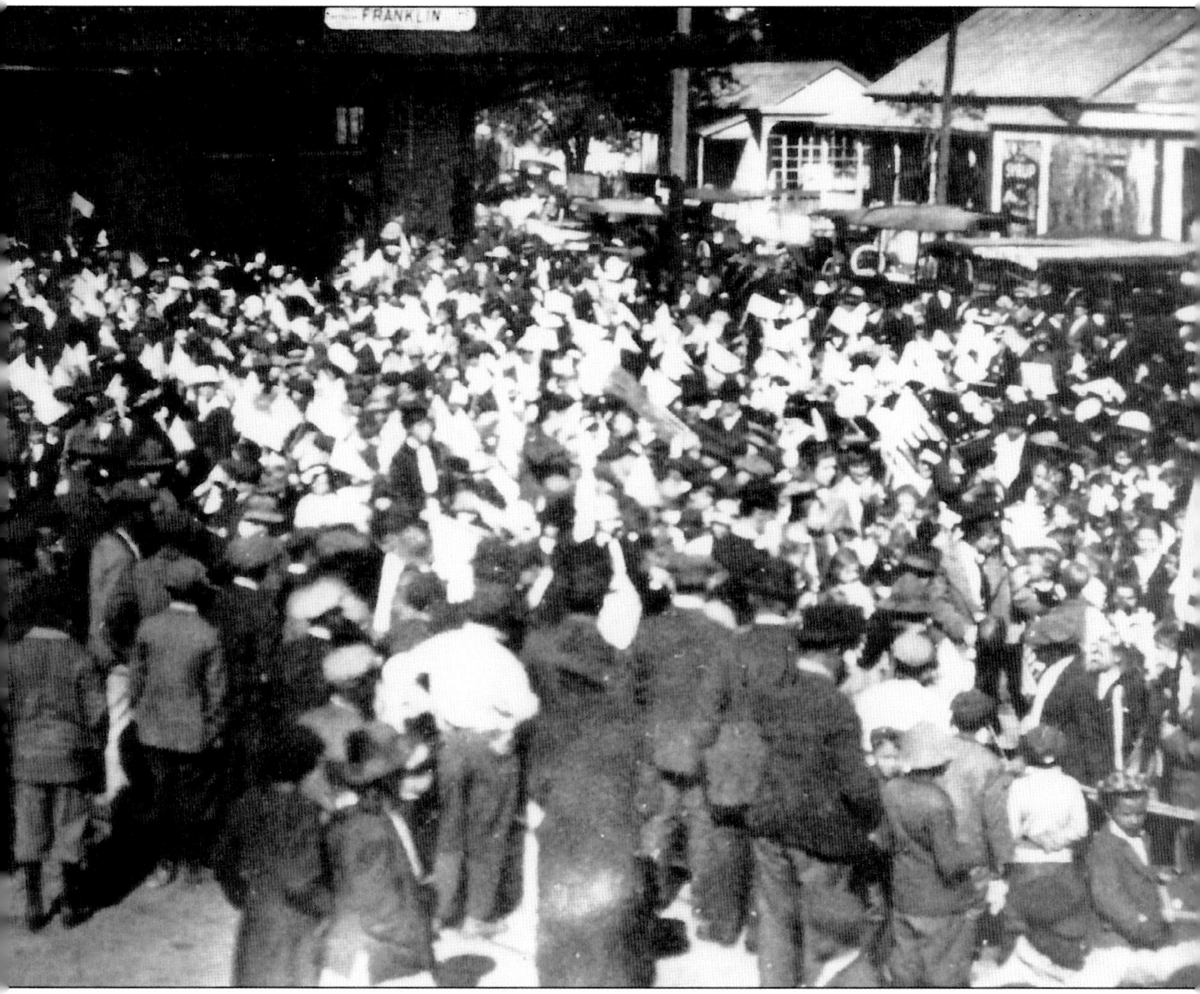

A great throng of people gathered at the depot to greet the Liberty Bell on its journey across the country in 1915. The atmosphere was described in the *Franklin Banner*: "With patriotic reverence to gaze upon this precious emblem of liberty which rang out to a listening world the glad tiding of the birth of the grandest republic in history." (Courtesy Perry Lowery.)

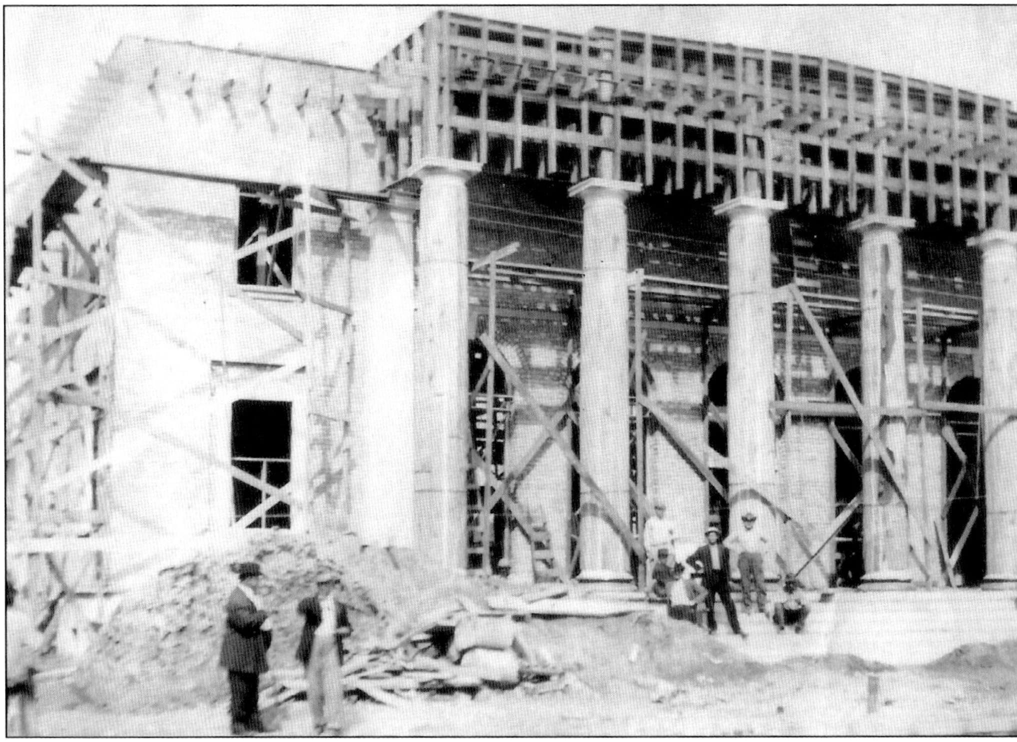

The Franklin post office has had several locations since services were first established in 1811, all within the business district of Franklin. With each new location, it increased in size as the town and population in the surrounding areas grew. The first noted postmark was April 1, 1811, according to records from the National Archives. (Courtesy Perry Lowery.)

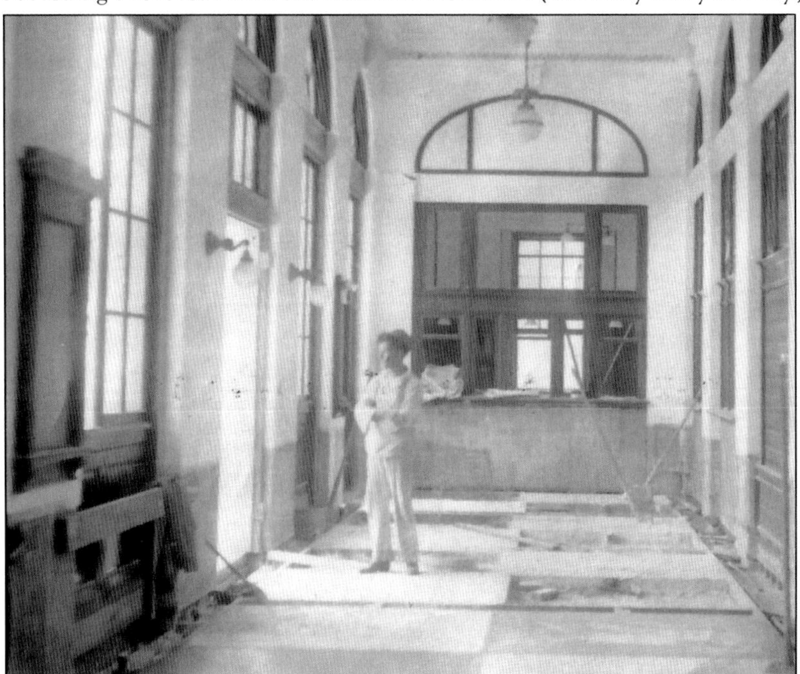

The interior of the Franklin post office was spacious, with tall ceilings, ample light, and clean lines. This building remained in use until the early 2000s, when the postal service yet again needed more space to accommodate patrons and better parking facilities, and moved two blocks down Willow Street to a metal building. (Courtesy Perry Lowery.)

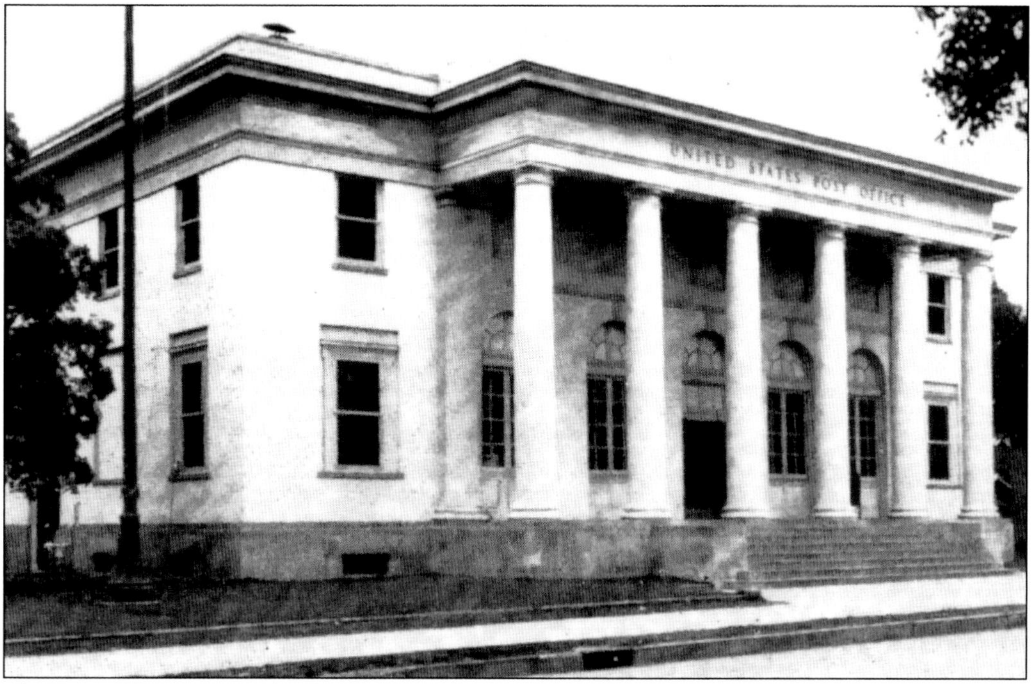

This post office was completed in 1913. With its massive Greek columns and impressive presence, it also served for many years as a gathering place for the community. Fortunately, through the efforts of three local citizens, it has been lovingly preserved and renovated and is currently available for parties or functions in the downtown area.

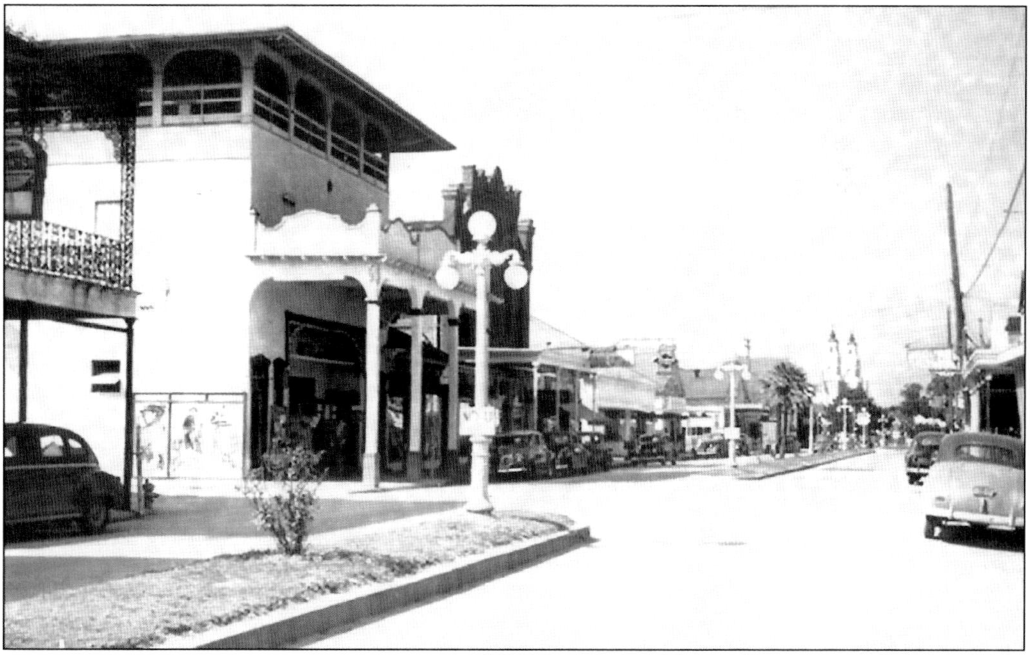

In 1913, the Opera House was opened by Lauve-Bodin Amusement Company. Stars like Charlie Chaplin, Lillian Gish, and Mary Pickford entertained the public. The rooftop garden of the Opera House was known for dancing and romance until 1917. (Courtesy Perry Lowery.)

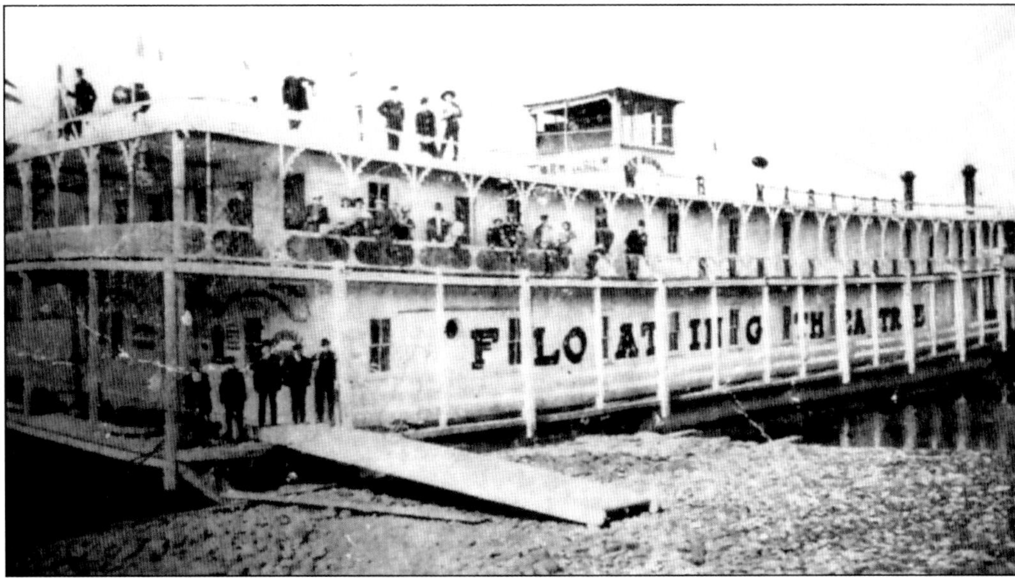

Floating theaters with names like *Sensation*, *Swallow*, and *Cotton Blossom* arrived on Bayou Teche to entertain citizens with lively and colorful shows. Showboats stopped at places such as Calumet, Shadyside, Garden City, and all the large plantations, where they presented night performances to the delight of their audiences. (Courtesy Perry Lowery.)

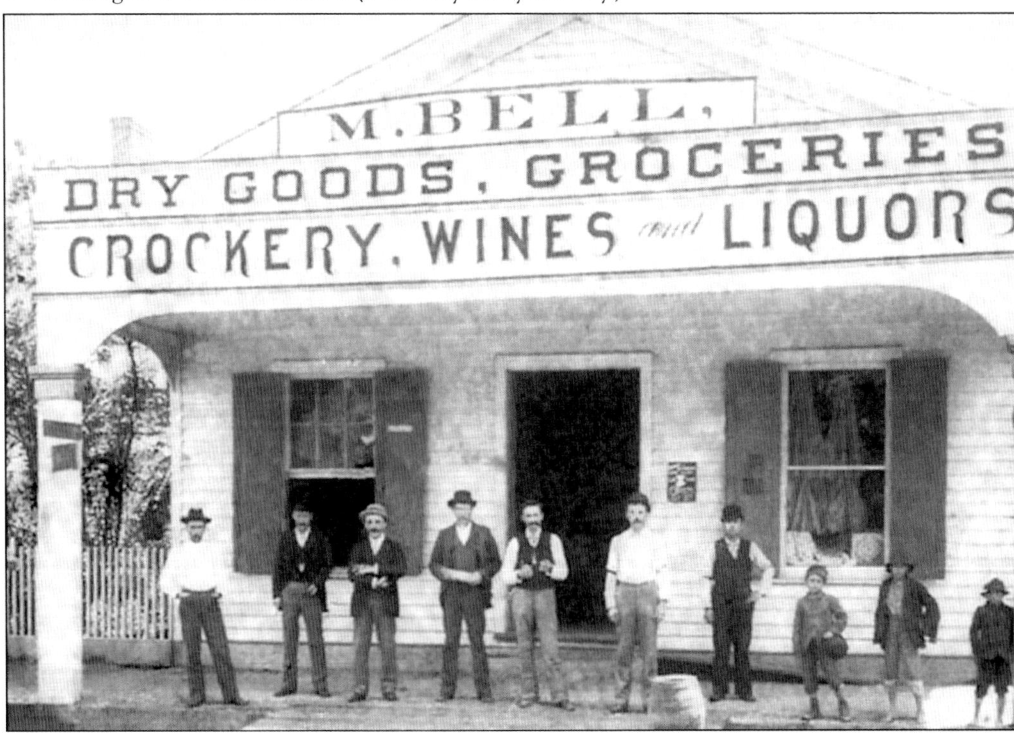

The sign out front of the M. Bell store on Main Street boasts of dry goods, groceries, crockery, and wines and liquors. A furniture store was attached to M. Bell, a leading retail establishment. According to an article by J.S. Glass, "the polite and obliging ladies and gentlemen supervise and fill the wants of the patrons of the Bell establishment." (Courtesy Perry Lowery.)

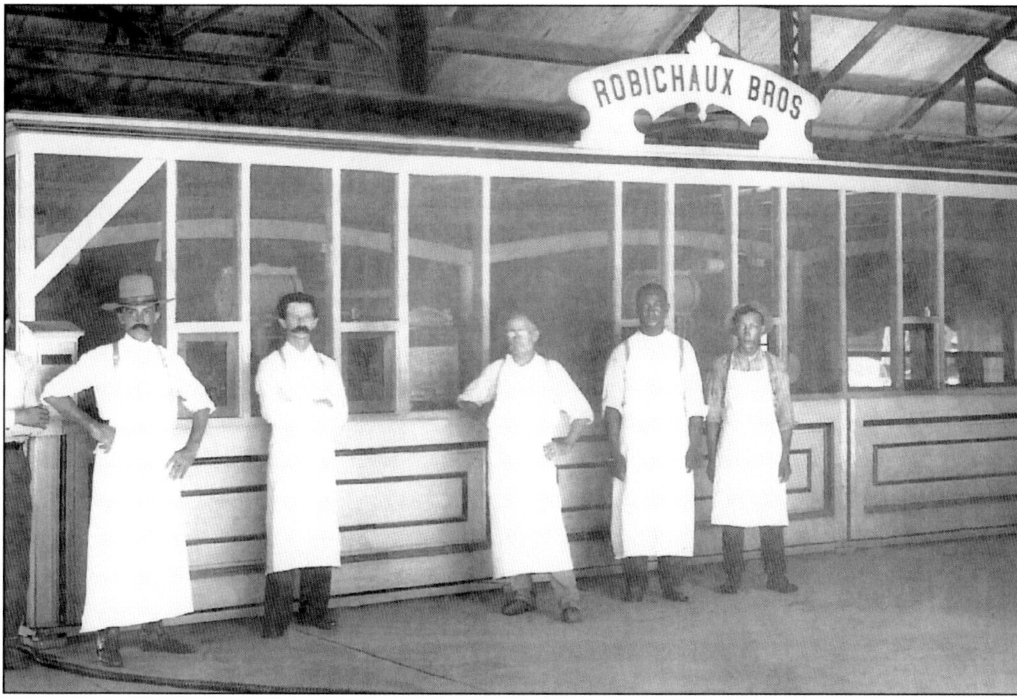

The Robichaux Bros meat market under the Old City Market was a popular local establishment offering farm-fresh meats. In those days, people went to their local butcher daily for cuts of meat to be cooked and served for that evening's meal. (Courtesy Perry Lowery.)

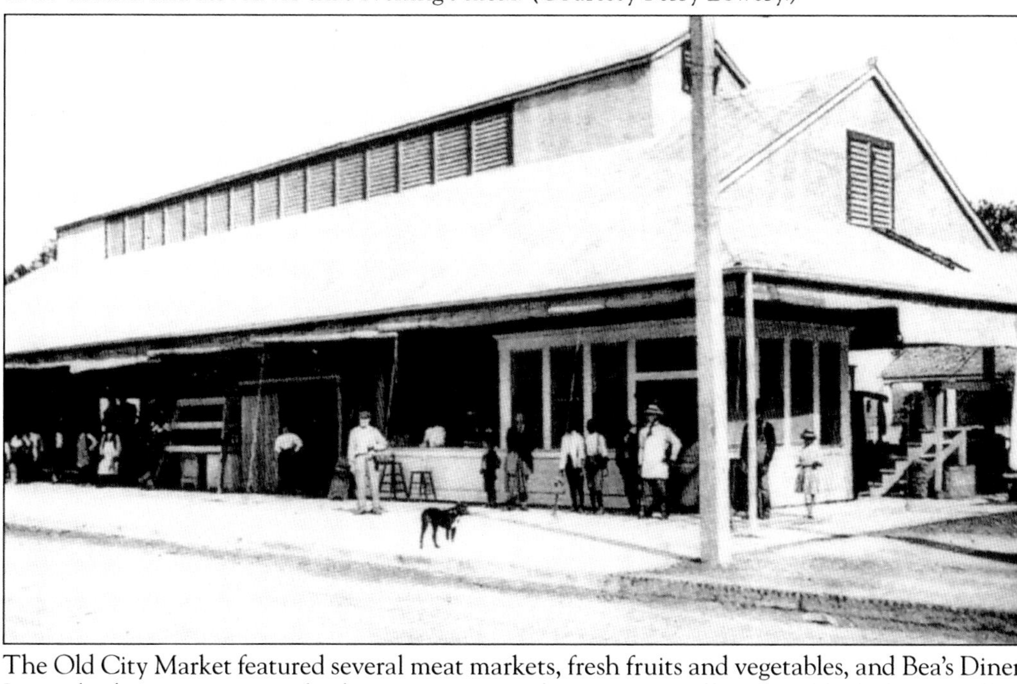

The Old City Market featured several meat markets, fresh fruits and vegetables, and Bea's Diner. It was built at approximately the same time as the new post office, one block down Willow Street. This open-air structure has been used for functions, parties, and the local farmers' market. (Courtesy Perry Lowery.)

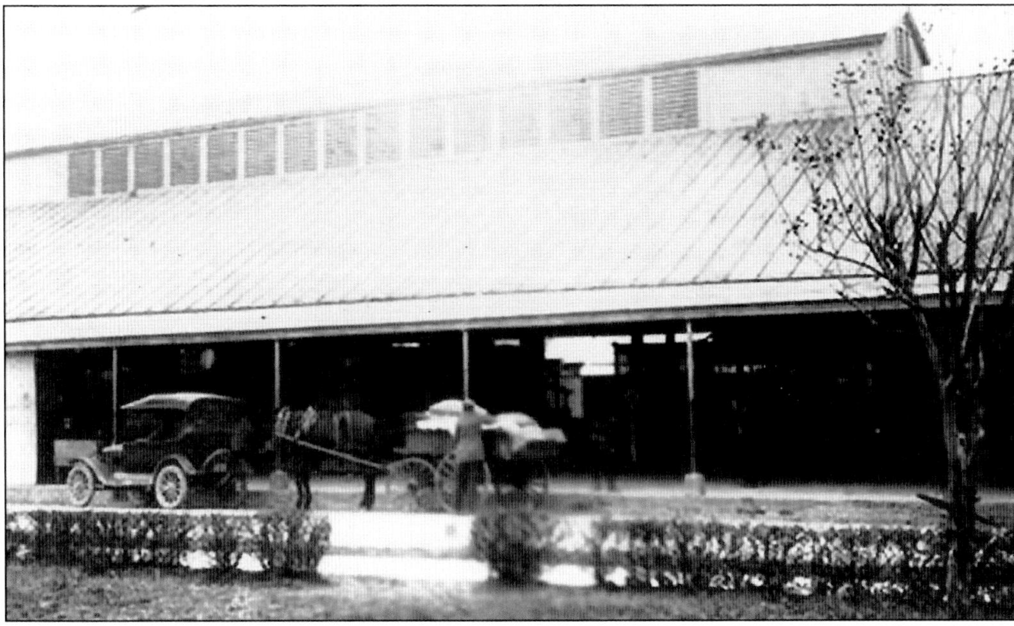

This is a wonderful photograph of the old, the new, and the things that endure: the Old City Market, a newfangled gas-powered vehicle, and a man with a horse and cart loaded with supplies. Some photographs are worth a thousand words, but some speak quietly on their own. The market was built during John C. Lewis's tenure as mayor, from 1900 to 1910. (Courtesy Perry Lowery.)

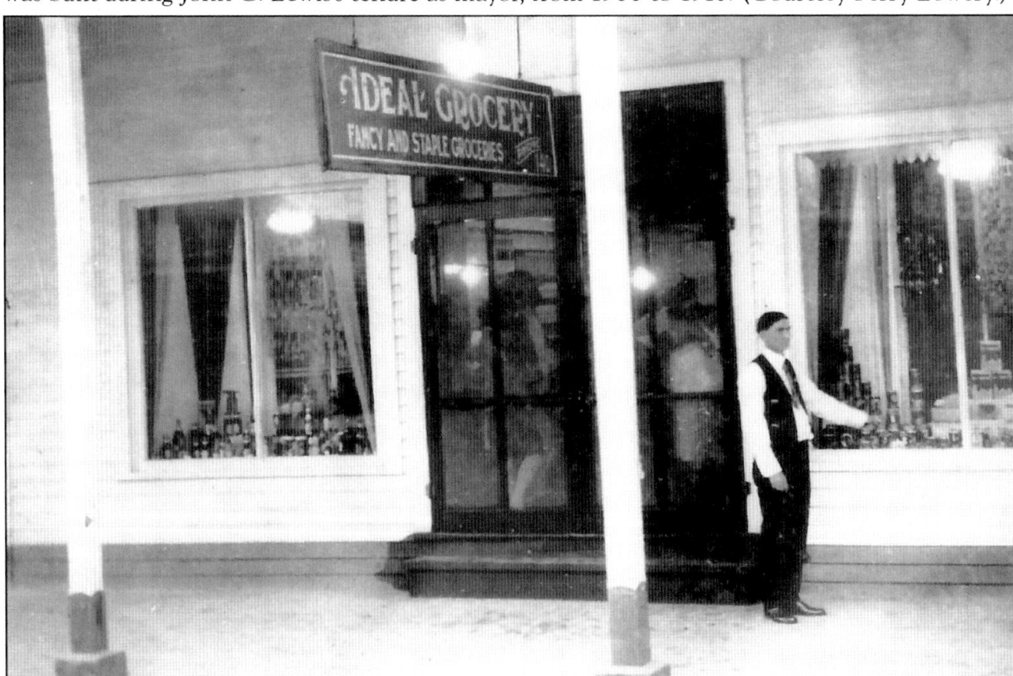

Ideal Grocery, on the corner of Main and Commercial Streets, was a grand example of a fine upscale grocery and one of the first buildings with electric lighting. The gentleman in front of the store is Samuel Romero. (Courtesy Perry Lowery.)

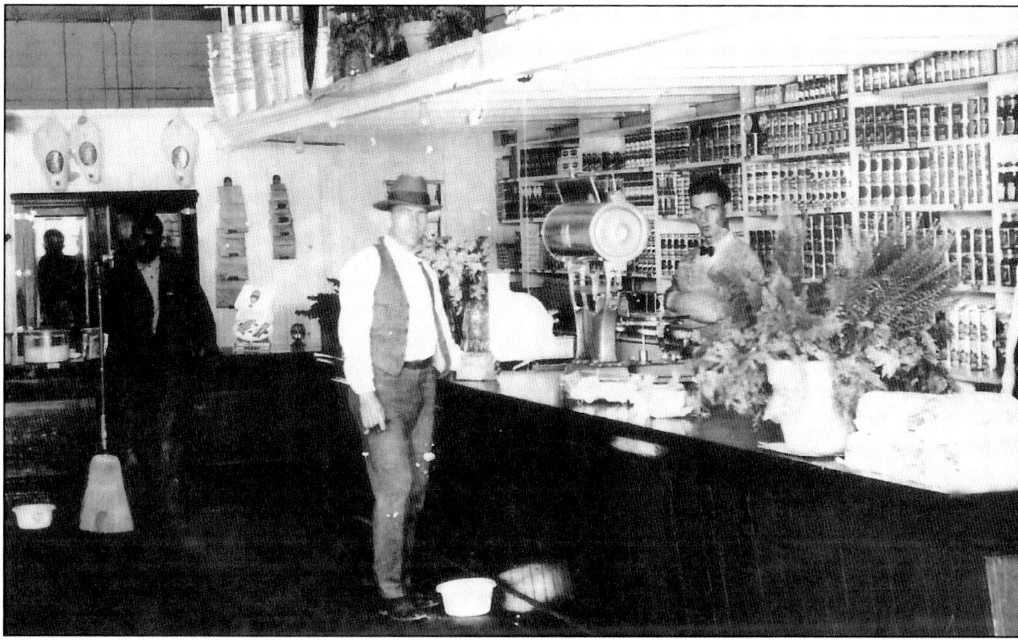

Ideal Grocery was known for offering fancy and staple groceries in a modern and beautiful store. The opportunity to shop in a clean store with stocked shelves and newfangled lighting was an exciting development for the community. (Courtesy Perry Lowery.)

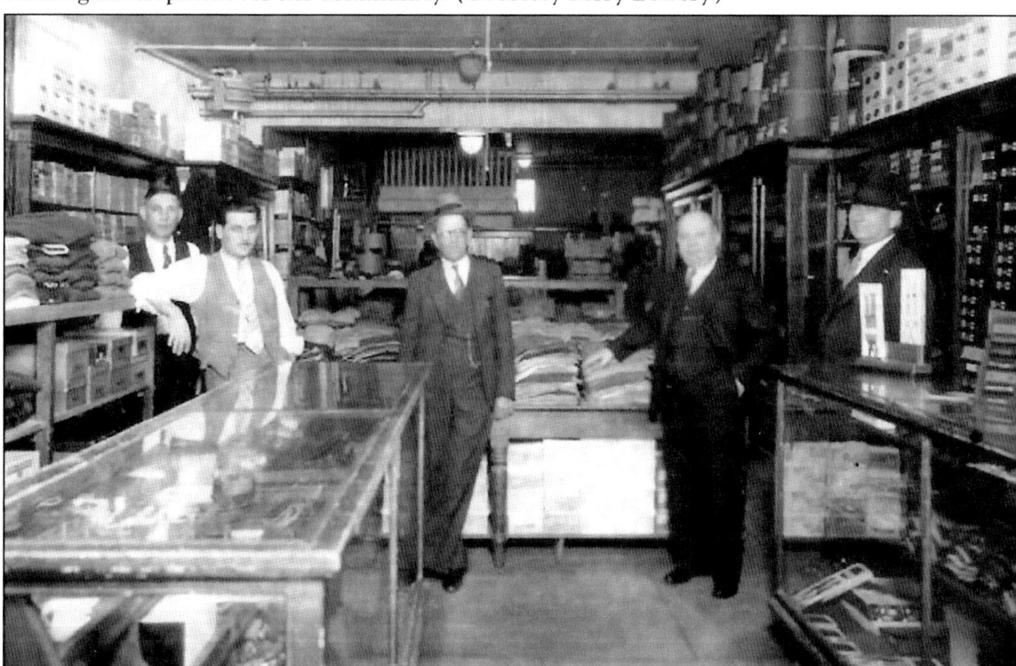

What is today known as the Lawless Building once housed Wormser's department store. Sewing and household supplies, gifts, and clothing for men, women, and children could be found there. The owner, Louis Wormser, is second from the right; Joe Cusimano is second from the left in the vest. (Courtesy Perry Lowery.)

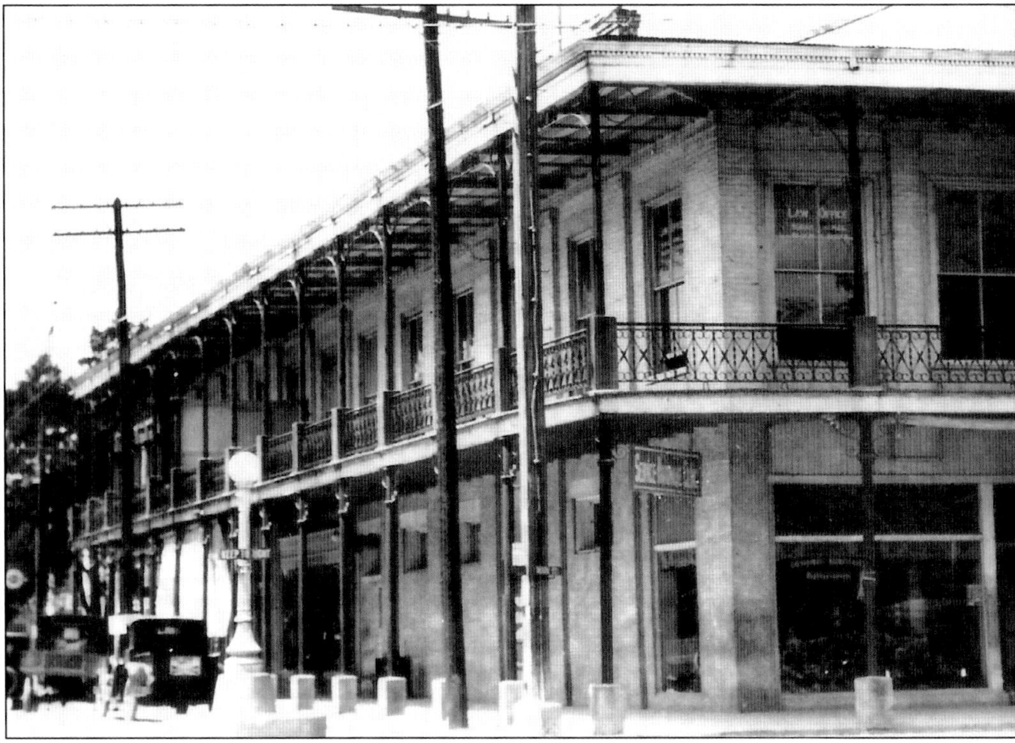

Wormser's department store was on the corner of Willow and Main Streets. This photograph was taken looking down Willow towards the new post office and the Old City Market. Wormser's occupied the old Union Hall (the original Old Opera House) with an interesting old roundabout used for traffic control. (Courtesy Perry Lowery.)

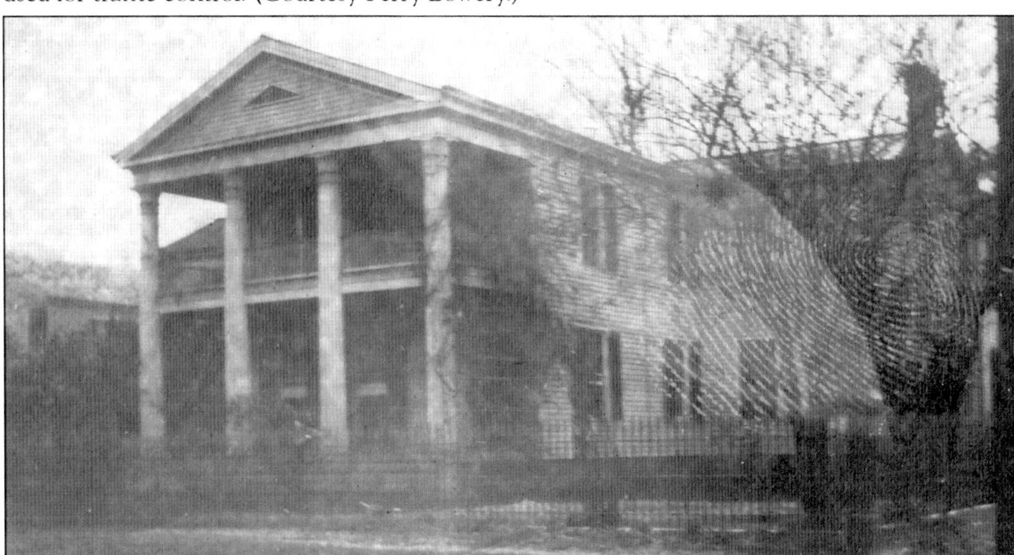

St. Mary Sanitarium was on Willow Street across from the post office. Built in 1835, it was Franklin's first hospital and was owned by Dr. Beverly Walker Smith from 1904 until his death in 1925. He was the first to own a horse-drawn ambulance and the first to own an automobile. (Courtesy Stephen Stirling.)

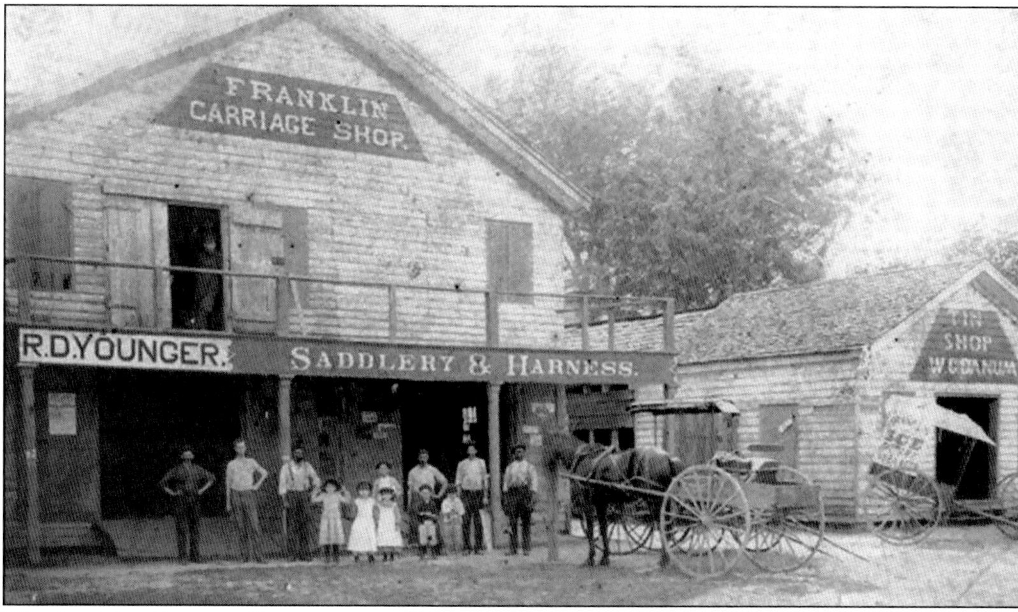

The Franklin Carriage Shop was a significant business entity in Franklin. Robert Wilson, the editor of the *Planters Banner*, had this to say about it in the May 1847 edition: "Resounding hammers wielded by blacksmiths and carriage makers beat out the tempo of the day as Franklin's business activity moved steadily forward during the decades before the Civil War." (Courtesy Perry Lowery.)

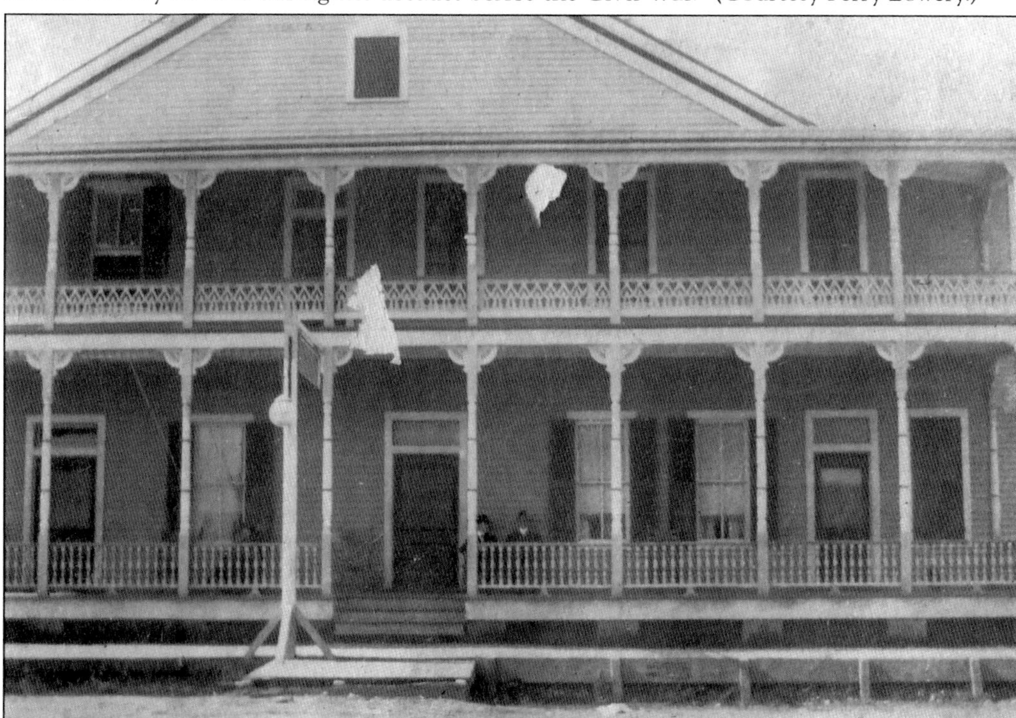

The original Commercial Hotel was located on Main Street. An article from the May 6, 1847, *Planters Banner* stated, "He had enlarged and improved his hotel and would be prepared to accommodate ladies and families in such a manner as to *ensure every comfort*." (Courtesy Perry Lowery.)

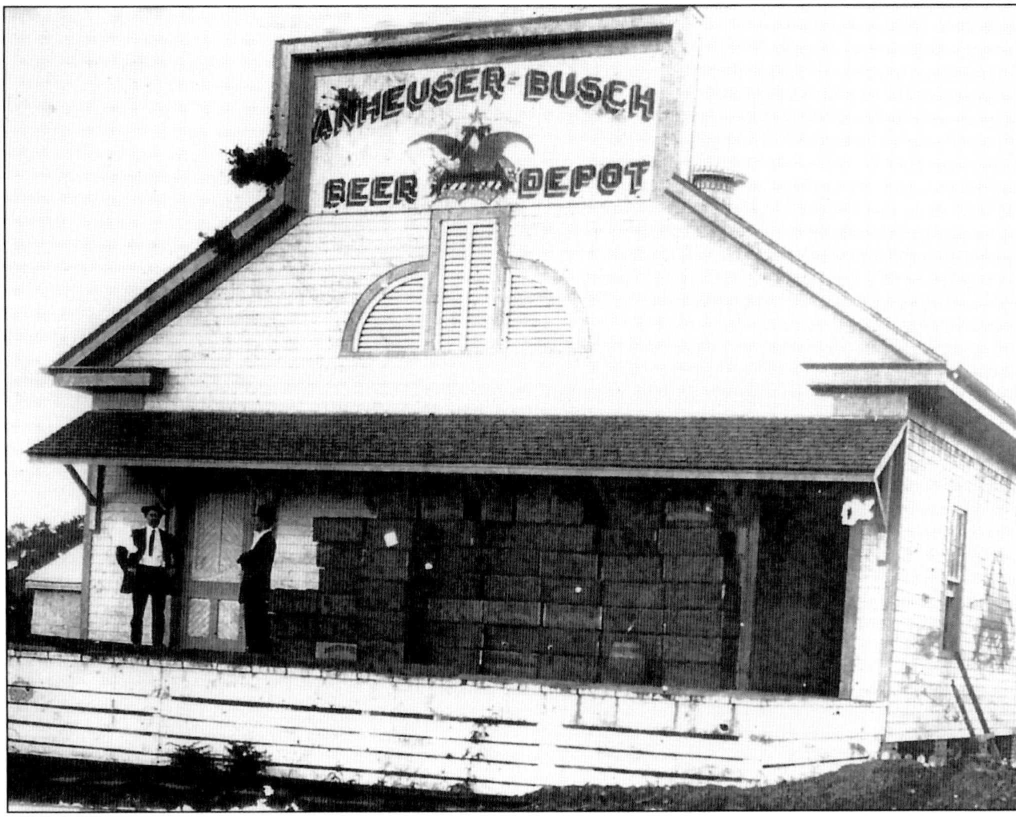

The Anheuser Busch depot was located on Anderson Street in Franklin next to the Southern Pacific Railroad depot. The Peerless Exchange, established in July 1886, was next to the depot in Baldwin. It boasted a line of first-class liquors, wines, cigars, cigarettes, and tobacco, as well as Anheuser Busch beer on tap. (Courtesy Perry Lowery.)

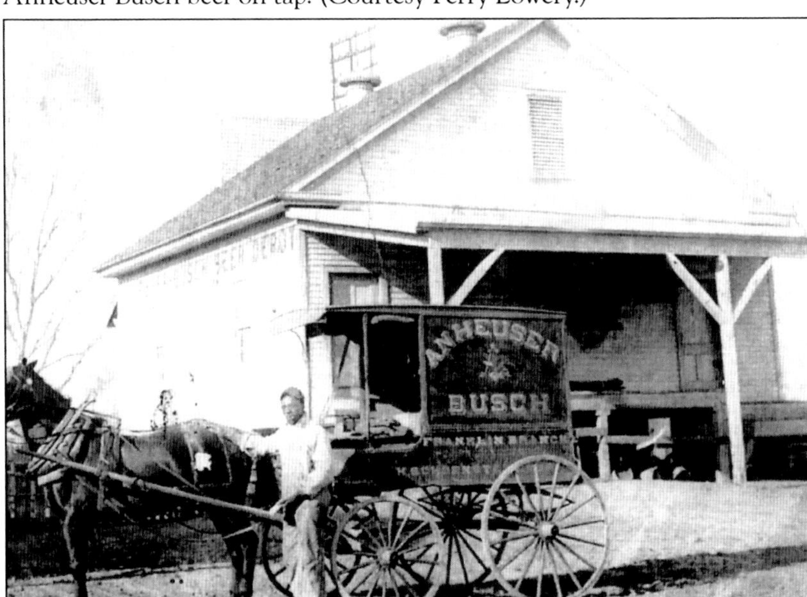

This is a rear view of the Anheuser Busch depot, on Anderson Street by the Southern Pacific tracks. The beer deliveryman shows off with his horse and delivery buggy, which served customers in the Franklin area. (Courtesy Perry Lowery.)

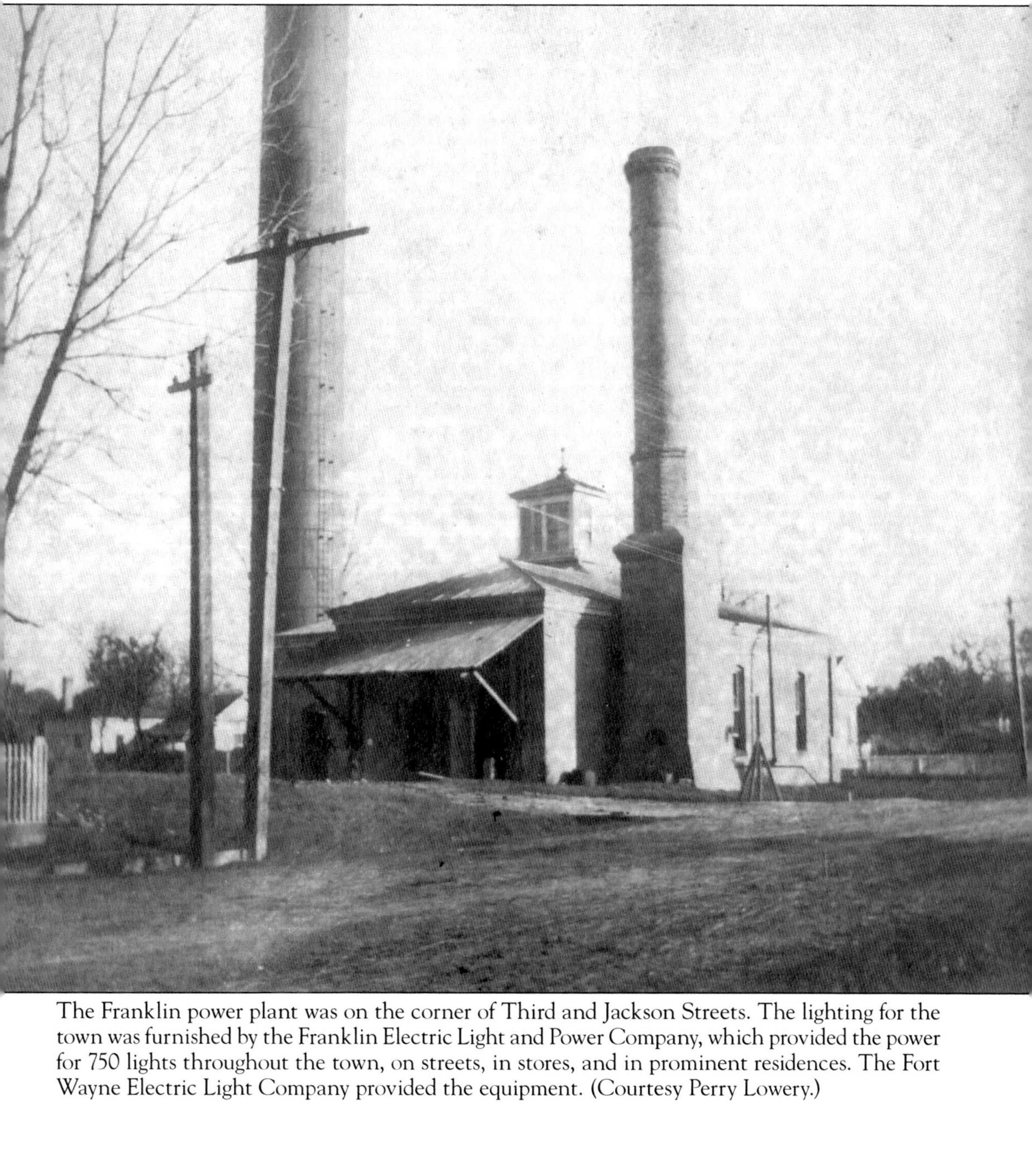

The Franklin power plant was on the corner of Third and Jackson Streets. The lighting for the town was furnished by the Franklin Electric Light and Power Company, which provided the power for 750 lights throughout the town, on streets, in stores, and in prominent residences. The Fort Wayne Electric Light Company provided the equipment. (Courtesy Perry Lowery.)

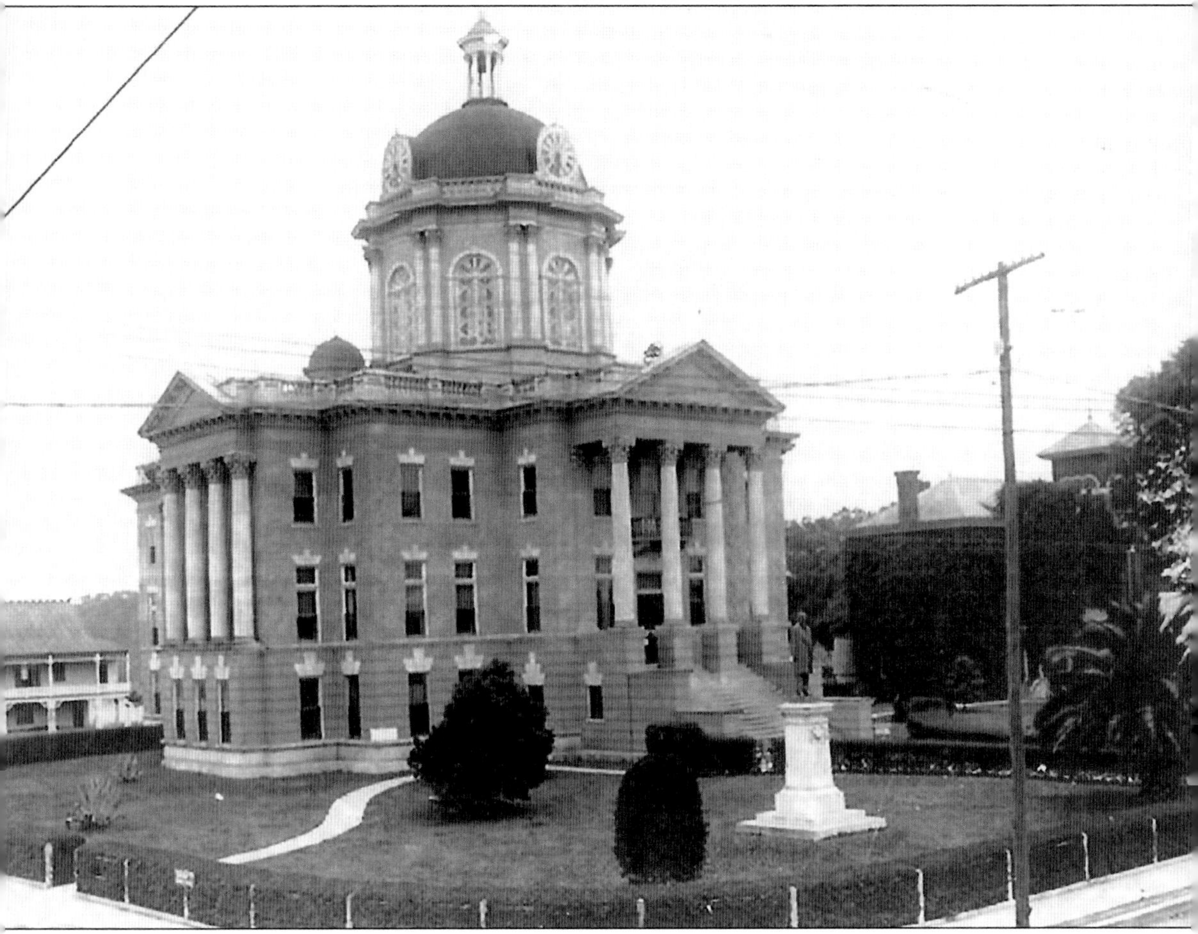

The first parish courthouse, which preceded the 1908 courthouse seen here, was a venerable relic of antebellum origin and was the center of jurisprudence in St. Mary Parish for more than 57 years before succumbing to the pressure of progress. At the beginning of the Civil War, the St. Mary Cannoneers organized all the soldiers on the steps of the first courthouse, which was 11 years old at the time, in a very impressive ceremony. With great patriotic pride, Louise McKerrall presented a silken flag of the Confederacy made from pieces of the town's ladies' petticoats, and told the soldiers, "Return with it and may its folds forever shield you." In 1908, the old courthouse was torn down and this new courthouse was constructed amid much dissenting opinion. The architecture was reminiscent of the renaissance period, with three floors built of tan brick and concrete and an open center rotunda crowned with a copper dome and topped by the tin figure of Justice. (Courtesy Perry Lowery.)

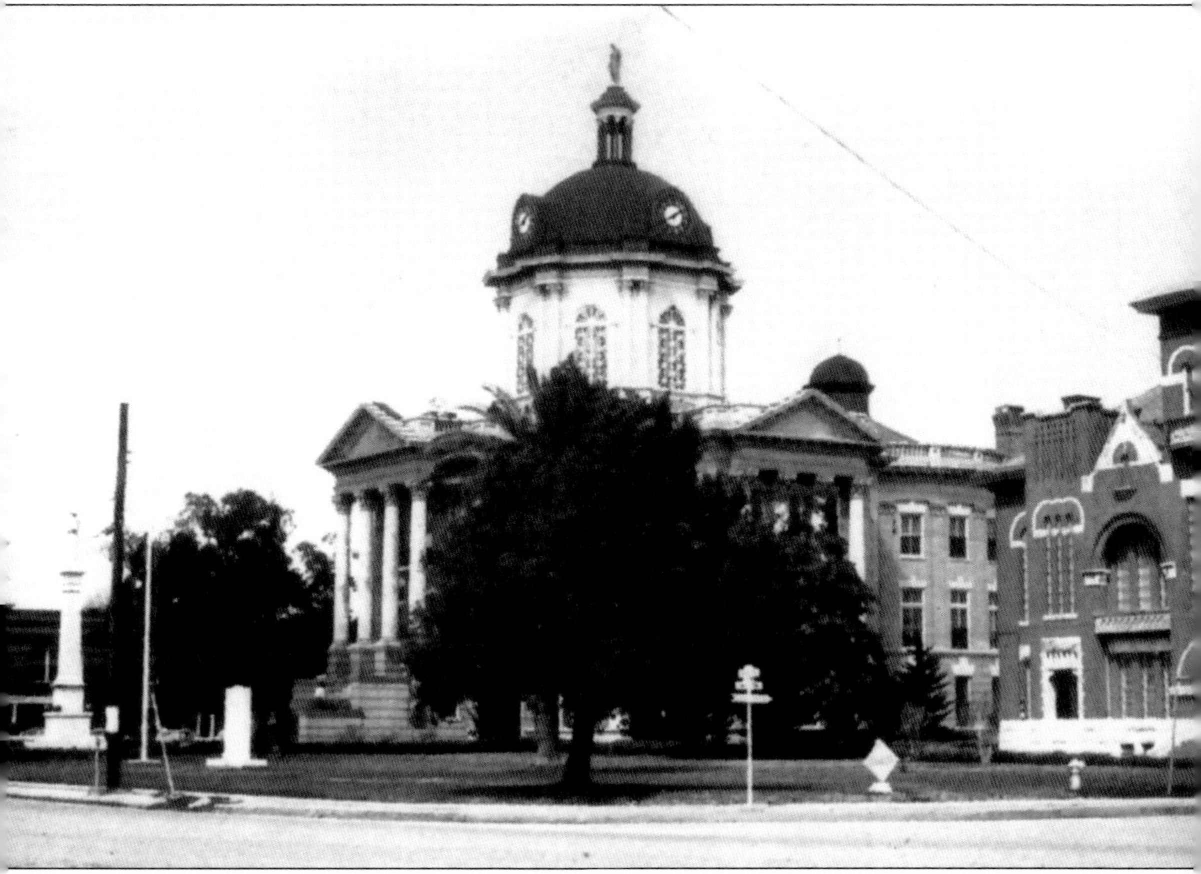

The courthouse complex contained the courthouse, the jail, and the health unit. Franklin's 1847 jail is reported to have adequately provided for the necessities of the prisoners, according to a description in the May 20, 1847, issue of the *Planters Banner.* The new jail, built in 1896, was the site of the hanging of convicted murderers Ada Bonner Leboeuf and Dr. Tomas Dreher on February 1, 1929. (Courtesy Perry Lowery.)

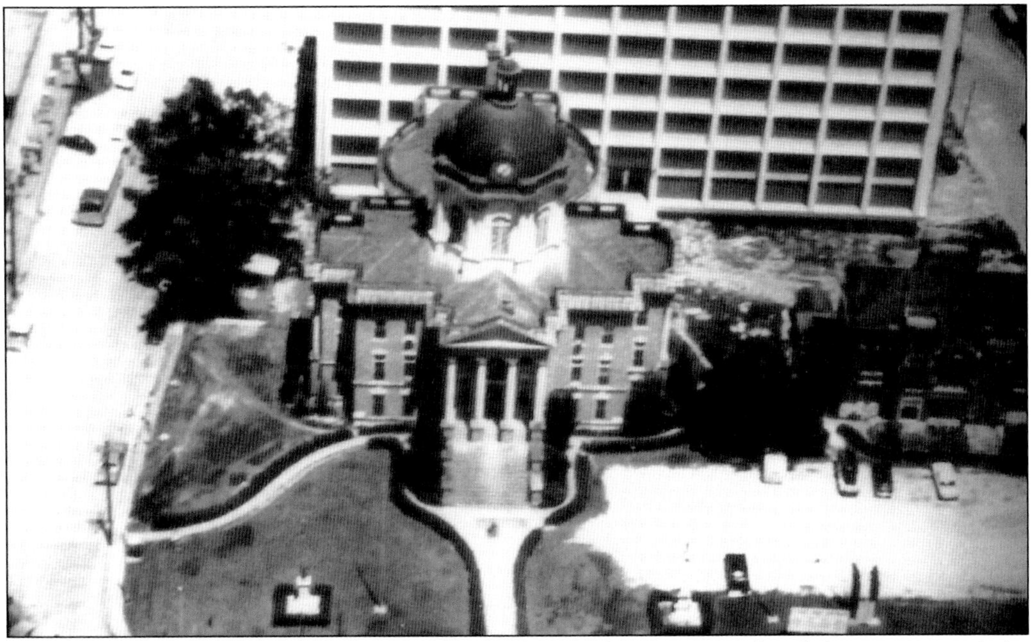

In Alexander Guinea Lewis's land donation to the parish, it was stipulated that it must only be used for a courthouse. In 1969, the 1908 Franklin courthouse was replaced with the third, present-day courthouse. In this photograph, the older building sits in stunning contrast to the new, more modern complex. (Courtesy Perry Lowery.)

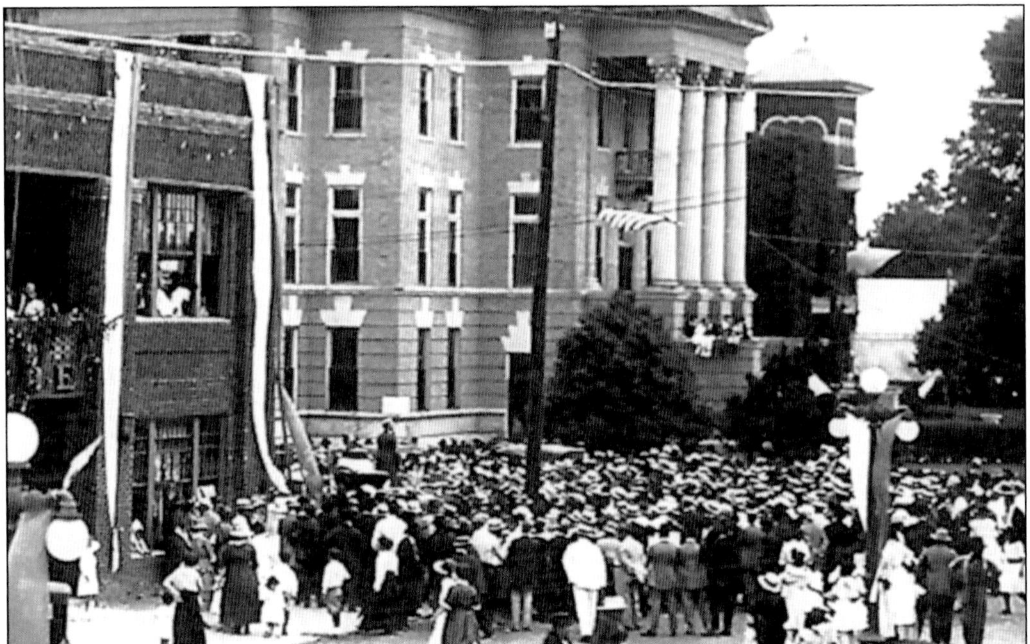

The Elks have been a moving force in Franklin and St. Mary since 1920. Having used the Max Silverman building for a number of years as well as the Blevins Building, the Elks eventually built their own facility on Commercial Street. A celebration of the dedication of the Elks Lodge was held in the courthouse square. (Courtesy Perry Lowery.)

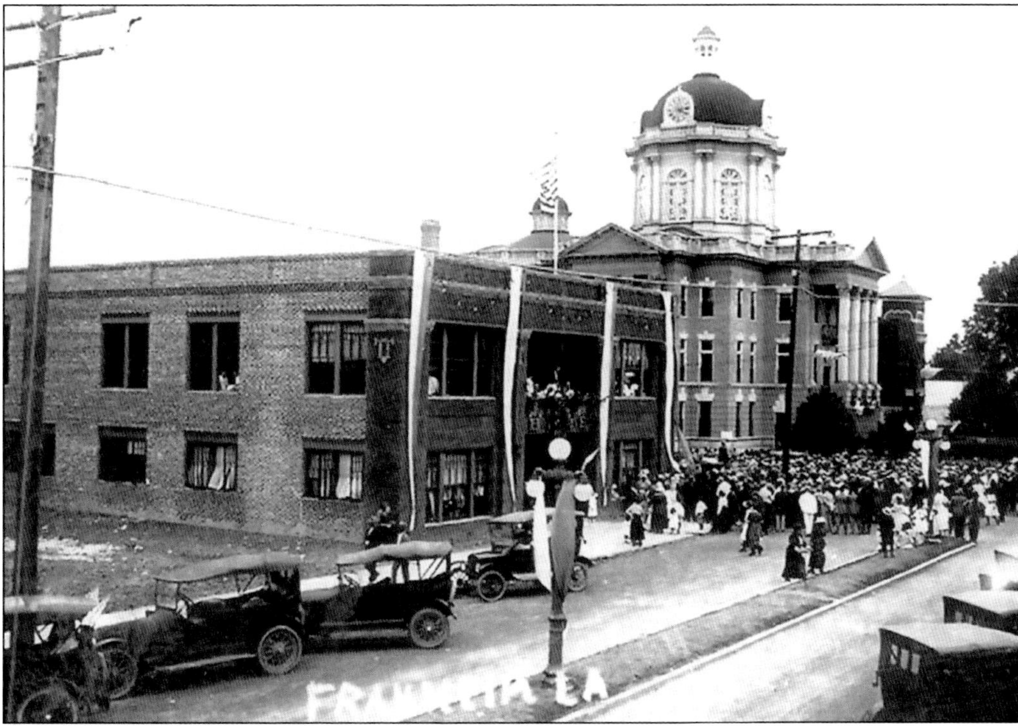

Before building on Commercial Street, the Elks lodge met in the building on the left, before the courthouse, now known as the Blevins Building. A long-time favorite program was "Bucktown," an annual fair and festival held to raise money to finance construction of the first Elks Home. (Courtesy Perry Lowery.)

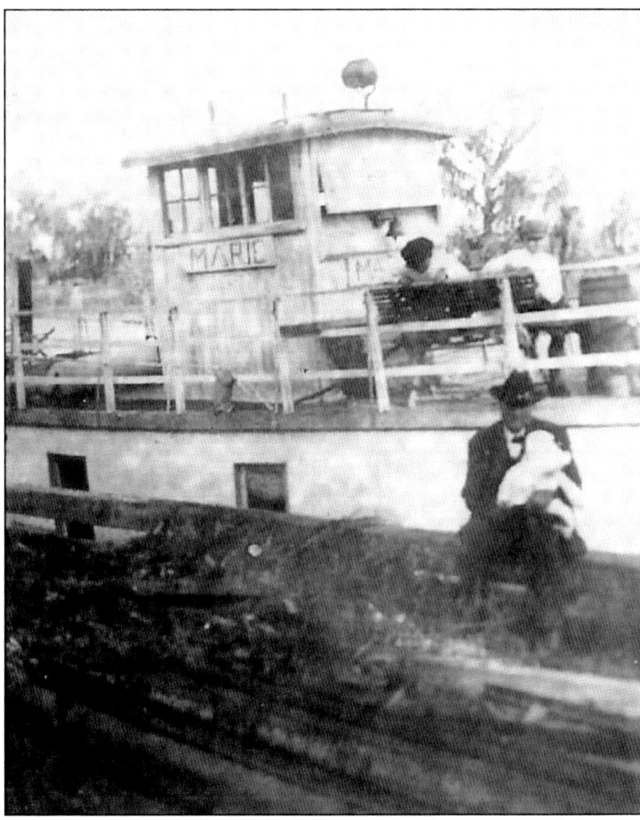

The Sternwheeler *Marie* was owned and operated by Capt. Eugene Carl Tyler. It often docked at the foot of Adams Street in order to load and unload passengers and cargo. (Courtesy Stephen Stirling.)

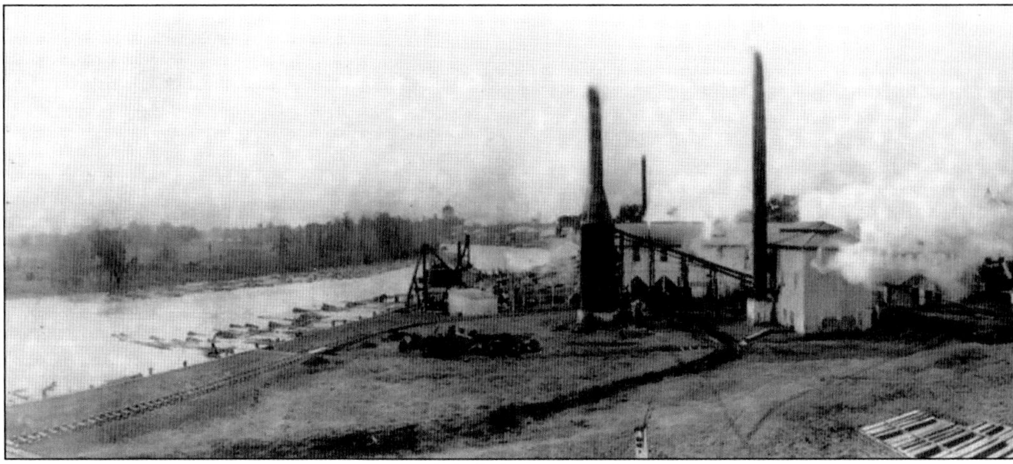

The Kyle Lumber Company employed more than 75 people in its Franklin operation, with a peak capacity of 75,000 to 80,000 board feet of lumber daily. It was founded by William Kyle on February 4, 1896, along the banks of the Bayou Teche. (Courtesy Tony Scelfo.)

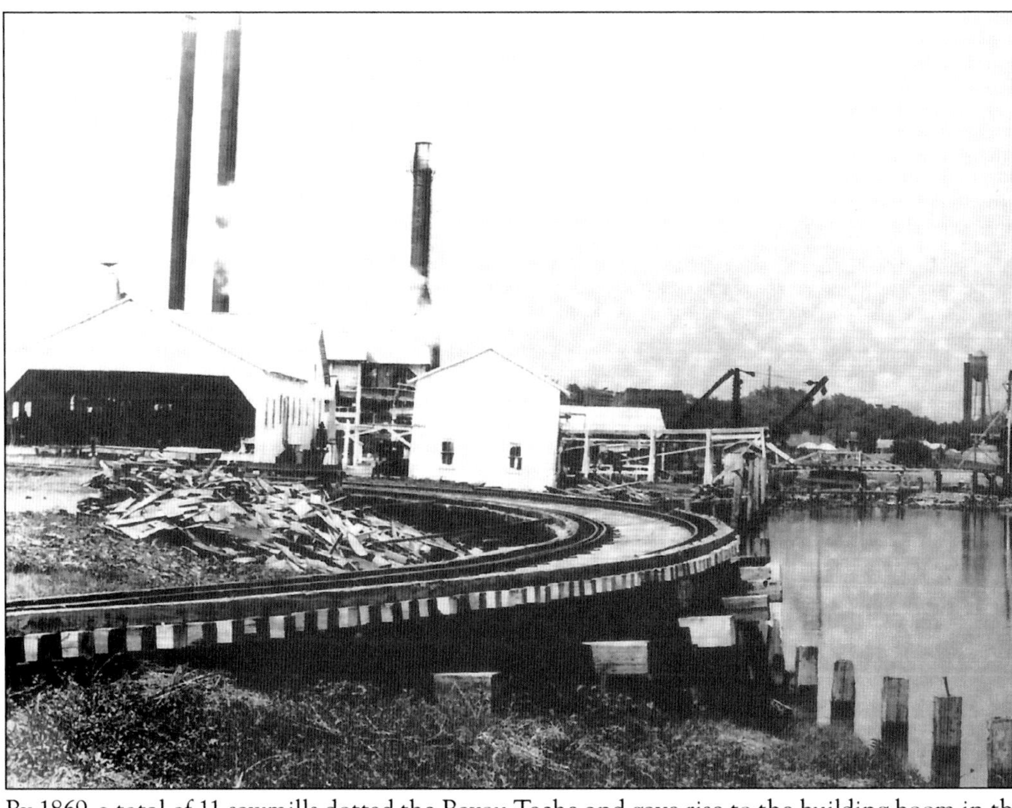

By 1869, a total of 11 sawmills dotted the Bayou Teche and gave rise to the building boom in the community and surrounding states. (Courtesy Perry Lowery.)

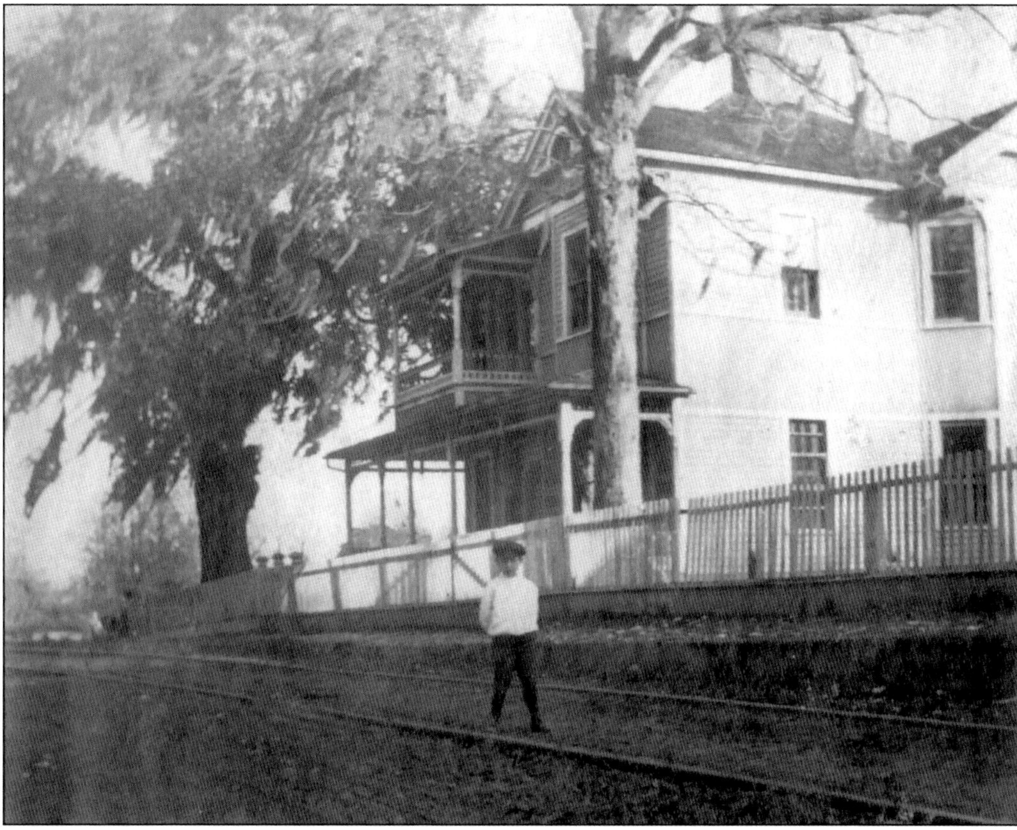

The Dummy Rail was a narrow-gauge railroad track carrying lumber from Kyle Lumber Company at the end of Adams Street, near Shadowlawn, down Adams Street to the Southern Pacific Railroad depot on Anderson Street. (Courtesy Stephen Stirling.)

This was the labor force working at the Kyle-Taylor lumber mill, which unfortunately burned in 1897 and was not covered by insurance. Thanks to the assistance of Edward Hanson and Frank Williams, credit was extended and the mill was rebuilt that year. It later became the Blakesley–St. John Lumberyard. (Courtesy Perry Lowery.)

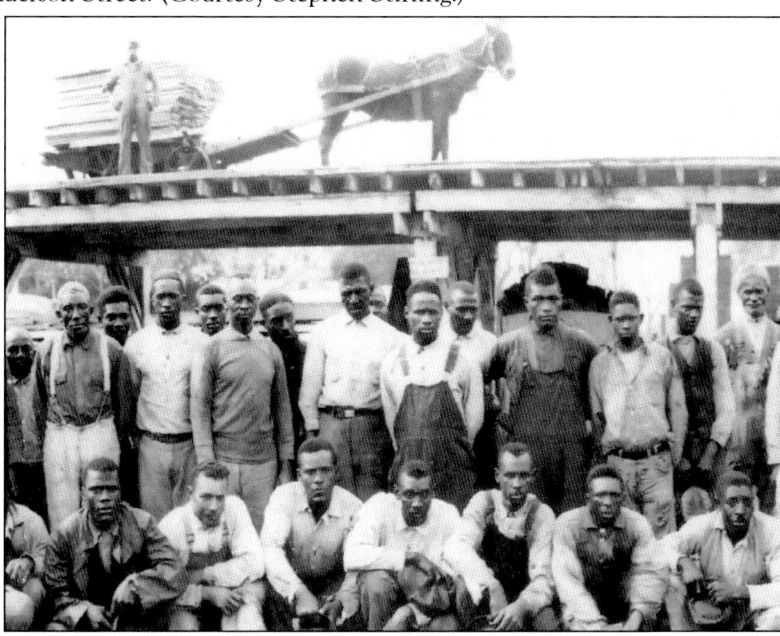

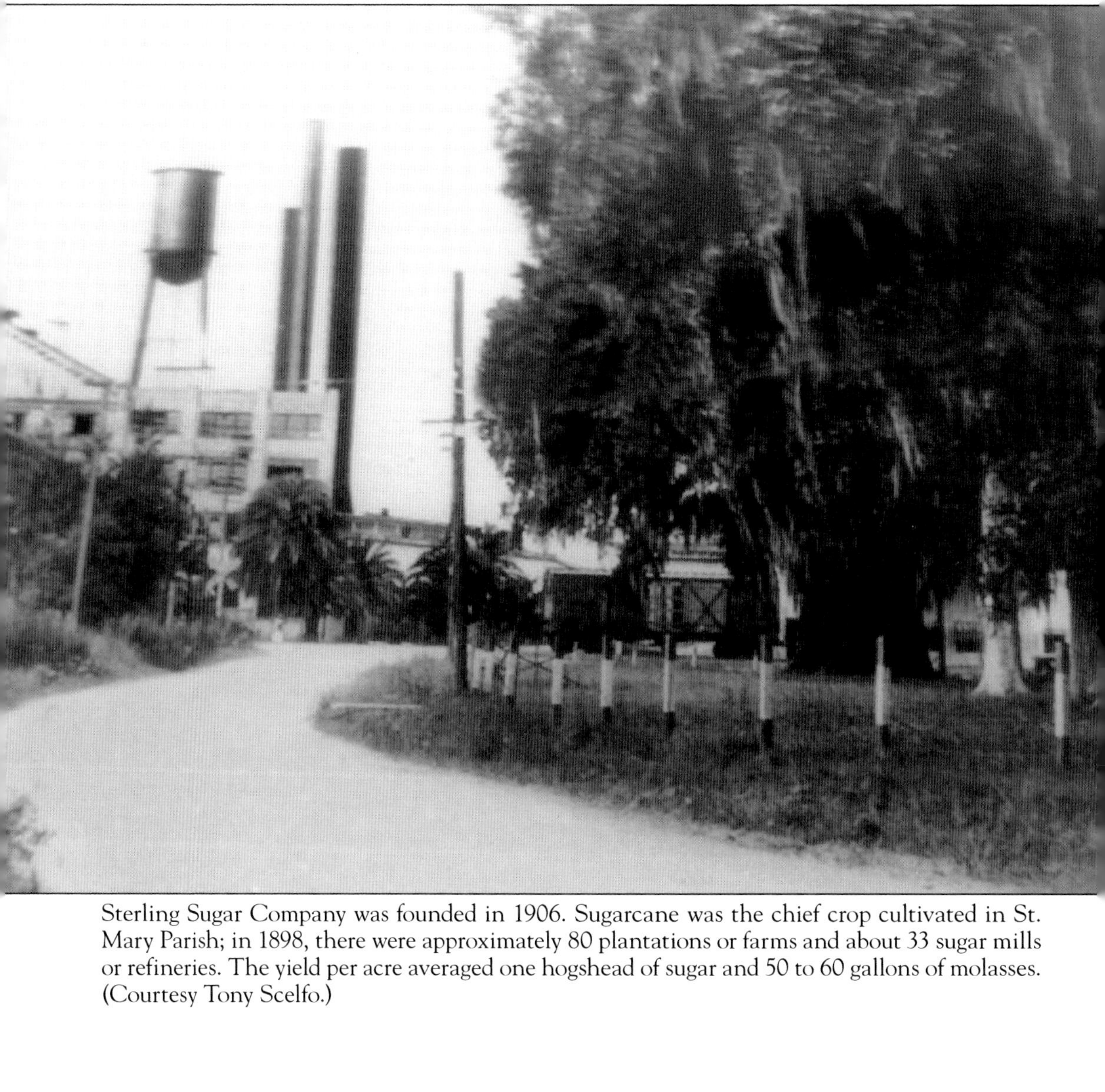

Sterling Sugar Company was founded in 1906. Sugarcane was the chief crop cultivated in St. Mary Parish; in 1898, there were approximately 80 plantations or farms and about 33 sugar mills or refineries. The yield per acre averaged one hogshead of sugar and 50 to 60 gallons of molasses. (Courtesy Tony Scelfo.)

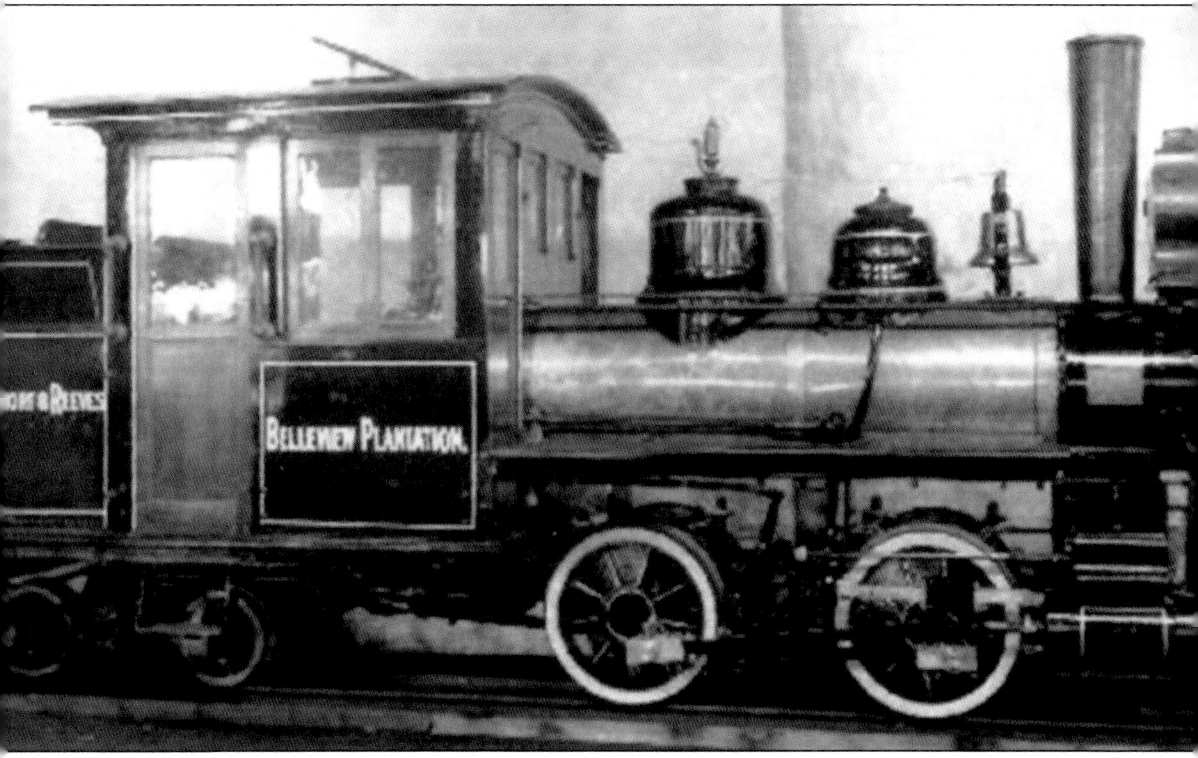

Small steam locomotives were used in the sugarcane fields for hauling cut cane to the refinery for processing. The tracks would be laid down by hand by the field workers before the locomotive from field to field, and then moved to the next location. (Courtesy Perry Lowery.)

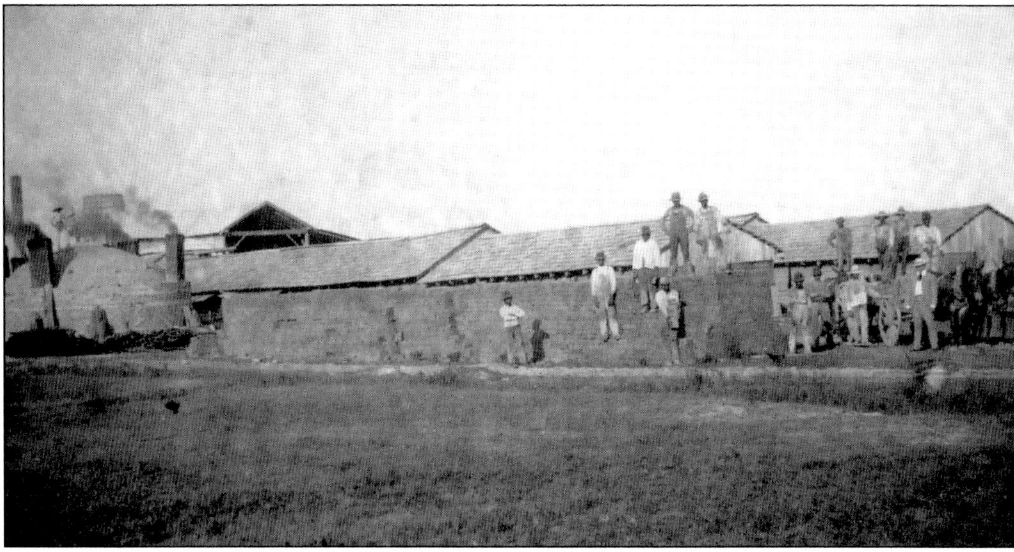

Tom Bodin Brickyard was near Dixie Plantation, the home of Murphy James Foster (1849–1921), a prominent St. Mary Parish landowner and lawyer during Reconstruction. Employees are seen here standing on finished bricks around 1925. This plant consisted of an improved common brick press, with 35,000 bricks, and four sheds containing 150,000 bricks. There was blue, yellow, and white clay in the plot of ground from which the bricks were made. There were shipping facilities for both rail and water transport. (Courtesy Perry Lowery.)

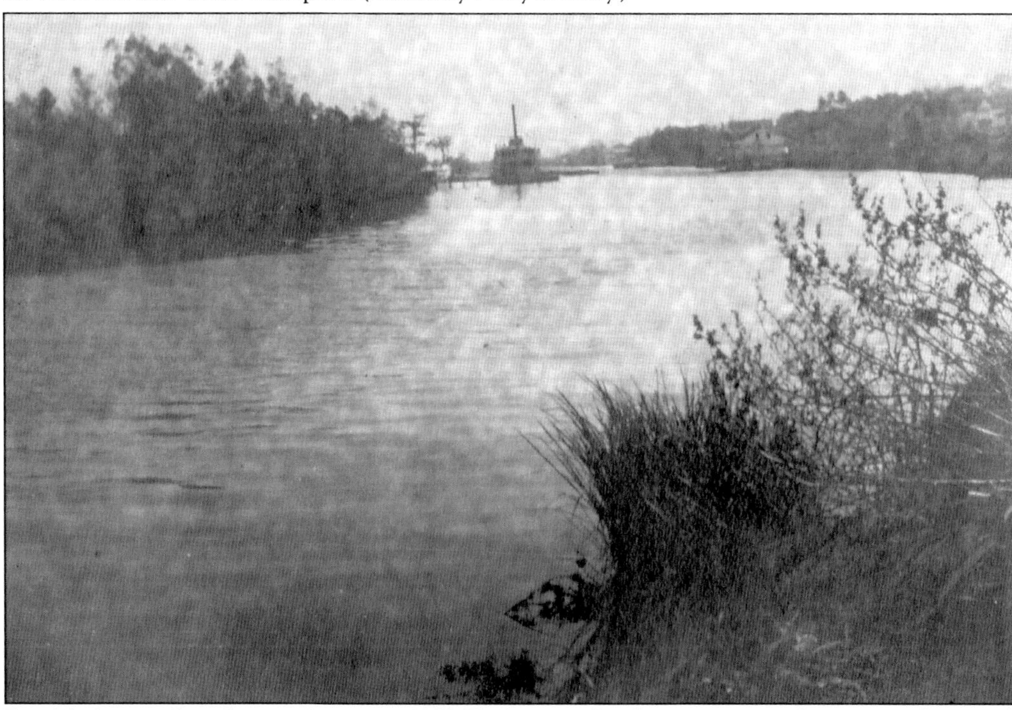

Franklin's steamboat history began in 1835. Early in its development, steamboats were frequently seen heading up or down the Bayou Teche. Boats with names like *Experiment* and *Belle of Attakapas* traveled the waterways with supplies and passengers until 1879, when the railroad was completed. (Courtesy Stephen Stirling.)

This steam locomotive is moving finished lumber through a field. Before highways and automobiles came into the picture, seemingly everyone rode the train. The railroad offered good freight and passenger service and the trains usually ran on time. (Courtesy Stephen Stirling.)

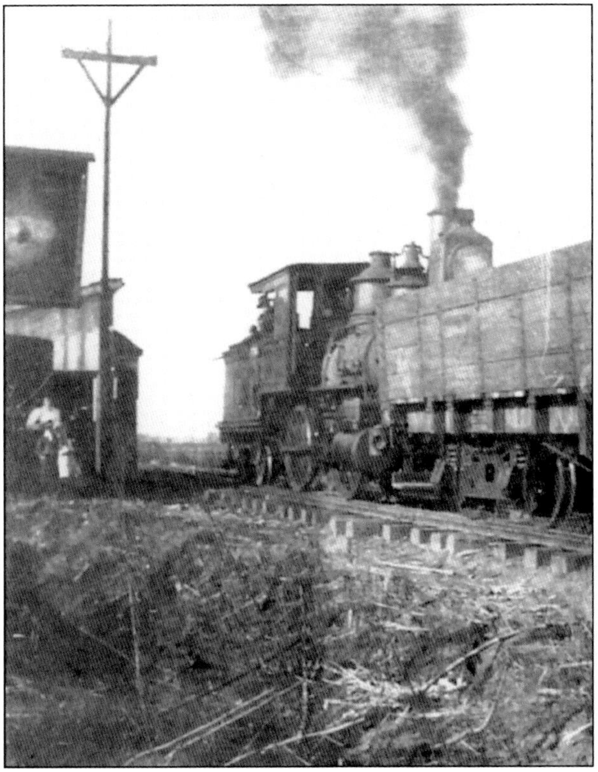

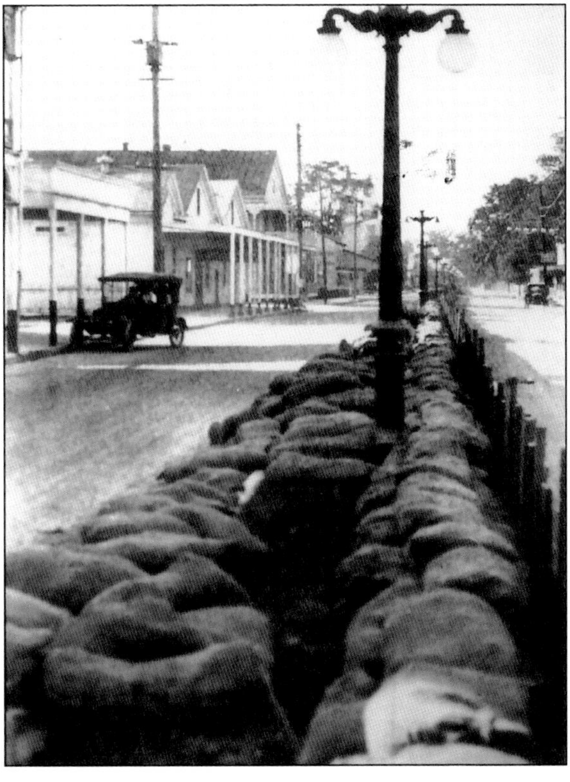

Much of St. Mary Parish lies within a 100-year floodplain, and over the years, it has seen its share of rising waters. Here, on Main Street in Franklin, hundreds of sandbags are piled against wooden stakes next to the boulevard to create a flood-protection barrier. (Courtesy Perry Lowery.)

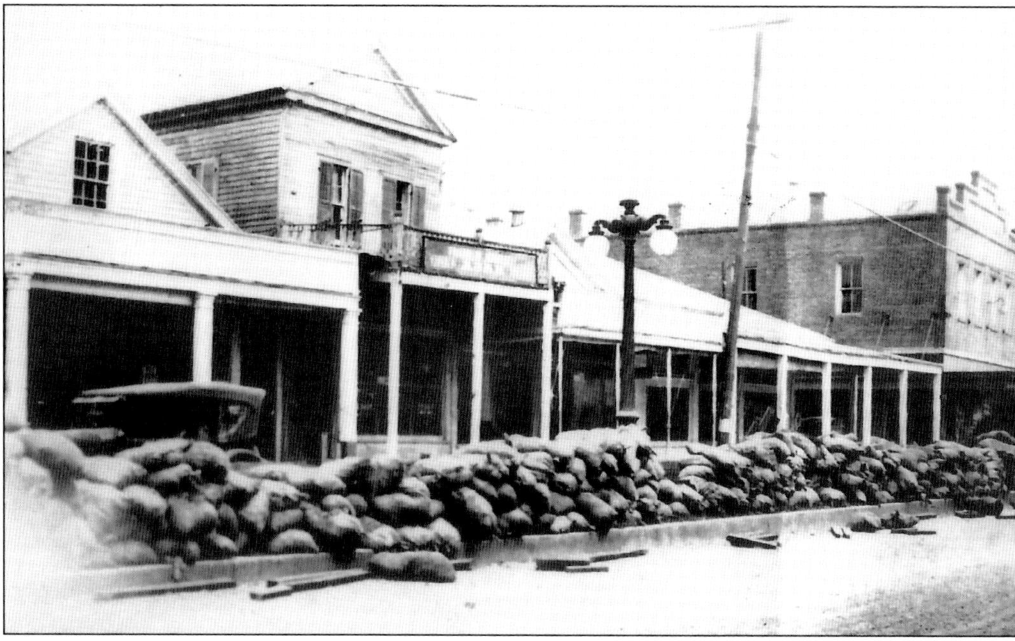

Flood damage was a threat to many buildings along Main Street during the flood of 1927. These lampposts had movable arms that could be rotated to avoid damage during sugarcane season or times of heavy traffic. (Courtesy Perry Lowery.)

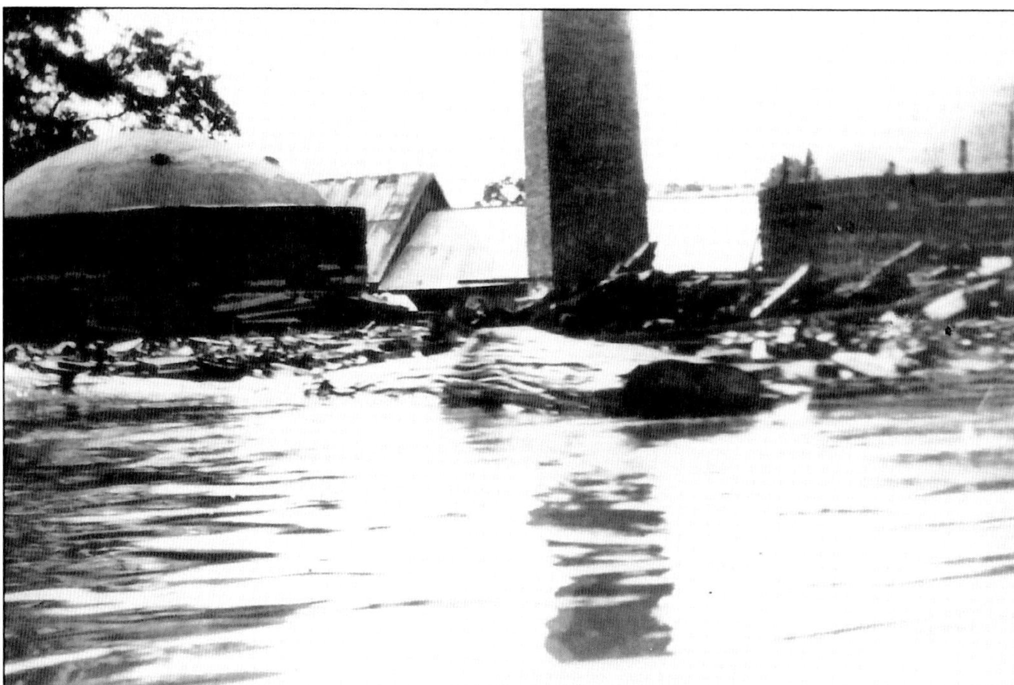

Millholland Brickyard, on Sterling Road, was one of many businesses that depended upon the waterway for commerce and faced the threat of severe flooding that could damage or totally destroy the business. In the foreground, the kilns of the brickyard are surrounded by floodwaters. (Courtesy Perry Lowery.)

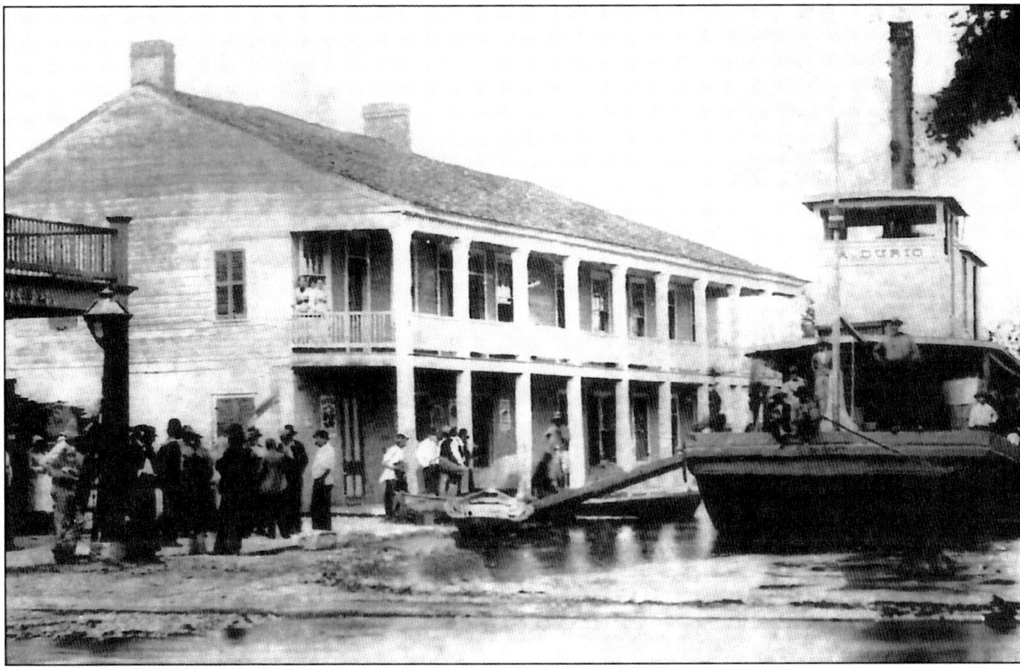

The famous O'Niell Hotel was on Willow Street near the Bayou Teche. The floodwaters of 1927 came high enough over the bank that a boat came within a few feet of the door. Thankfully, the high water generally receded quickly and life resumed its normal leisurely pace. (Courtesy Perry Lowery.)

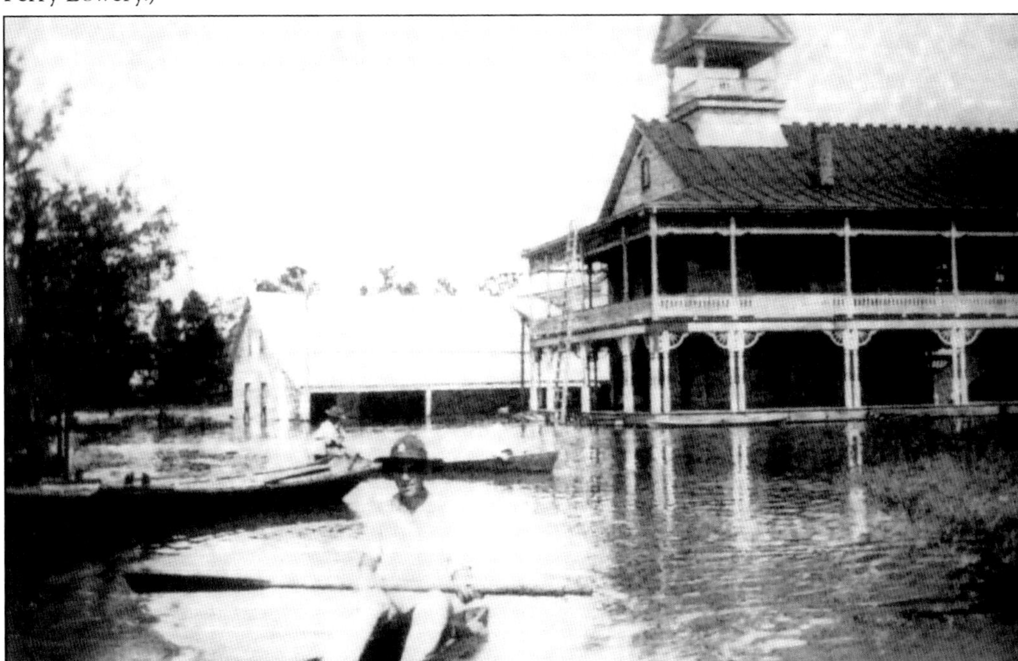

The flood of 1882 engulfed the town hall and what would become the *St. Mary Banner* newspaper office, which started in 1889 on Willow Street near the Bayou Teche. The town hall building was sold by the St. Mary police jury and torn down in April 1959. (Courtesy Perry Lowery.)

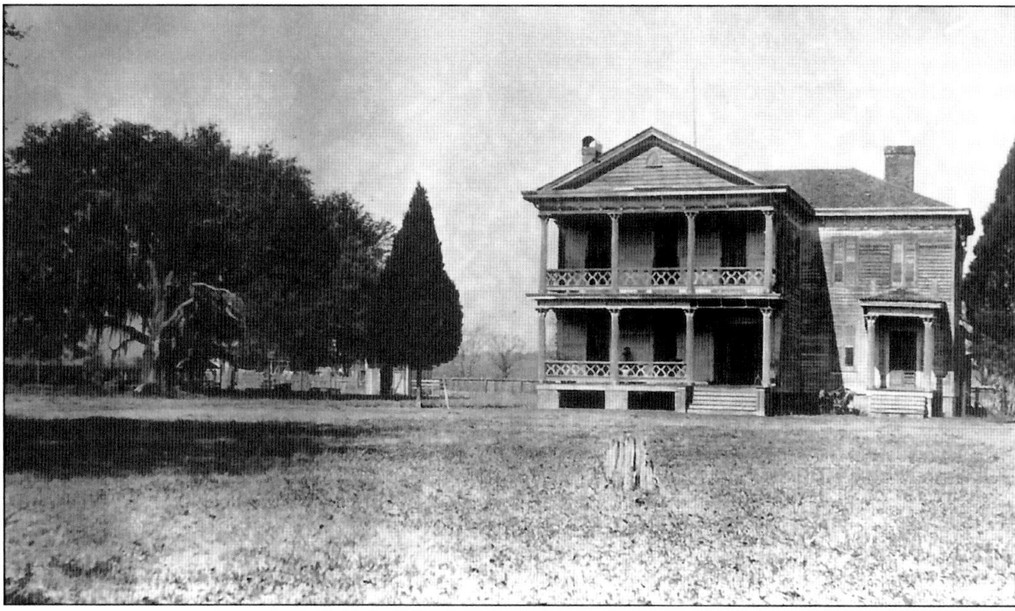

The Gibbons House, on Sterling Road, was one of many large homes dotting the landscape outside of town, but still within a comfortable carriage ride to church or shops. As was typical of most homes in south Louisiana, it was made of cypress wood and had wide cooling galleries with decorative millwork railings. Sadly, this home burned in 1938. (Courtesy Perry Lowery.)

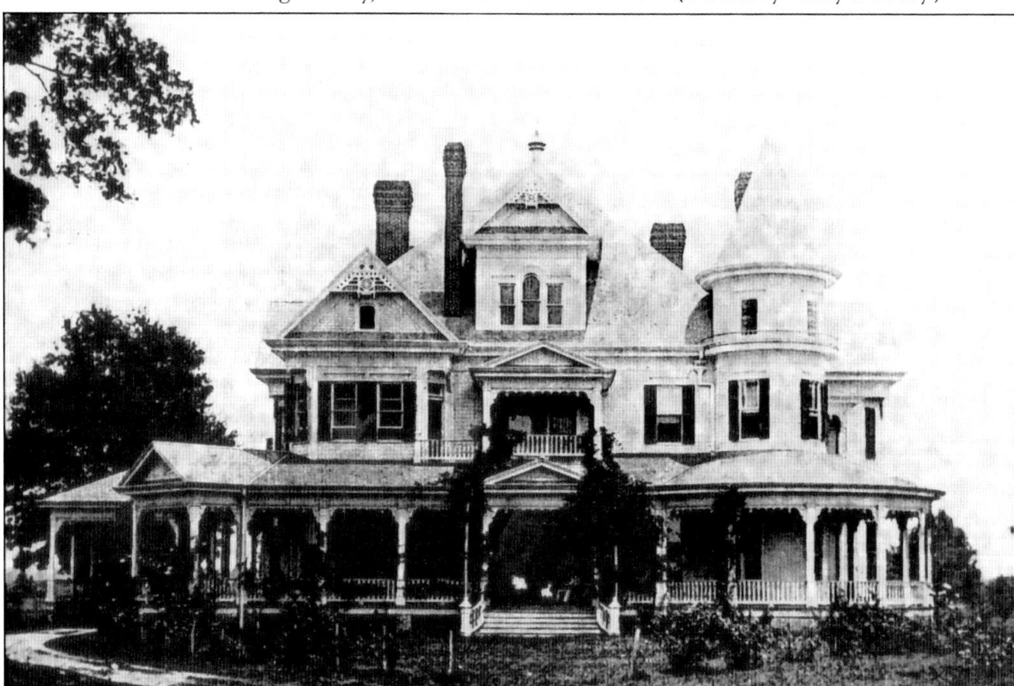

The Schaffer House, on Irish Bend Road near Medric Martin's store, was a charming, unique Victorian. The home had multiple gabled roofs, a turret, expansive front and side galleries, and bracketed turned posts. It was certainly a house of immense and grand proportions and was sadly torn down in the 1930s. (Courtesy Stephen Stirling.)

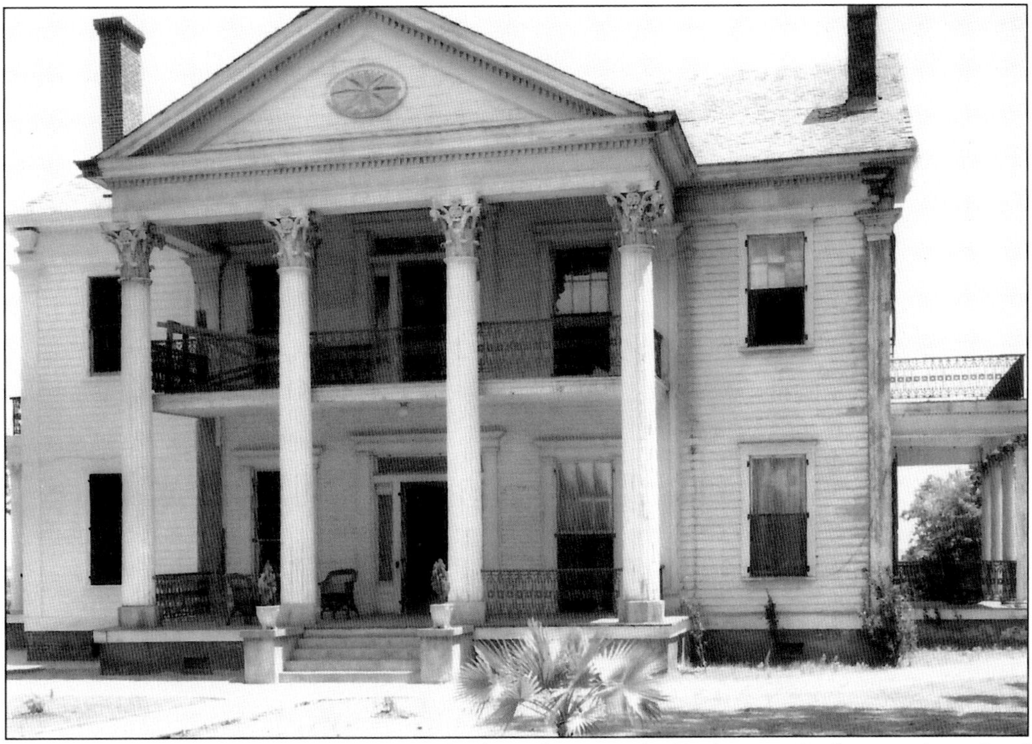

The antebellum mansion Arlington was built in the 1830s by Euphroisie Carlin on a large land grant from Spain. This magnificent Corinthian-columned home is on Highway 182 just east of Franklin and dates to the early plantation history of the area. (Courtesy Perry Lowery.)

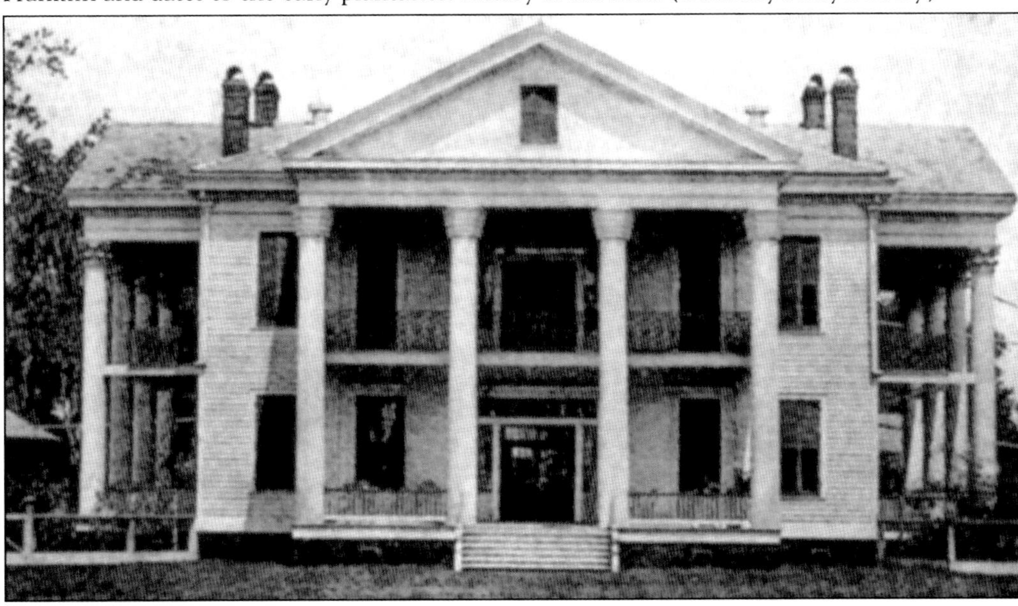

Haifleigh House was the home of Sen. Donald Caffery in the early 1900s. The Greek Revival home was made of cypress and had large Corinthian columns, matching side porticos, and lower and upper galleries. The house was occupied by Senator Caffery's son, Ralph Earl Caffery, at the time it was destroyed by fire in 1940. (Courtesy Perry Lowery.)

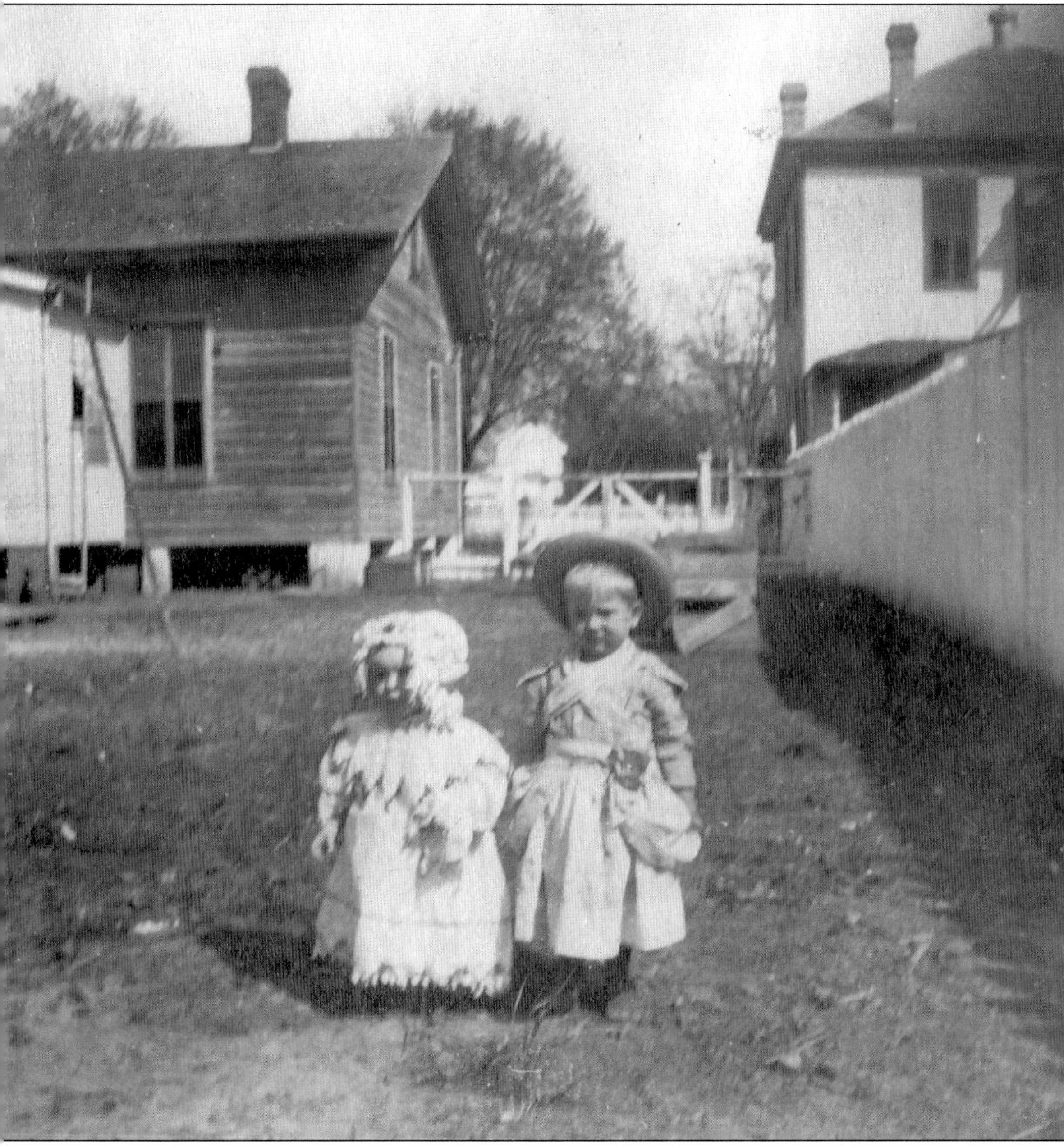

The young boy on the right in this photograph is Paul Taylor. The photograph was most likely taken by Caroline Gertrude Lyman, a prolific photographer in the late 1800s and early 1900s, at her home on Adams Street. Lyman was credited with having opened a private school in 1895 in a one-room cabin. (Courtesy Stephen Stirling.)

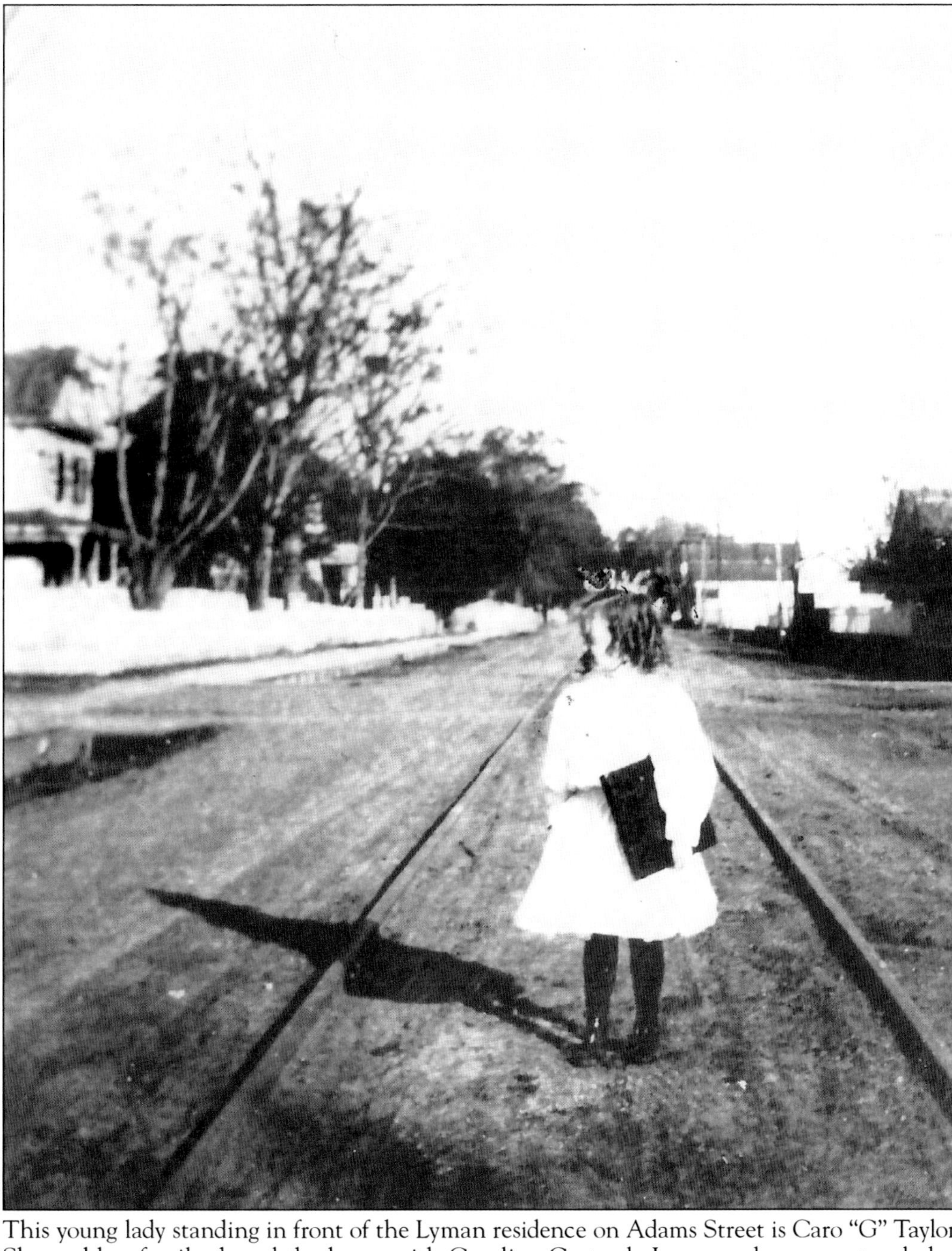

This young lady standing in front of the Lyman residence on Adams Street is Caro "G" Taylor. She and her family shared the home with Caroline Gertrude Lyman, who was not only her namesake, but also her aunt and godmother. Caro "G" Taylor was Stephen Stirling's grandmother. (Courtesy Stephen Stirling.)

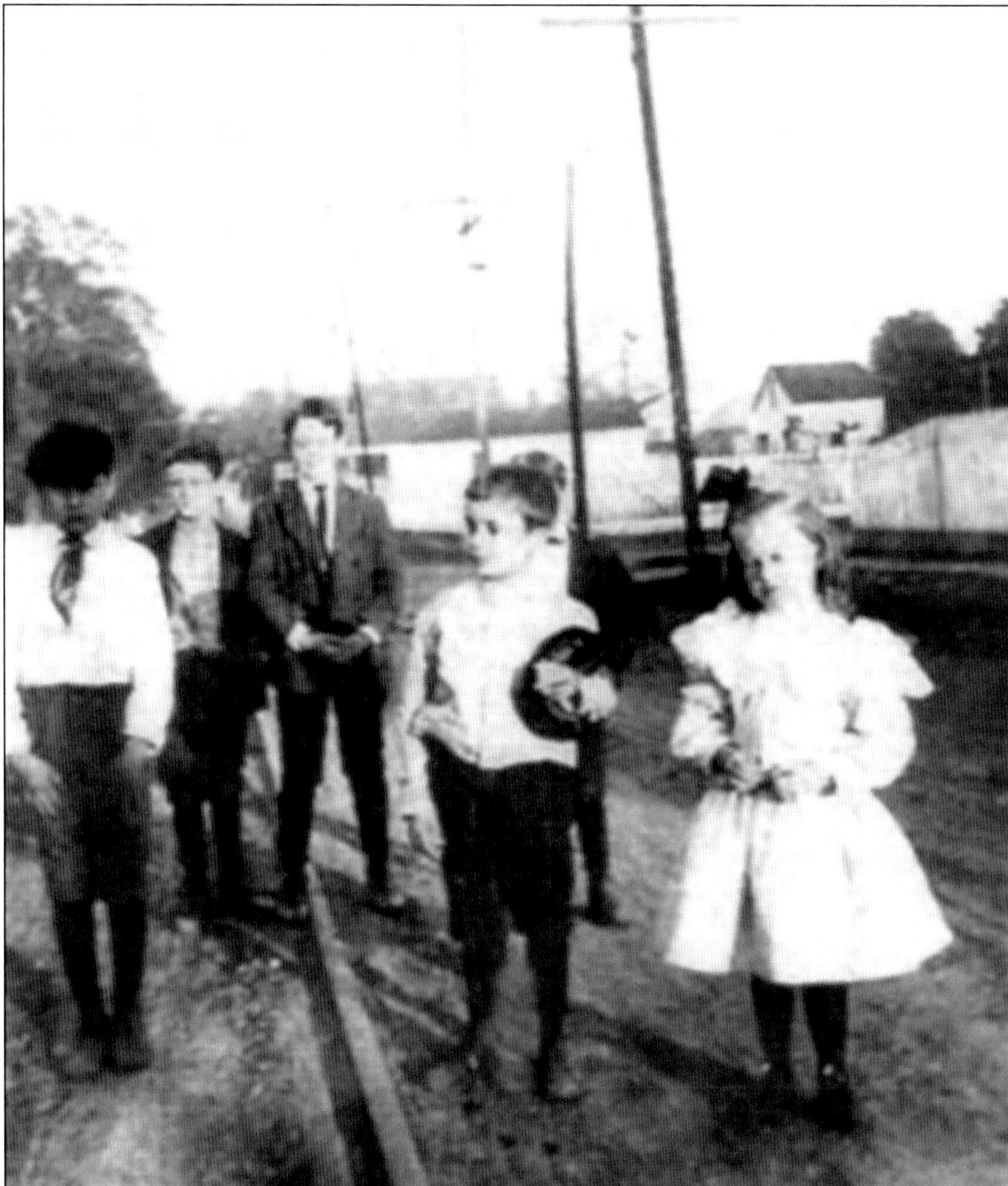

A young Caro "G" Taylor, on the far right, and George Taylor, with hat, pose with a group of children on Adams Street between First and Second Streets. Notice the rails that ran down Adams Street, connecting the Kyle Lumber Company on the Bayou Teche to the Anderson Street railway depot. (Courtesy Stephen Stirling.)

Caro "G" Taylor, on the left in her new Easter dress, strikes a pose outside her home on Adams Street. In custom millinery in the finest styles of the day, the young ladies were as beautifully dressed as their mothers for Easter Sunday services. (Courtesy Stephen Stirling.)

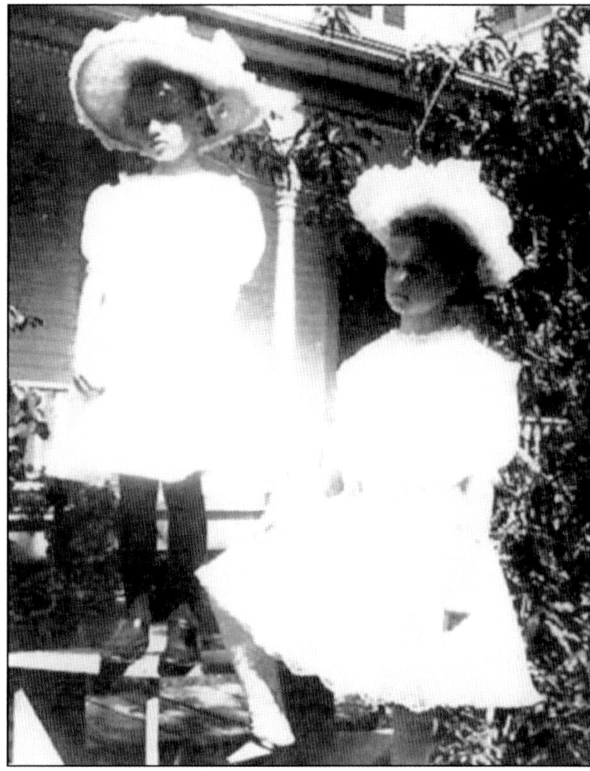

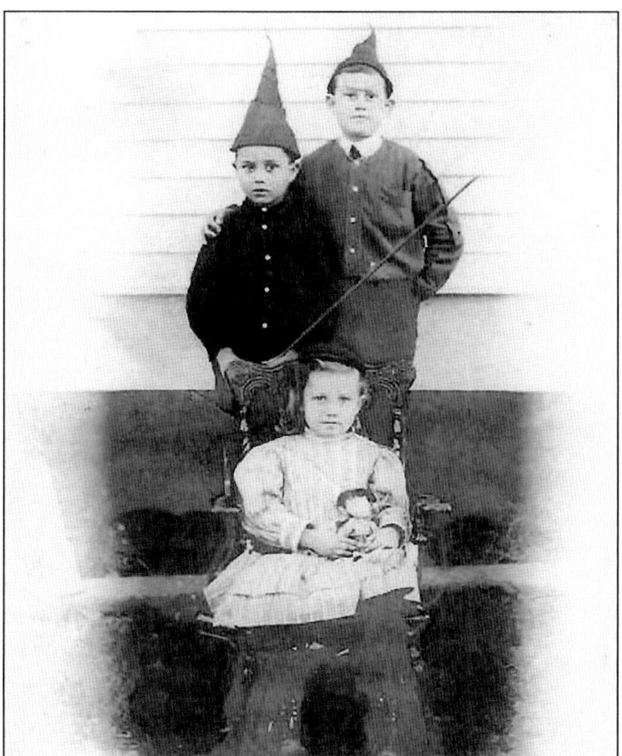

The Taylor children loved to dress for all occasions, as in this Christmas card photograph, where they pose in their finest elf hats. From left to right, the children were George Creed Taylor, Caro "G" Taylor, and Warren Lyman Taylor. (Courtesy Stephen Stirling.)

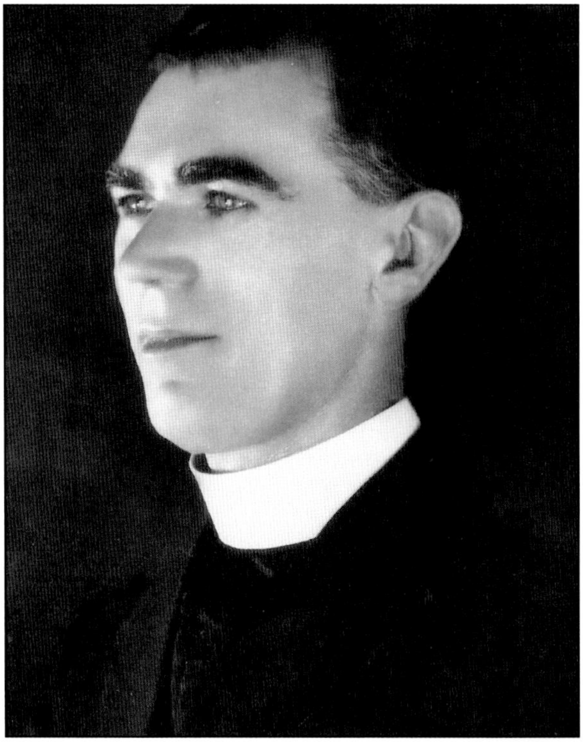

Msgr. J.J. Rousseau was pastor of the Church of the Assumption from July 1914 to July 1953, when failing health necessitated his retirement. He was closely identified with the history and growth of the church parish during his lifetime. (Courtesy Perry Lowery.)

In 1854, Father James Blank built the Church of St. Anthony. After the church was blown down in the storm of 1879, a new wooden church, named St. Mary, Patronal Feast–Assumption (pictured), was built in 1880. The cornerstone for the larger, brick Church of the Assumption of the Blessed Virgin Mary was laid in 1913 on the corner of Main and Iberia Streets. (Courtesy Perry Lowery.)

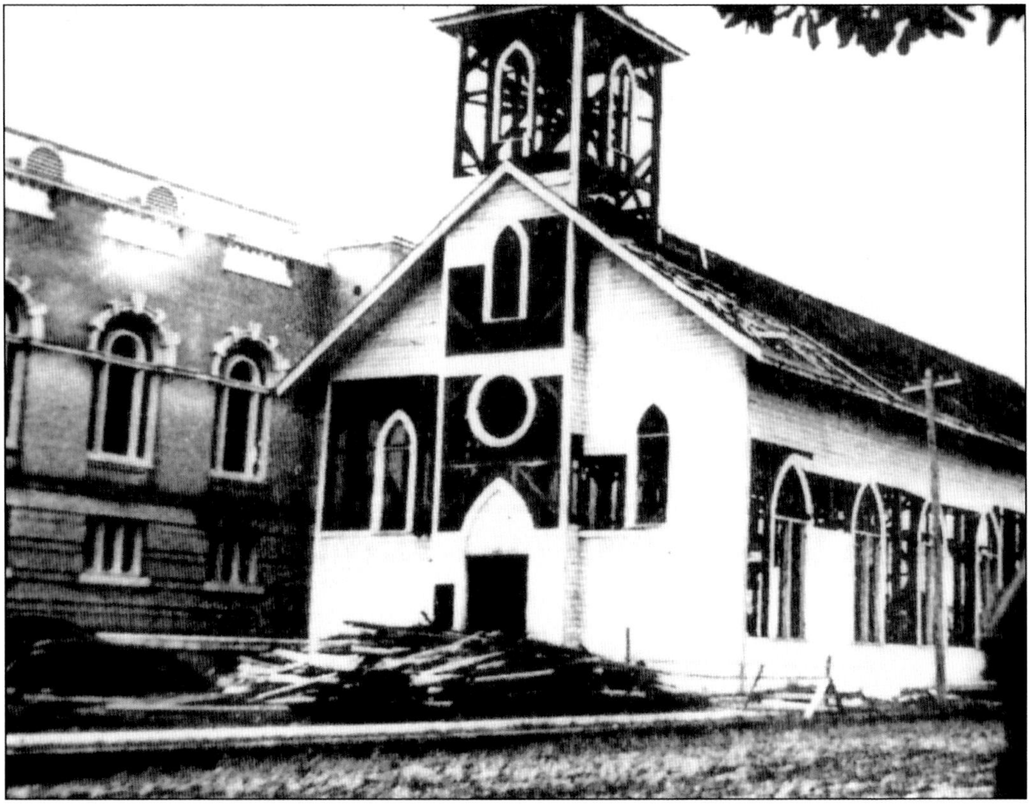

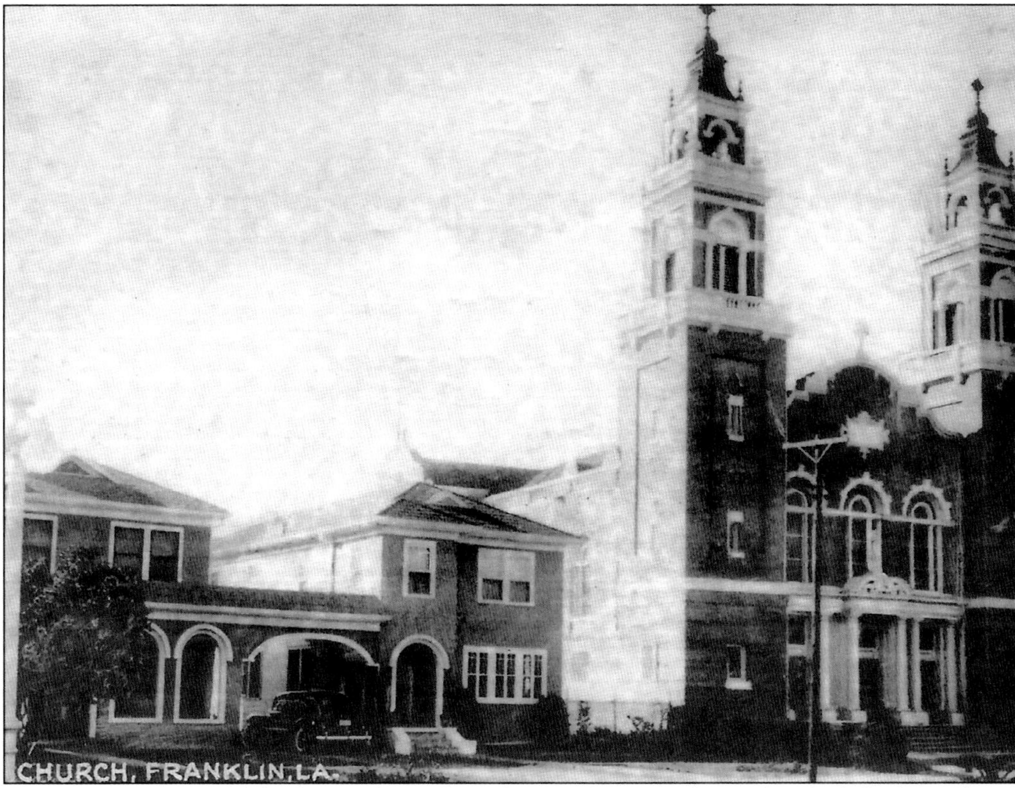

Ibert's Mortuary, established around 1860 by Valentine Ibert, was located to the left of the Church of the Assumption. By 1959, four generations of the Ibert family had served the Franklin area with nearly 100 years of dignified service. The property was purchased by the church in 1990 for use as a parish center. (Courtesy Perry Lowery.)

The Academy of St. John, under the direction of the Marianites of Holy Cross, was picturesquely built on Bayou Teche around 1871. The Sisters took great care in the happiness, moral preservation, and intellectual and religious instruction of the girls entrusted to them. (Courtesy Perry Lowery.)

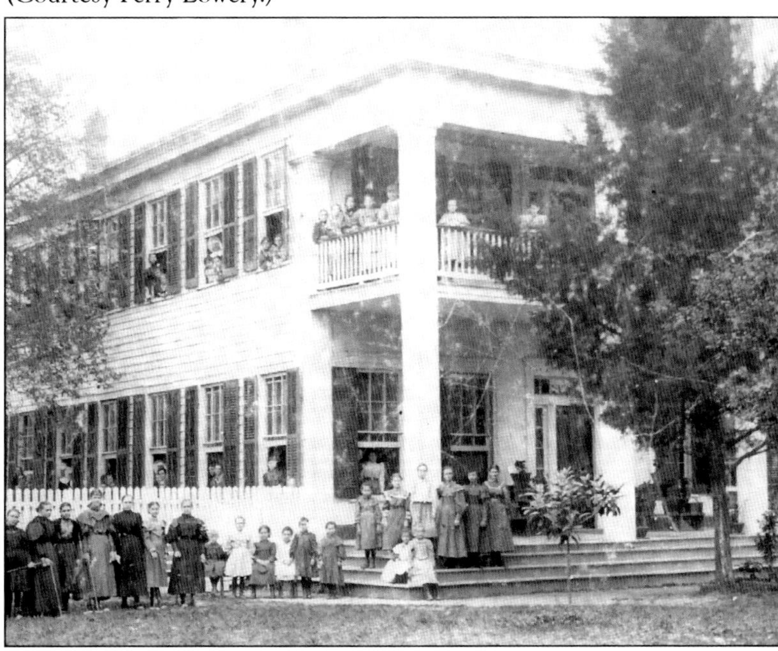

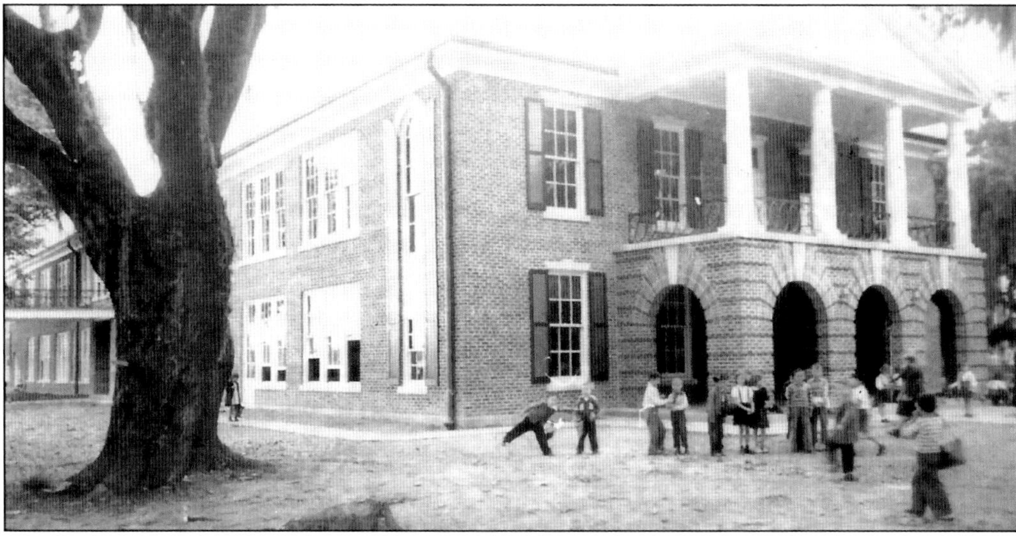

St. John Elementary, still located on its original site, is currently open to pre-kindergarten through fifth grade students and provides a solid education with strong Catholic values. Upon completion of their elementary studies, students move on to Hanson Memorial High School. (Courtesy Perry Lowery.)

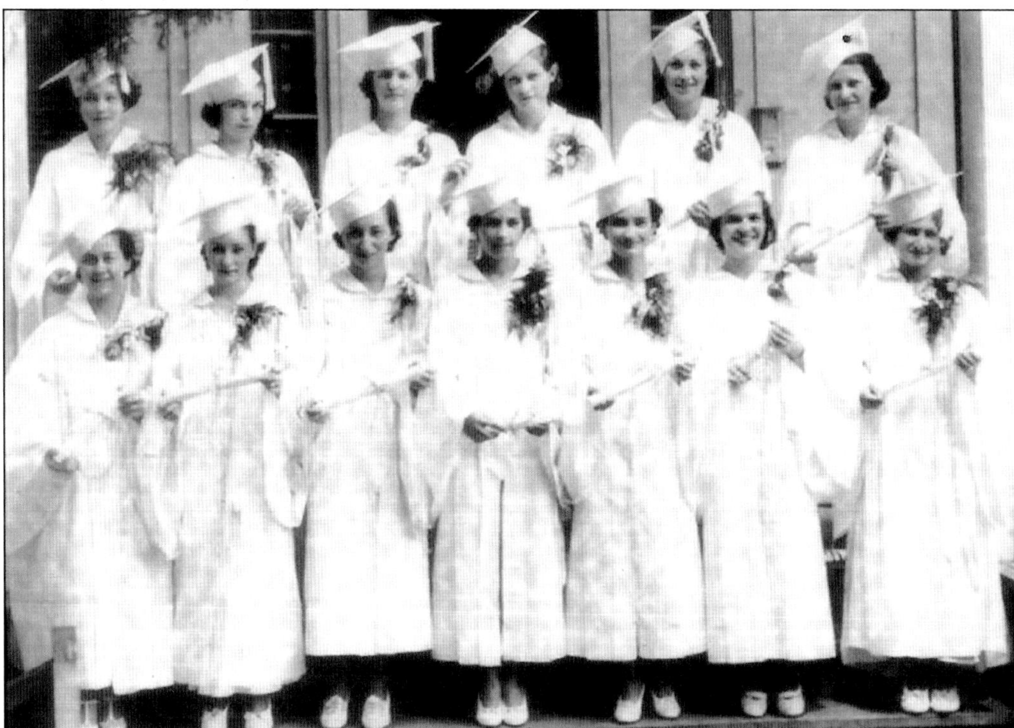

Graduates of the Academy of St. John, a Catholic school for girls established in 1871 and staffed by the Marianites Sisters of Holy Cross pose on the steps of their school. A new school building was built in 1950 and now houses St. John Elementary. In 1986, for the first time, the school came under the administration of a lay principal. The services of the Marianites ended completely in May 1991. (Courtesy Perry Lowery.)

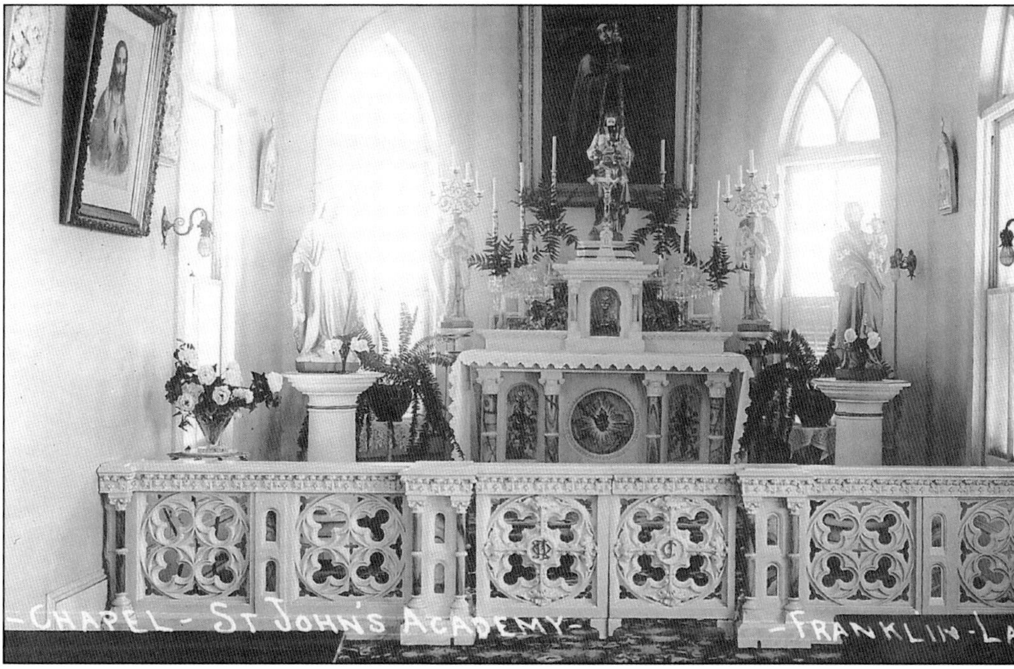

Students attended daily mass in the chapel at St. John's Academy. The sanctity of the chapel encouraged the young women to spend time in quiet meditation. (Courtesy Perry Lowery.)

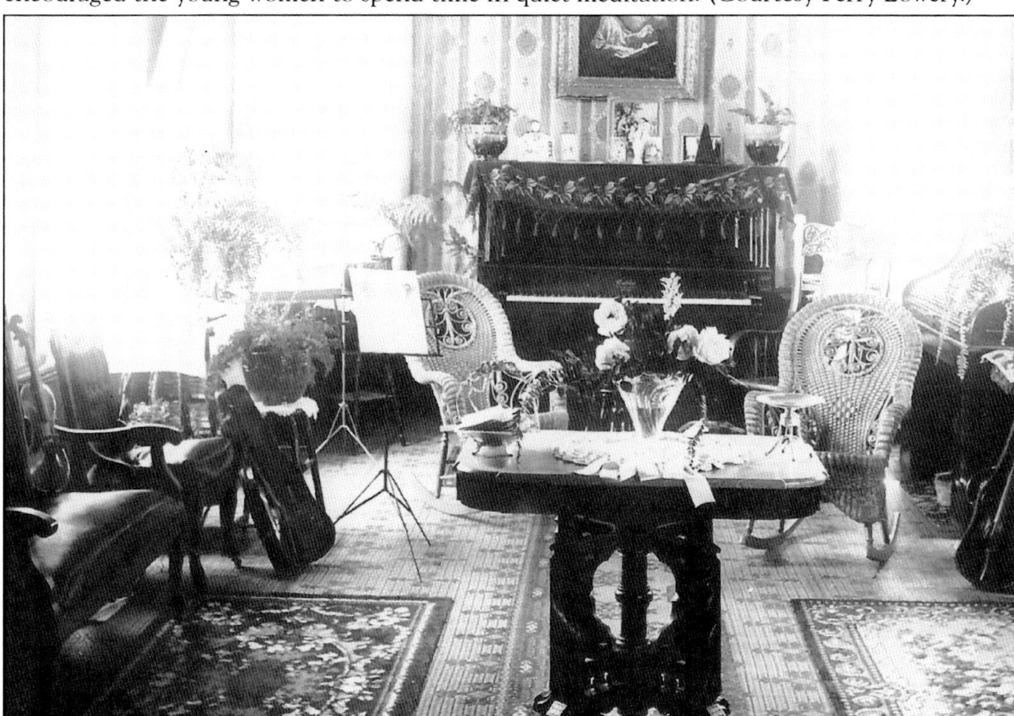

The curriculum at St. John Academy included the study of music and the arts in this beautifully appointed music room. The sunny, airy room encouraged the development of musical appreciation and skills. (Courtesy Perry Lowery.)

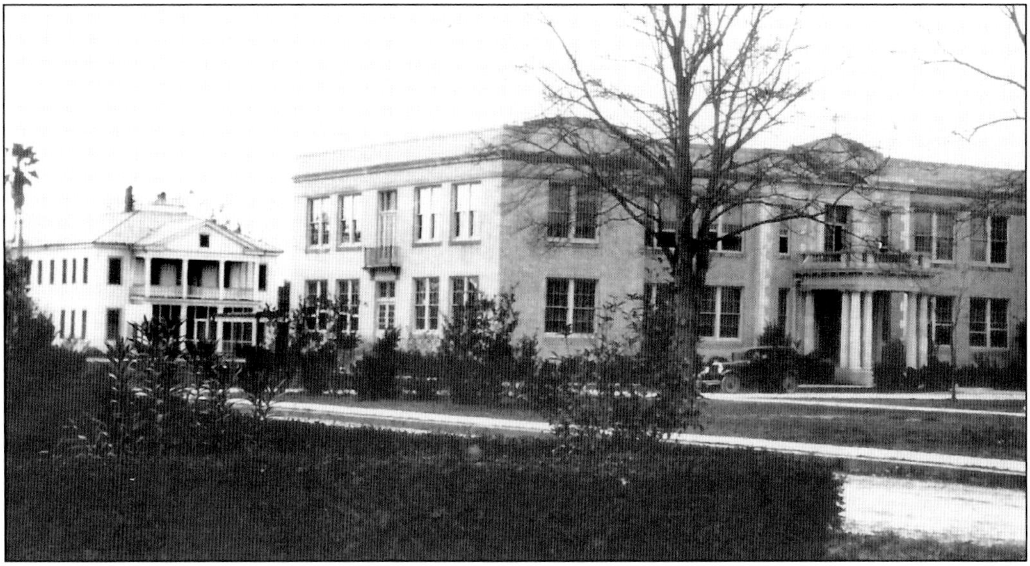

Hanson Memorial High School was built in 1925, largely thanks to the generosity of Minnie H. Conolly. Father J.J. Rousseau, the pastor and principal, made arrangements to have the Christian Brothers come to Franklin and direct the boys' school. The Brothers' home, once called Eaglesfield, was behind the school. (Courtesy Perry Lowery.)

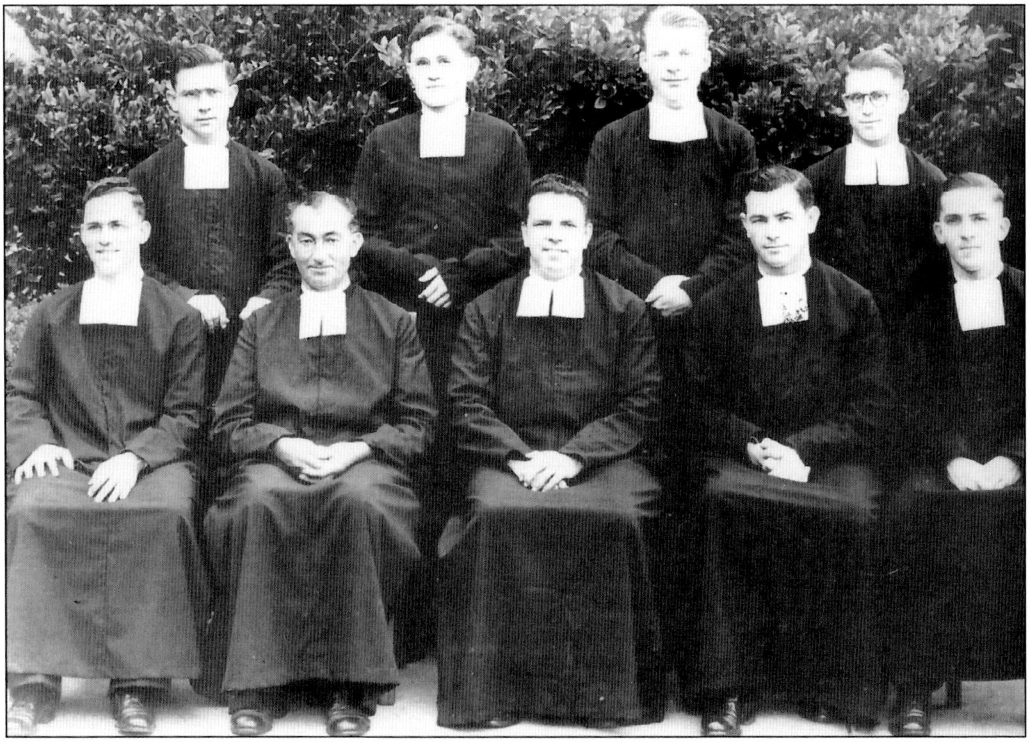

The Christian Brothers of Hanson Memorial High School posed for this faculty photograph in 1930. Brother Gauthier is seated second from the left. The principal said, "We have hopes that the new generation coming up will realize more fully the importance of a complete education of the physical, mental, and moral side of man." (Courtesy Perry Lowery.)

The Techeland Arts Council is a 501(c)3 nonprofit organization that presents its performances at the beautifully restored Art Deco–style Teche Theater on Main Street in Franklin. The vignettes are gathered from the local life experiences of our community and presented in folk-life theater. (Techeland Arts Council 2012.)

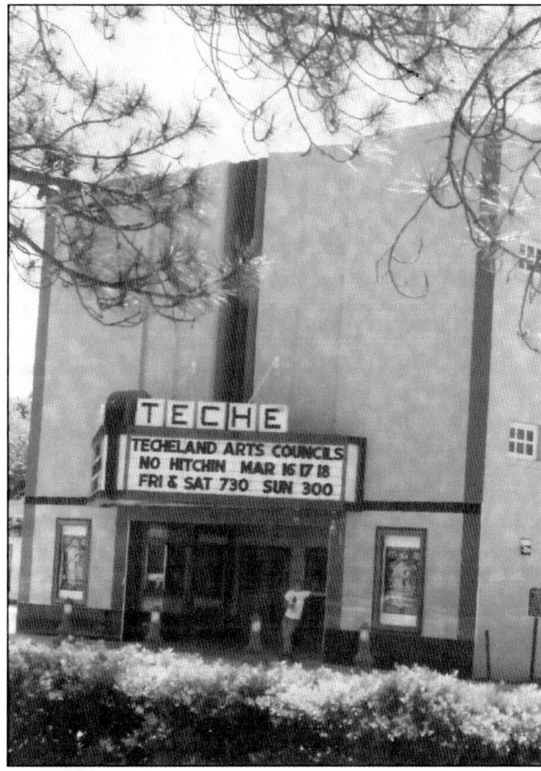

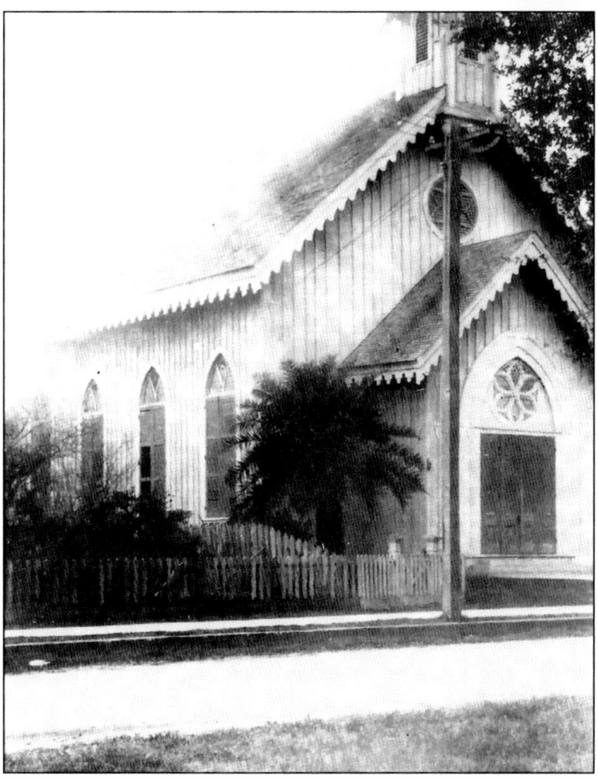

St. Mary's Episcopal Church held services as early as 1830. In 1870, the landmark was lost in a fire that started in a bakery on the bayou side and, fed by high winds, destroyed many buildings in its path. The bell from the gunboat *Diana* still hangs in the church tower and rings the Angelus at noon every day. (Courtesy Perry Lowery.)

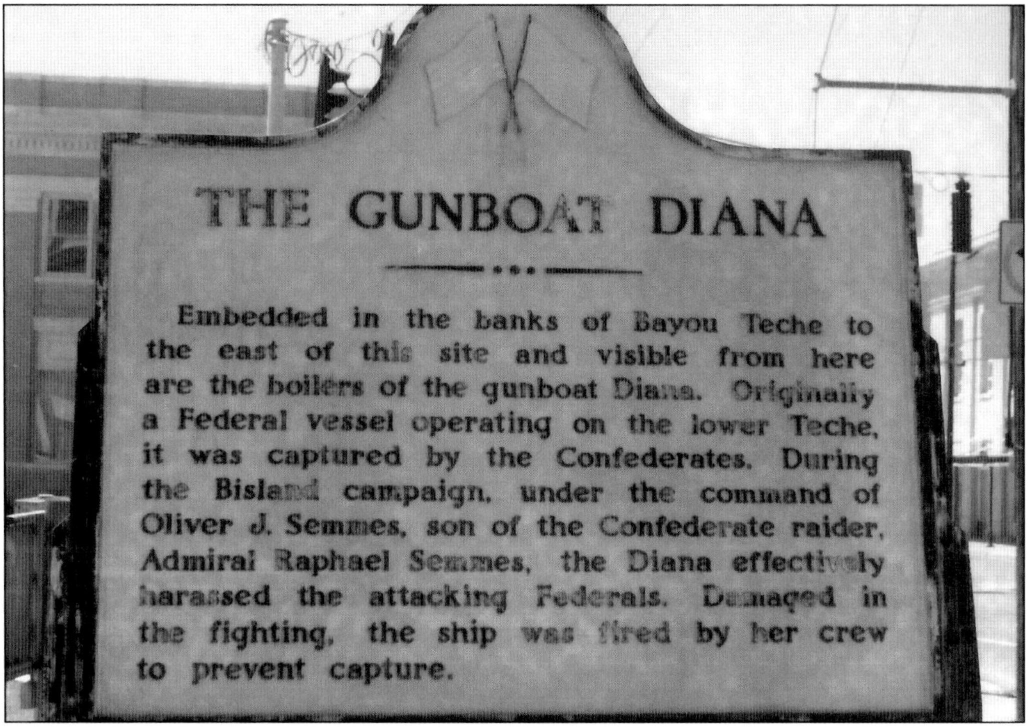

This historical marker about the gunboat *Diana* is in the courthouse square. Sunk in the Bayou Teche, for many years it remained a visible symbol of Confederate pride, having stopped the advancement of Federal troops. (Techeland Arts Council 2012.)

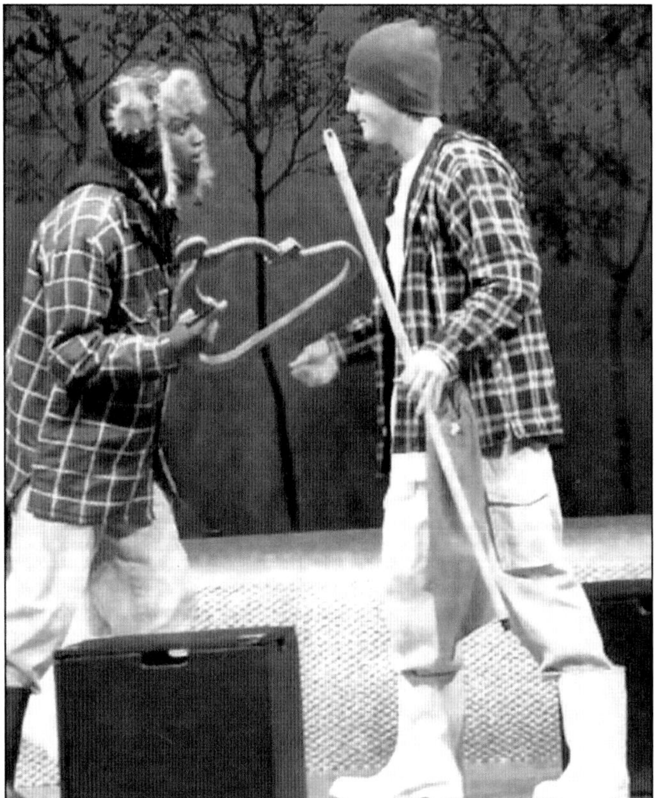

In *A Gunboat Named Diana*, Morris Raphael wrote, "For there is a spark of life which we hope shall never die for the bell from the Diana hangs in a church nearby. From the Episcopal steeple rings this bell so loud and clear a miraculous reminder of that tragic yesteryear. And maybe the bell of Diana which roused the blue and the gray will become a symbol of unity and ring on 'till judgement day." (Techeland Arts Council 2012.)

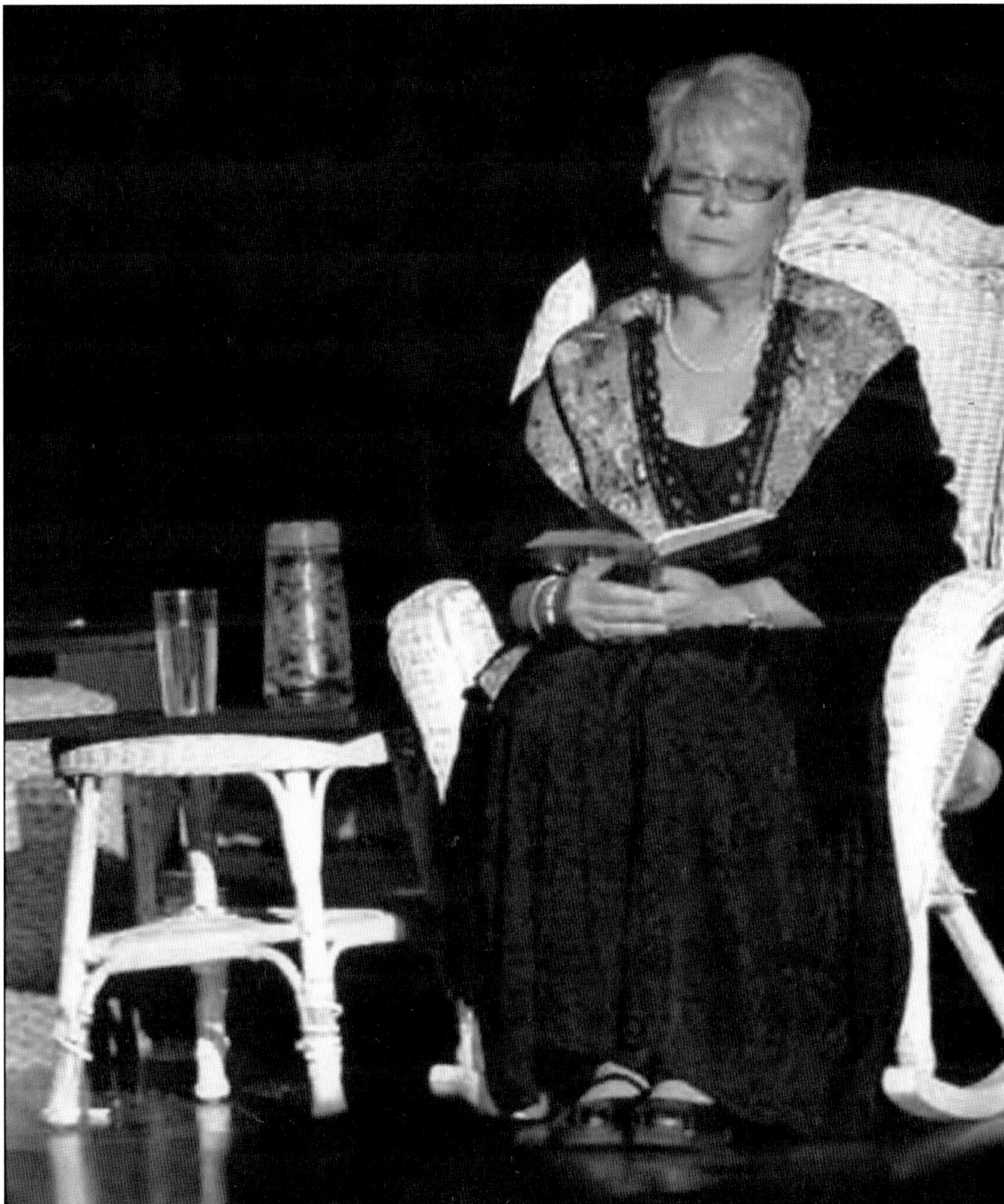

Denise Hodge tells a heart-wrenching story of a bus and train wreck in 1942. Jim Firmin was an infant traveling with his mother and siblings. As he fussed, a kind woman from the rear of the bus offered to take him and settle him down. Within minutes, the bus was hit by a train and Firmin's mother and siblings, sitting in the front of the bus, were killed. A total of nine people were killed and 14 were injured. This accident resulted in a rule making buses stop at railroad crossings. Jim Firmin was not aware of the details of the accident until Zeke Theriot shared his photographs and memories with him many years later and Firmin attended this performance of *No Hitchin'*, presented by the Techeland Arts Council for the 2011–2012 season. (Techeland Arts Council 2012.)

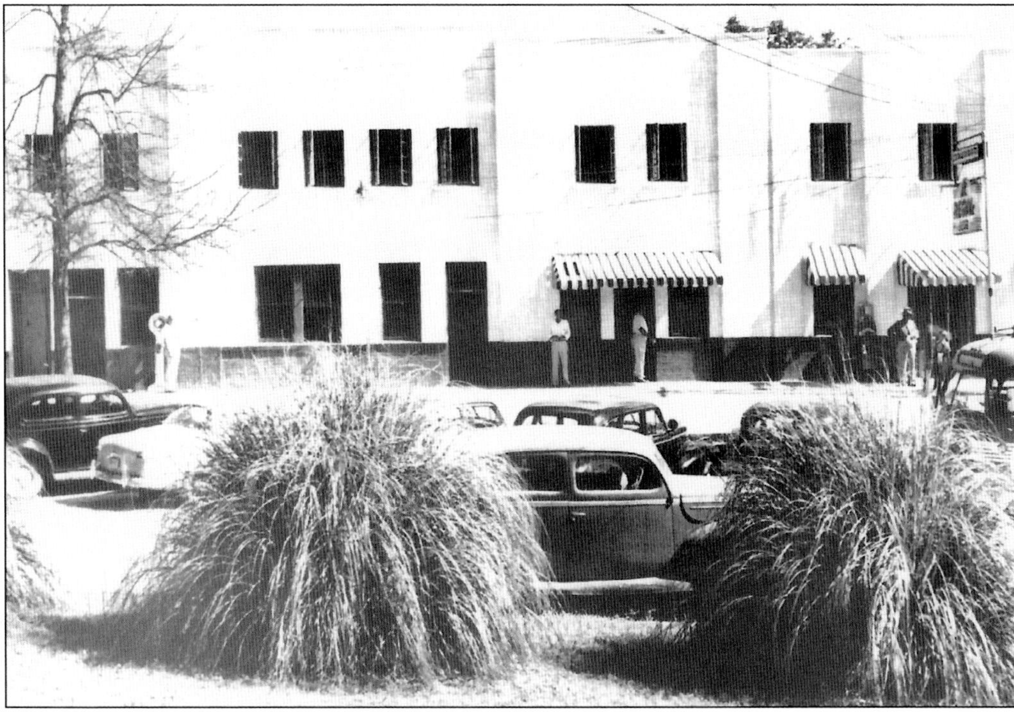

The old Greyhound bus station and Teche Breeze Café were located behind the Blevins Building, near the courthouse square on Willow Street and Teche Drive, along the bayou side. In the 1800s, this was the site of the O'Niell Hotel. (Courtesy Perry Lowery.)

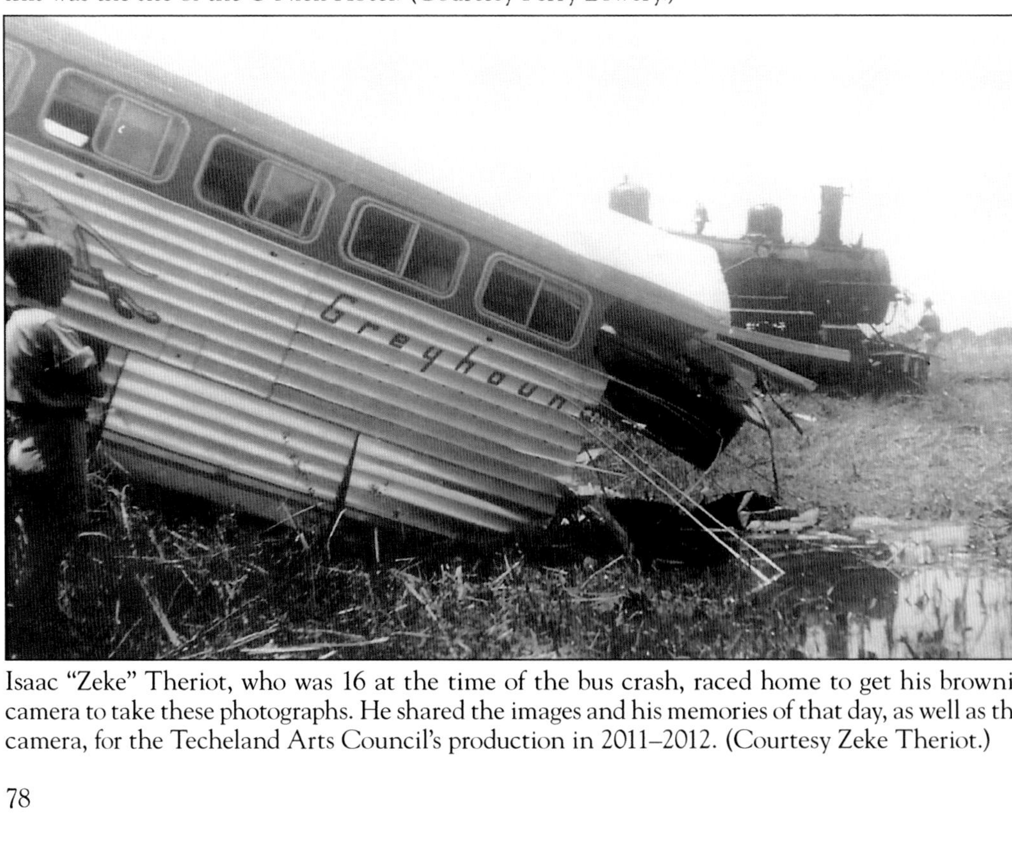

Isaac "Zeke" Theriot, who was 16 at the time of the bus crash, raced home to get his brownie camera to take these photographs. He shared the images and his memories of that day, as well as the camera, for the Techeland Arts Council's production in 2011–2012. (Courtesy Zeke Theriot.)

The standard-gauge Sterling Railroad was not the conventional-type plantation tram road, it was a common carrier line running to Milton, Louisiana, where it connected with the Abbeville branch of the Southern Pacific Railway. At right and below, the bus crash is investigated. Sterling owned the Franklin and Abbeville Railroad Company, later part of the Southern Pacific system, which originated at Sterling Junction, a short distance from the factory. The Franklin and Abbeville Railroad also offered passenger service, with one train each way daily. At 7:00 a.m., the train departed from Milton, arriving at Sterling Junction at 11:14 a.m. On the return, it departed Sterling Junction at 1:30 p.m. and arrived at Milton at 8:00 p.m.

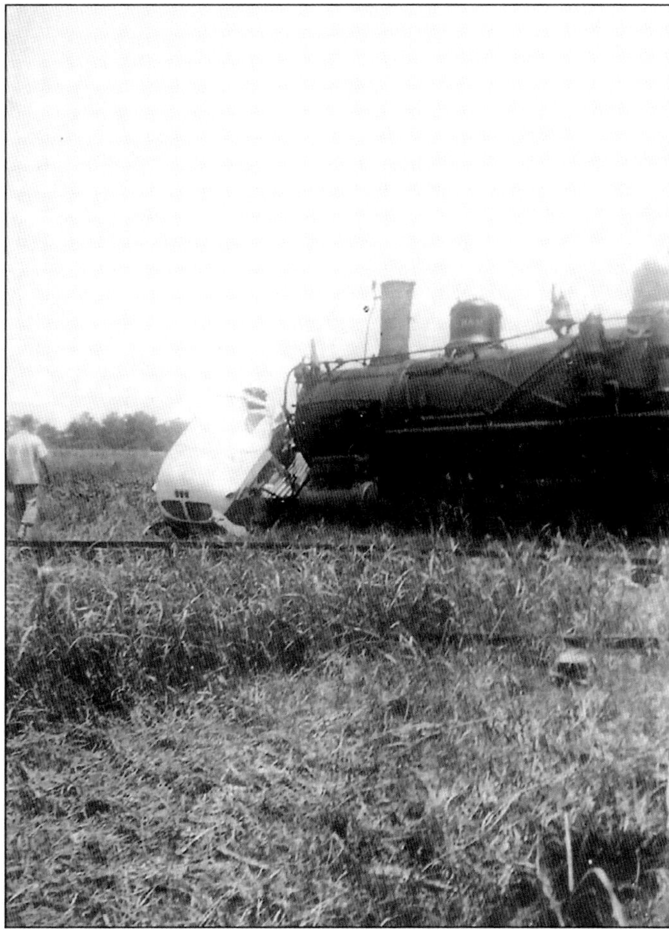

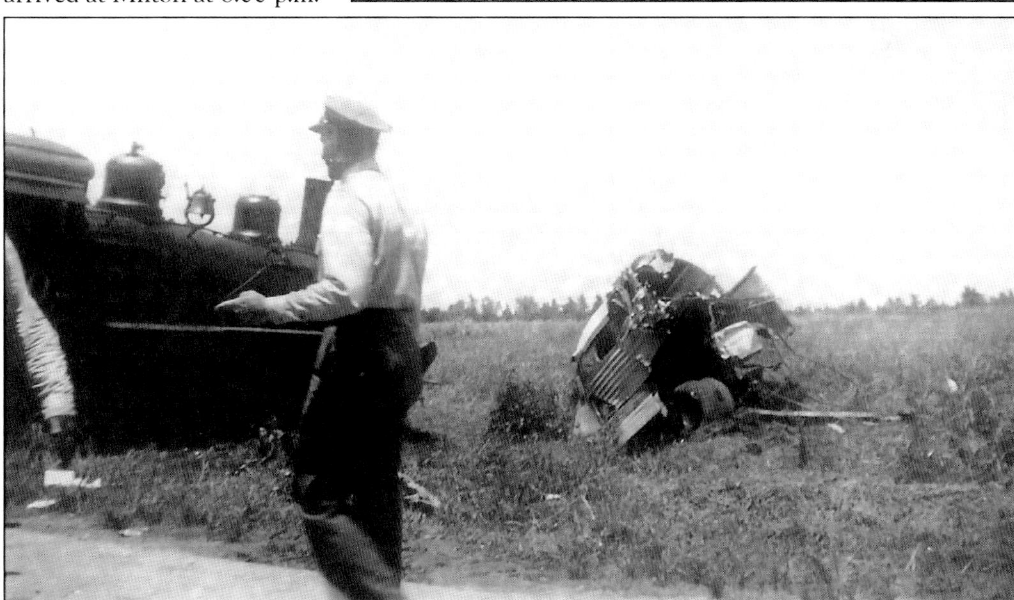

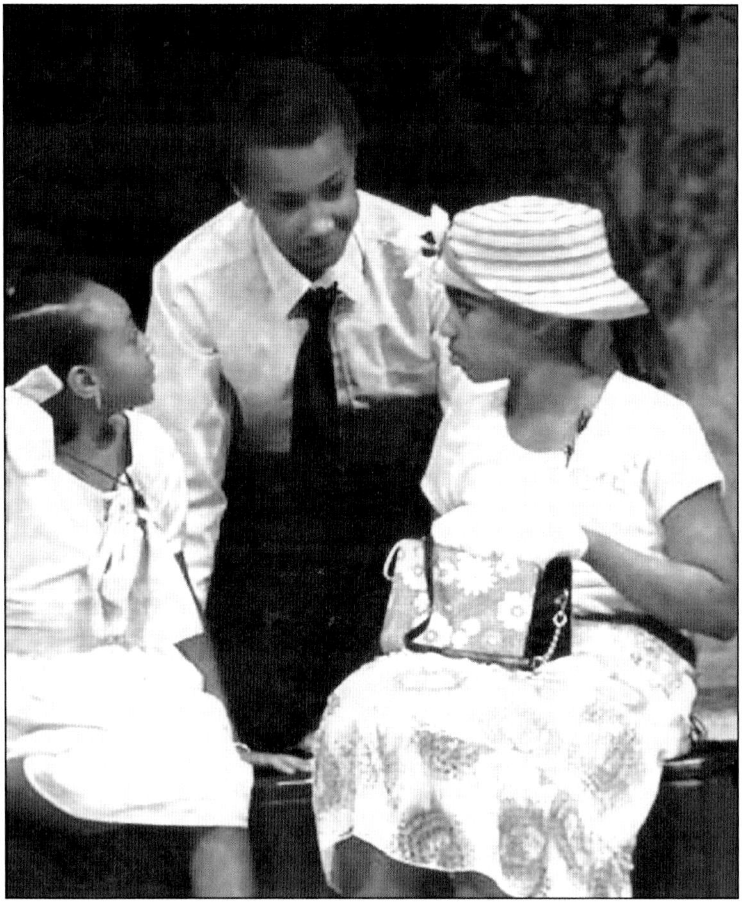

Amen Corner and Baptisms, Too was a vignette discussing the custom of baptisms in the Bayou Teche featuring, from left to right, Zoe LeGrier, RossAndre LeGrier, and Suhalya Chirdon. (Techeland Arts Council 2012.)

The baptism of African Americans in Bayou Teche was steeped in custom and passed on through the generations. It was a time of great joy, singing, and reverence. (Courtesy Perry Lowery.)

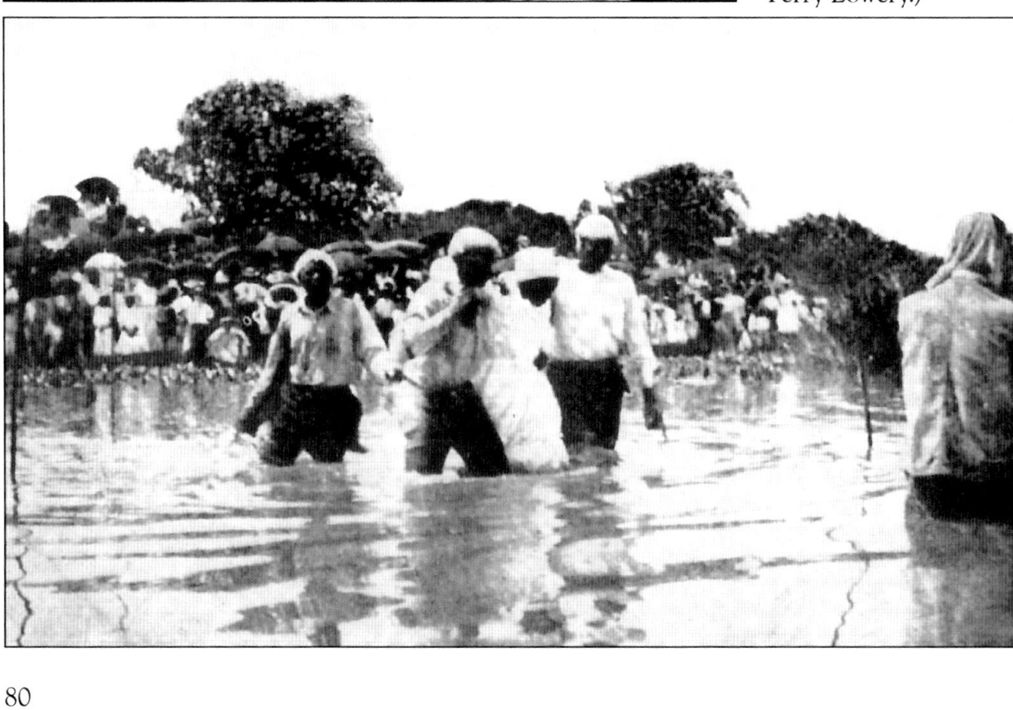

Four
GARDEN CITY

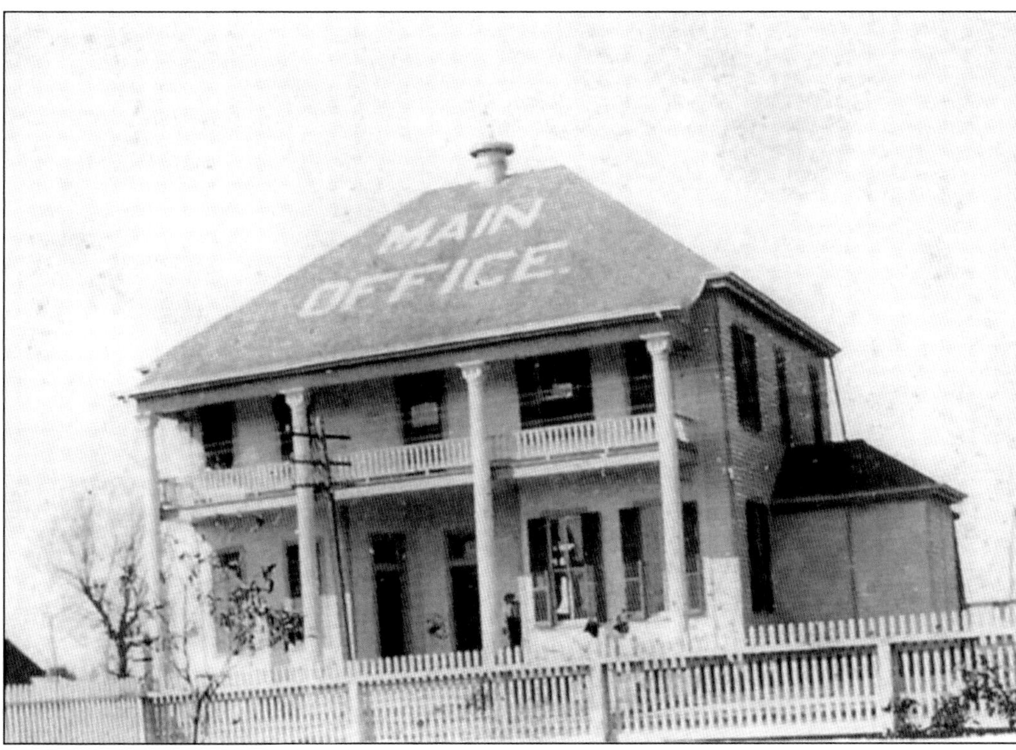

The main office for the Albert Hanson Lumber Company in Garden City, seen here, sat on 14 acres of land and boasted the very latest and most improved machinery in the industry, shipping lumber to St. Louis and Chicago. There was a tramway running from the mill to the Southern Pacific depot. It was later purchased by May Brothers. (Courtesy Stephen Stirling.)

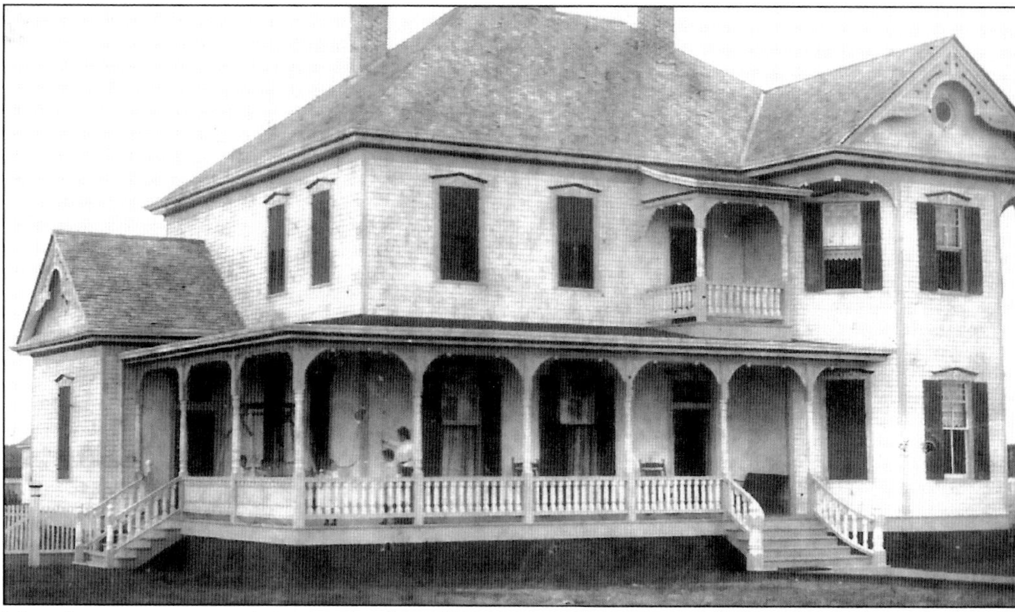

The charming manager's house for the Albert Hanson Lumber Company still stands in Garden City and has been lovingly restored to its former glory. The beautiful home in a grove of oak trees stands as a proud reminder of the lumber industry that built it and is listed in the National Register of Historic Places. (Courtesy Stephen Stirling.)

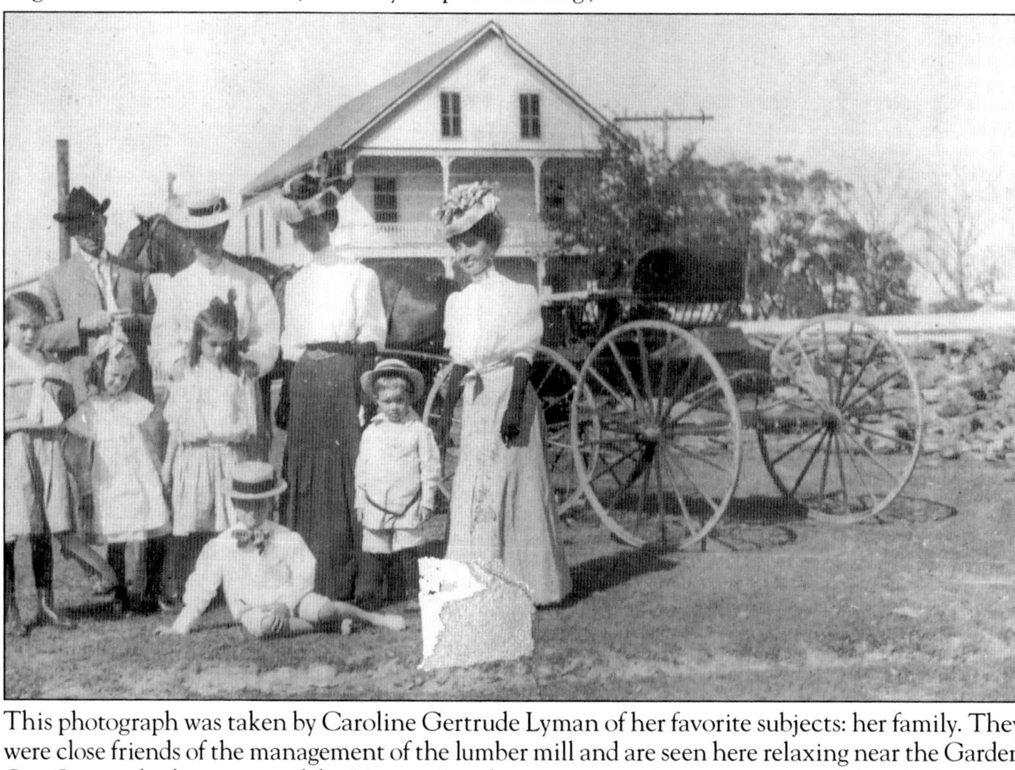

This photograph was taken by Caroline Gertrude Lyman of her favorite subjects: her family. They were close friends of the management of the lumber mill and are seen here relaxing near the Garden City Store, which was part of the Hanson Lumber Company. A store was operated in the building until recently, selling sandwiches, vitamins, and odds and ends. (Courtesy Stephen Stirling.)

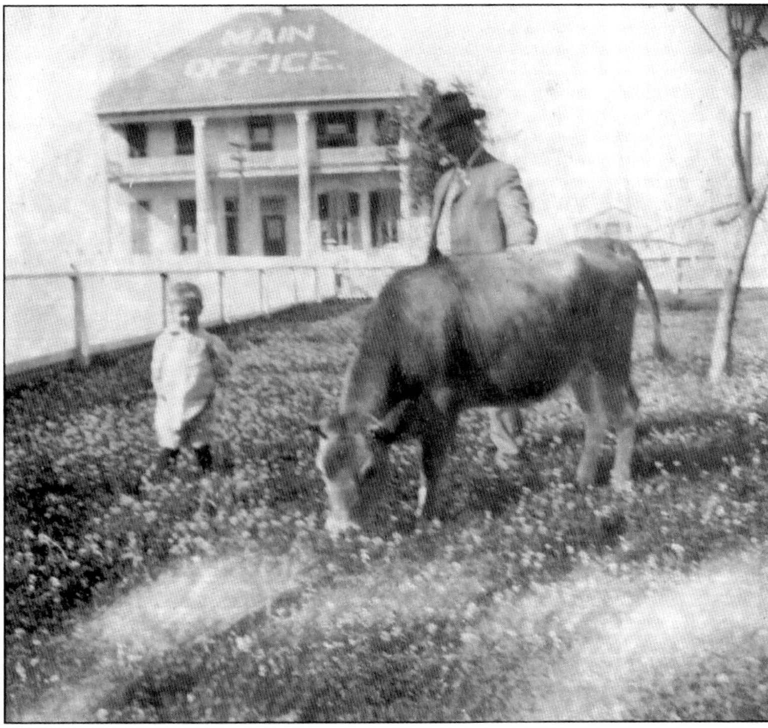

A man, a child, and a cow enjoy the outdoors in front of the Hanson Lumber Company main office. Another wonderful C.G. Lyman photograph, this peaceful and idyllic pasture scene leaves one calm and serene. The main office is now a private residence directly across Highway 182 from the manager's house. (Courtesy Perry Lowery.)

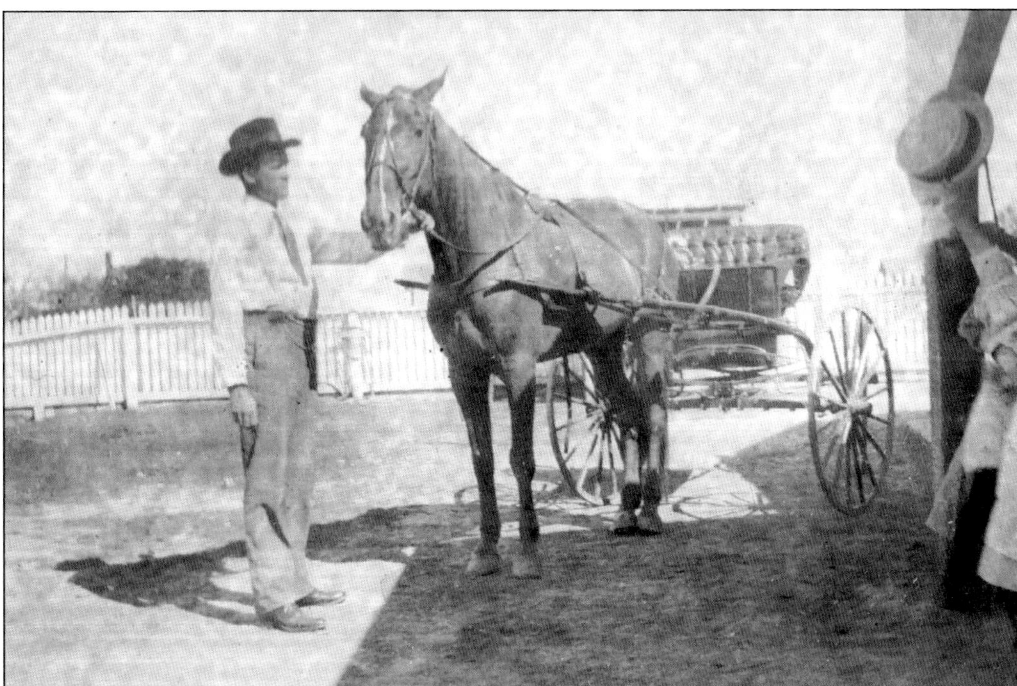

At the time of this photograph, taken near the Hanson Lumber Company in Garden City, a horse and buggy were the normal mode of transportation along the dusty unpaved roads of St. Mary Parish. A board walkway that many locals remember walking as a child used to extend from Garden City to Franklin. (Courtesy Perry Lowery.)

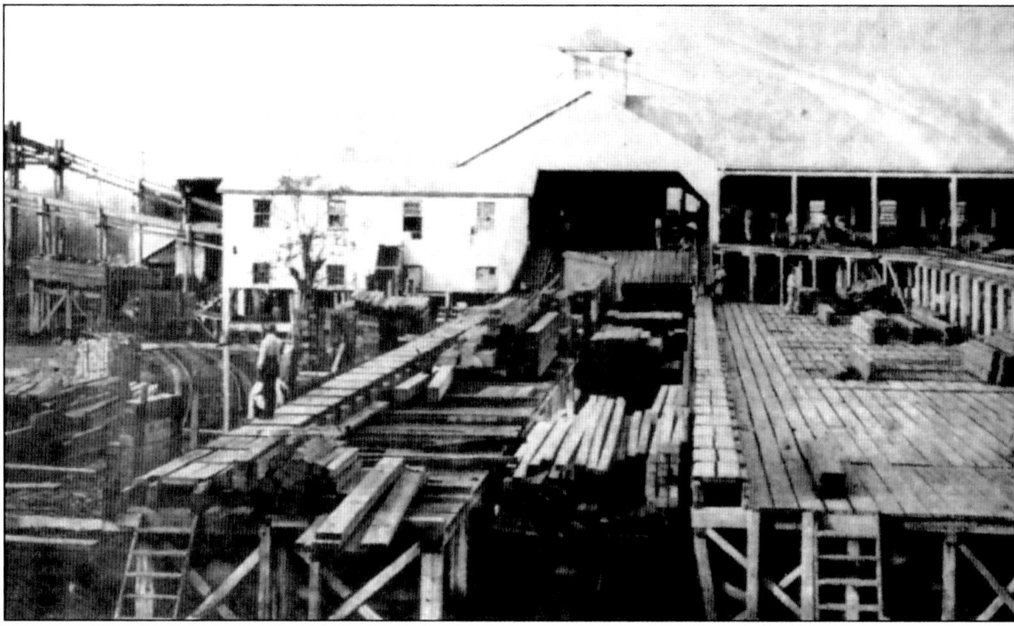

Originally on East Main Street in Franklin, the Hanson Sawmill was relocated to Garden City and is credited with building the once-thriving community between the Old Spanish Trail (Highway 182), the Southern Pacific Railway, and what is now Highway 90. (Courtesy Roland Laws.)

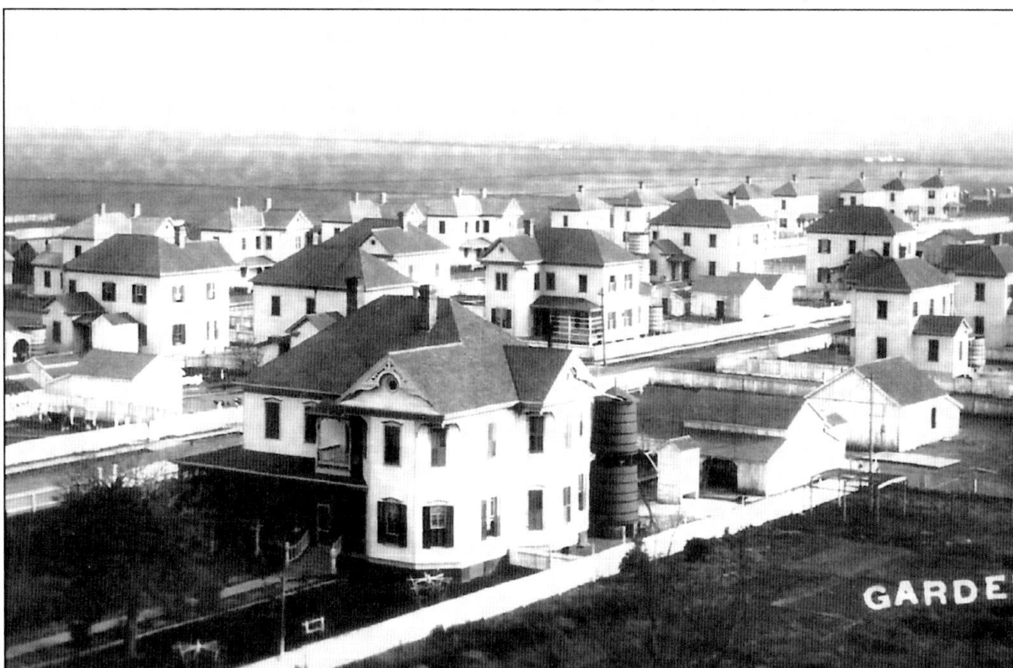

The Albert Hanson sawmill and the newly built housing for its labor force was set against the backdrop of tall, waving sugarcane. An entire community sprang up around the lumber industry in Garden City, including rows of houses, a school, and a general store—everything a growing family needed for work and play. Incredibly, only a handful of these houses still exist. (Courtesy Perry Lowery.)

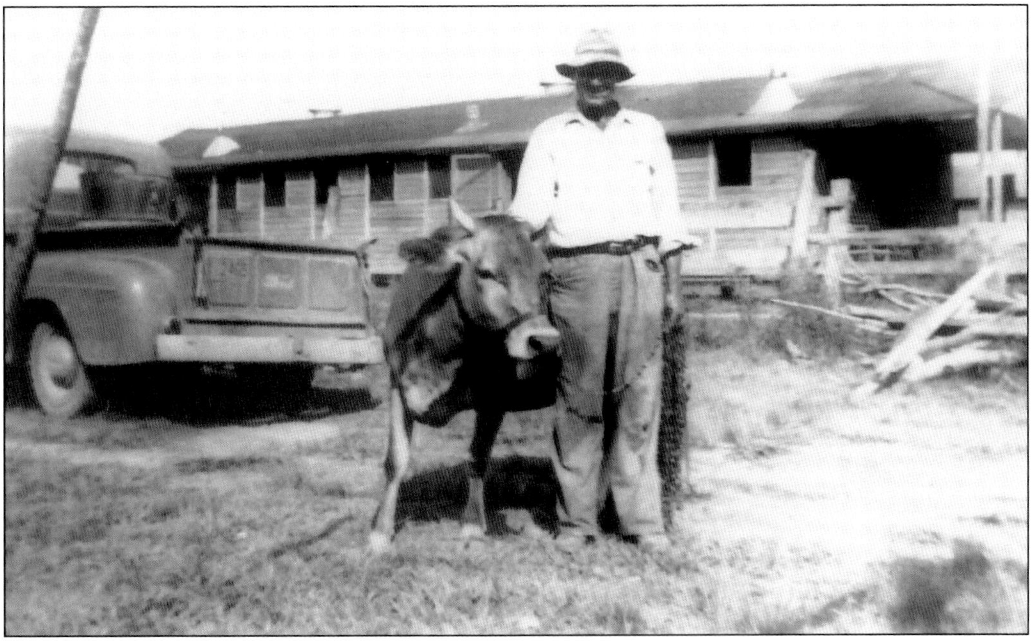

Even in the midst of the small, bustling community and active industry, the rural country setting still shone through, as this man and his prize cow demonstrate. Small family farms are still scattered along the Old Spanish Trail, reminiscent of the plantation days of the past. (Courtesy Perry Lowery.)

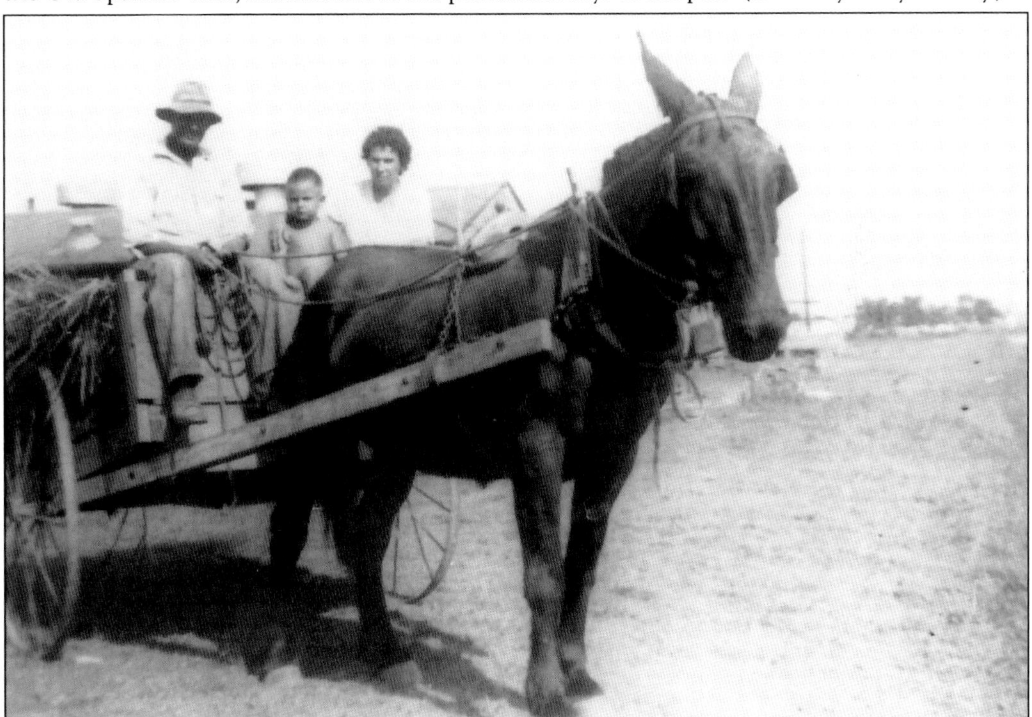

Old traditions mixed with the new, and as the modern age came to St. Mary Parish, many still lived the older, slower lifestyles of the past. The rural communities embraced their heritage and continued to thrive as farming held steadfast to its roots. (Courtesy Perry Lowery.)

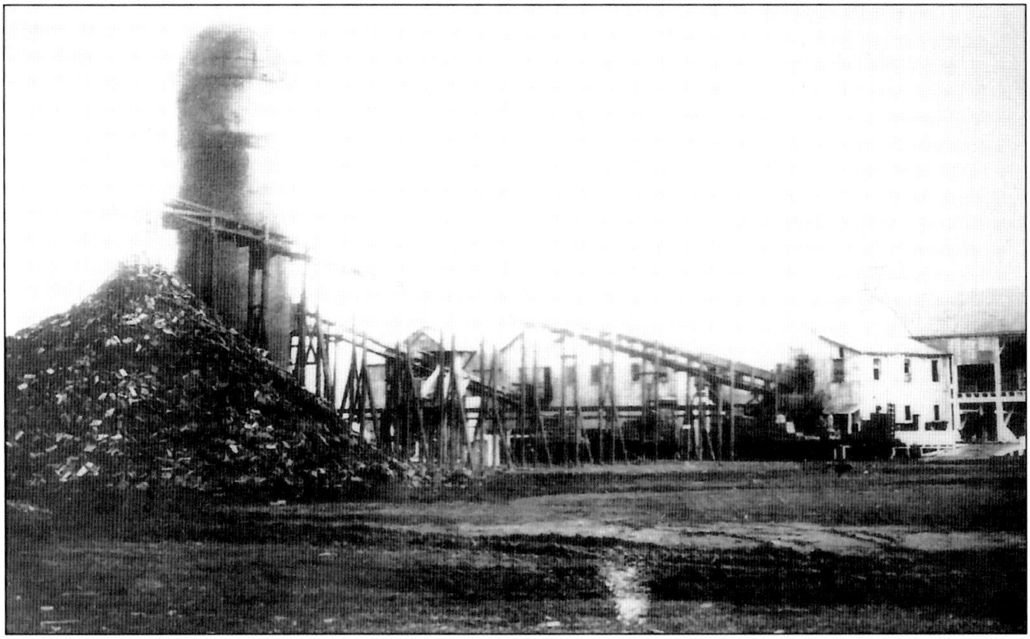

Garden City remained a lumber company town and the building continued to be used as the lumber industry remained an important historical force in the state. Industrial lumbering was one of the major historical forces in the development of Louisiana, and indeed the entire South. (Courtesy Perry Lowery.)

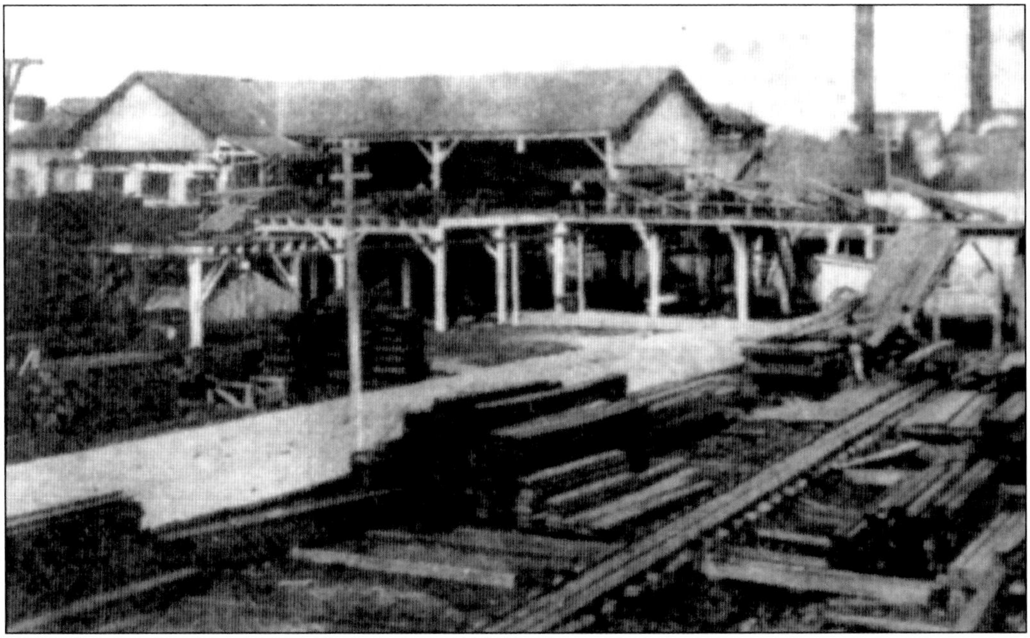

The May Brothers Lumber Mill replaced the Hanson Lumber Company. These Queen Anne Revival cottages and bungalows were found in many towns, representing the lumber boom and what it did for the state. Unfortunately, very few resources from the lumber boom survived. In many cases, lumber company buildings were dismantled and moved out of state when the timber played out. (Courtesy Perry Lowery.)

Five

Centerville and Bayou Sale

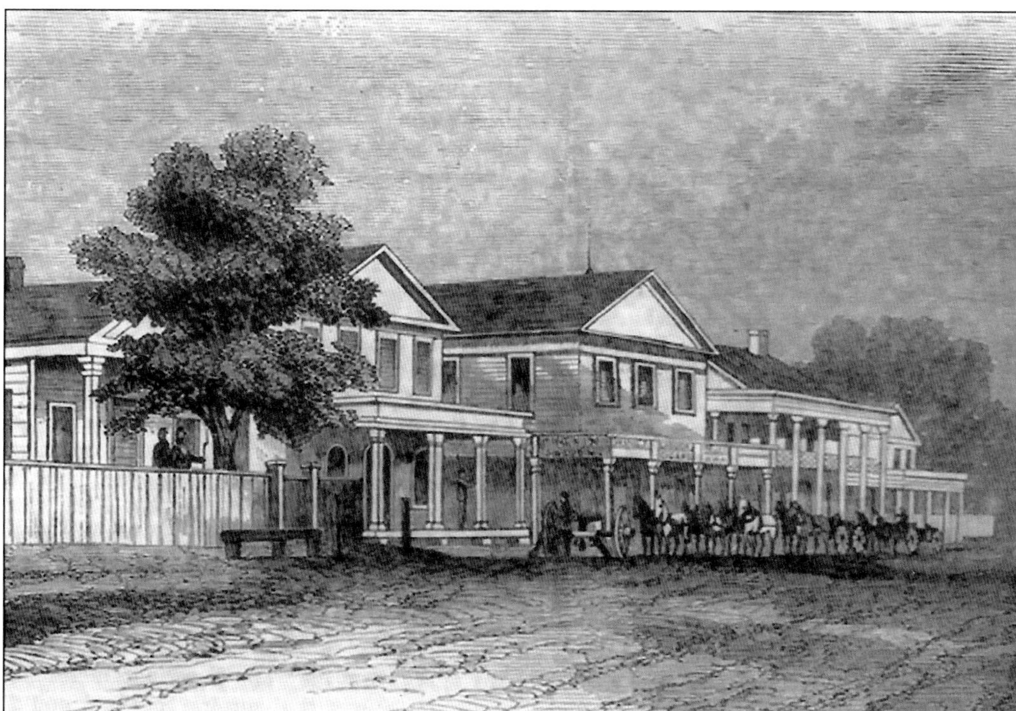

Centerville lies east of Garden City and was the center for much of the sugar activity concentrated in the Bayou Sale area during the steamboat era. The boats landed at Centerville docks on the Bayou Teche. At least one source credits this "center" of operations as the way Centerville got its name. In early 1848, Centerville had a sawmill, an icehouse, a hotel, a billiard hall, 17 businesses, two schools, and two physicians. (Courtesy Perry Lowery.)

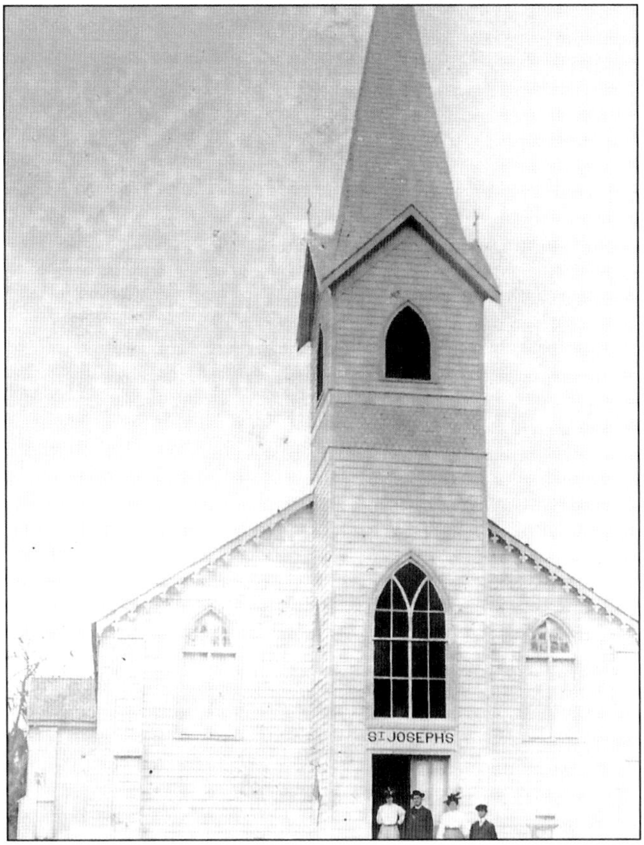

The history of St. Joseph's Church in Centerville dates back to the second half of the 1800s. It was enlarged in 1890, and during its existence, it changed back and forth from a mission to a parish church several times. Rev. John Hargrave served as pastor from 1894 to 1905, and from 1905 to 1915, the church was served by pastors from neighboring parishes in Franklin and Patterson. (Courtesy Perry Lowery.)

Centerville Mercantile Co. Limited was a full-service establishment offering staple items as well as agricultural items. From left to right are Willie Senette Sr., Everette Hayes, Justillian Aucoin, Willie Young Sr., two unidentified, John N. Miller, Clafey Boudreaux, unidentified, and Sam Carey. (Courtesy Ted Borne.)

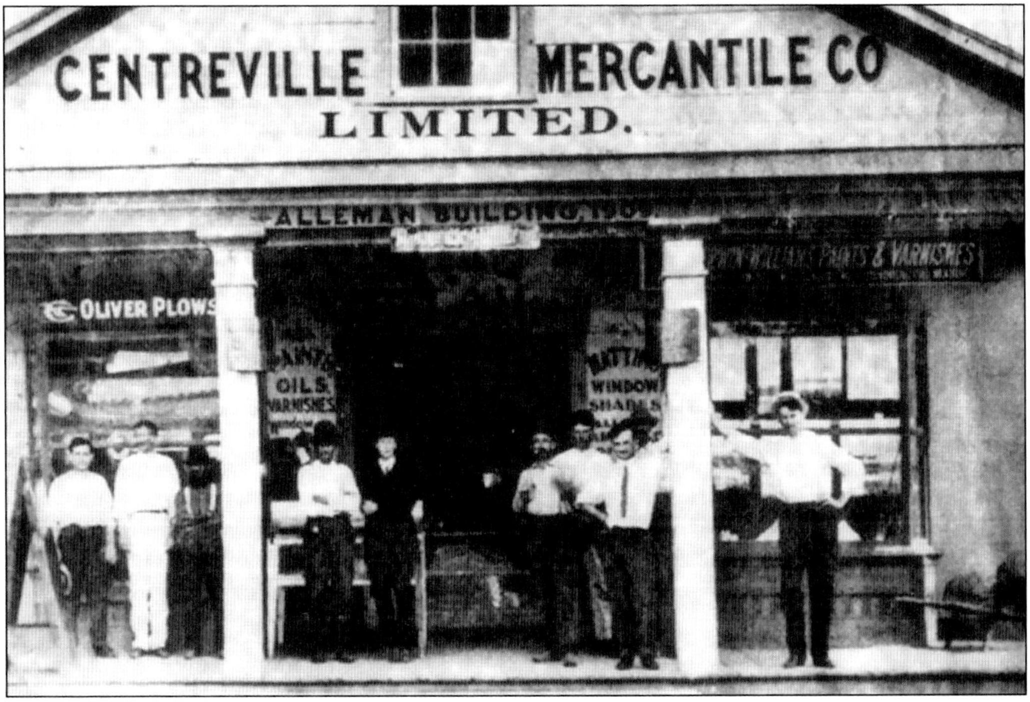

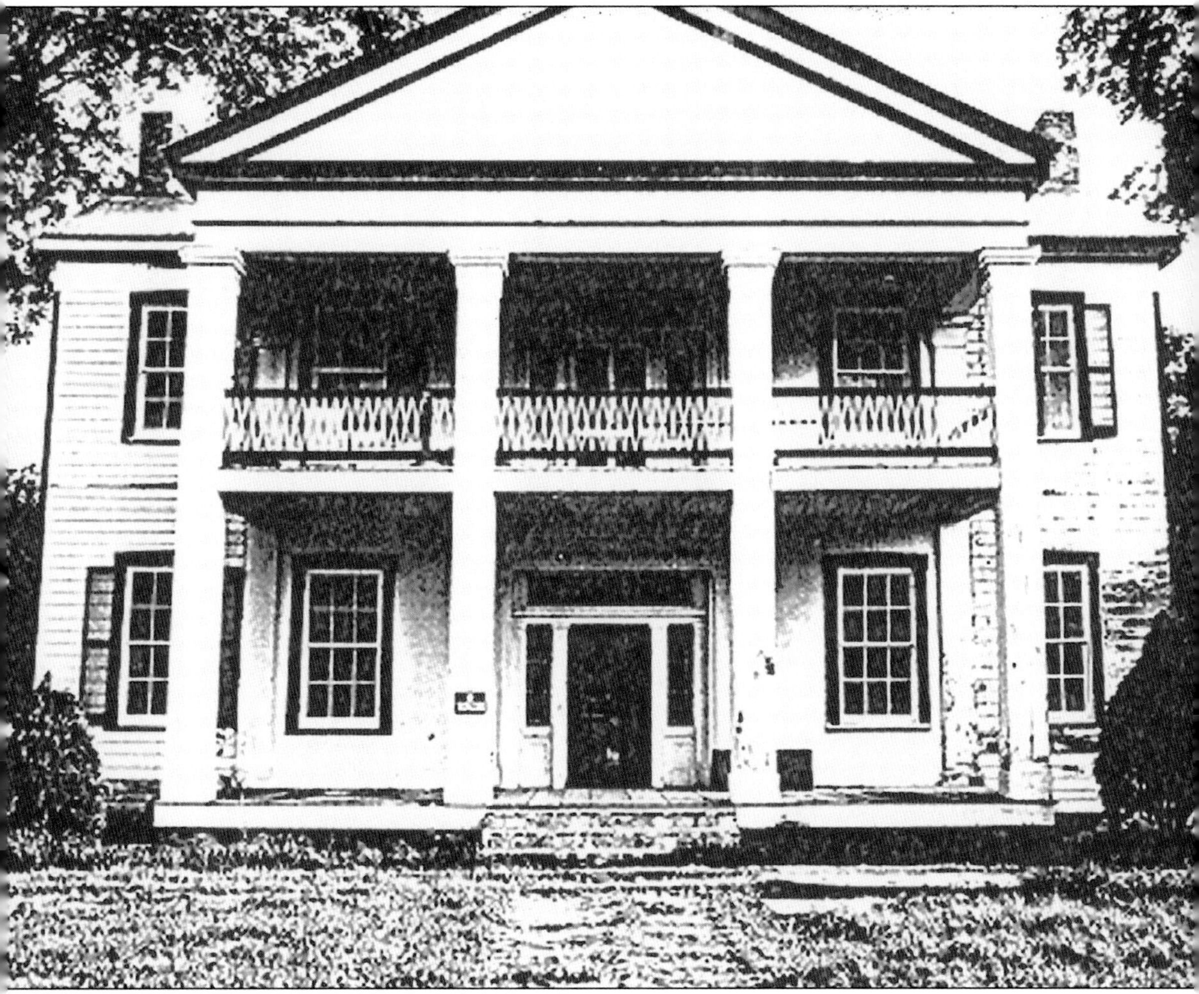

The Joshua B. Cary House, built in 1839, is one of the grand Greek Revival houses representing the distinctly Anglo-American architectural heritage of St. Mary Parish. According to Louisiana's standing structures survey, it is one of about a dozen grand temple-fronted Greek Revival residences in the parish, and it is listed in the National Register of Historic Places. (Courtesy Perry Lowery.)

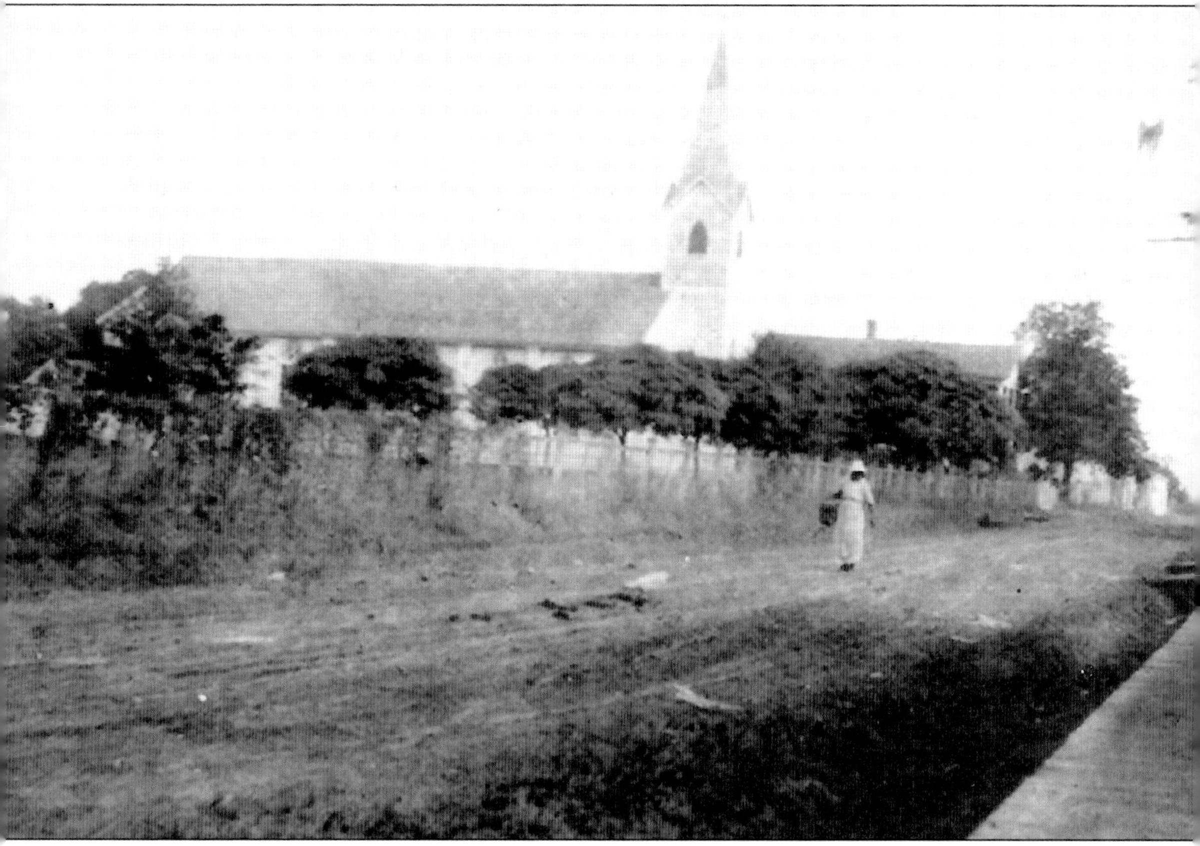

This photograph was taken looking down Bayou Sale Road towards the center of town with St. Joseph Church to the left. This charming scene shows a tree-lined street along the church property with a planked wood walkway on the opposite side of the unpaved street around 1800. (Courtesy Perry Lowery.)

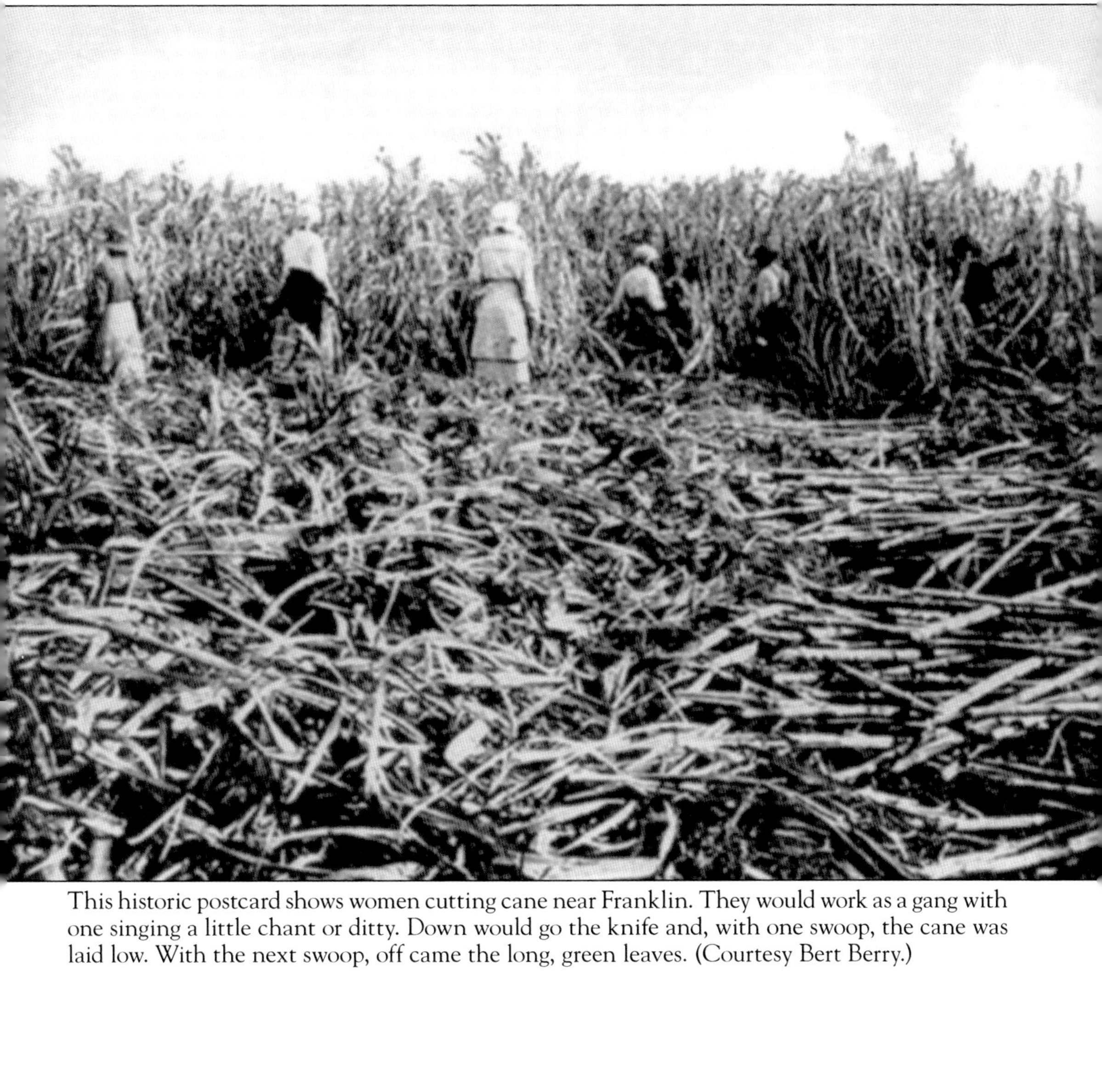

This historic postcard shows women cutting cane near Franklin. They would work as a gang with one singing a little chant or ditty. Down would go the knife and, with one swoop, the cane was laid low. With the next swoop, off came the long, green leaves. (Courtesy Bert Berry.)

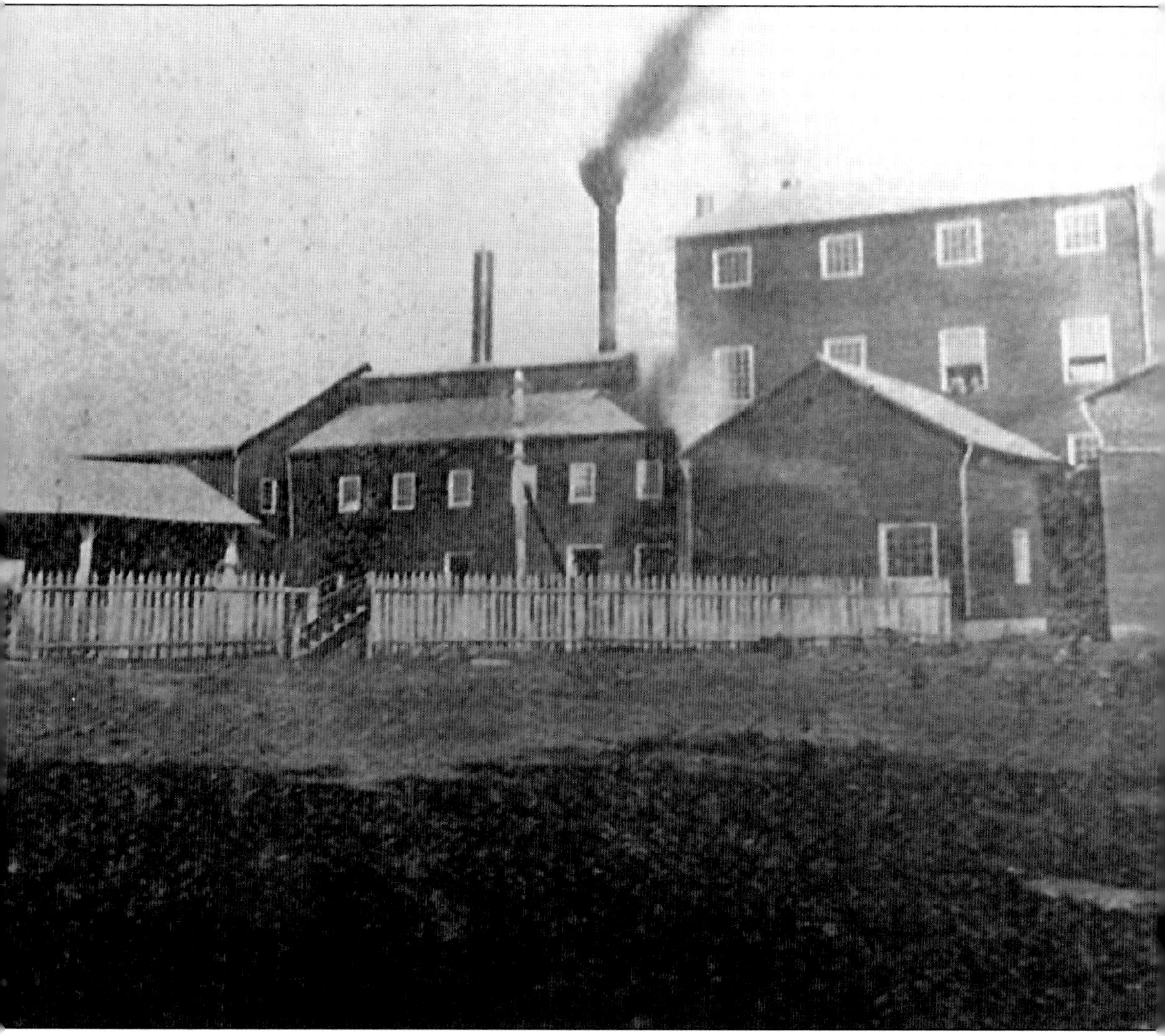

Before large mills, such as Germania Sugar Mill seen here, and before sugarcane was measured in tons and not hogsheads, the making of sugar was very different. Open kettles of varying sizes were set in brick and mortar, and open shed-like sugarhouses were built of pine with brick chimneys. As the sugar boiling process was refined, better sugarhouses were built with larger kettles, leading to increased output of hogsheads and continued industry growth. (Courtesy Perry Lowery.)

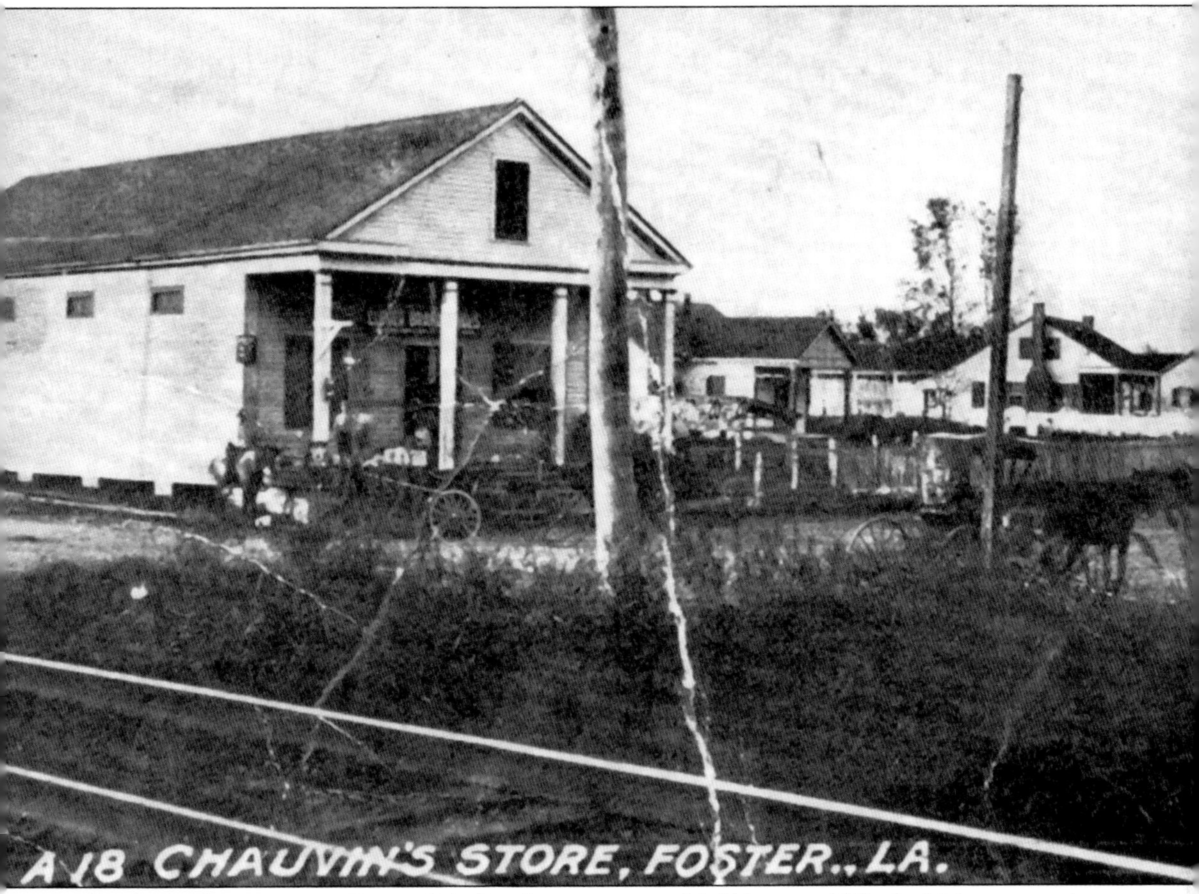

Maryland Plantation, on Bayou Sale Road, encompassed 1,300 acres, 500 of which were under cultivation, principally in cane. The sugarhouse building was cross-shaped, extending 100 feet by 100 feet each way. There was also an underground pipe connection to convey molasses to the Bayou Sale station. Seen here is the Chauvin Store, which was part of the plantation complex and supplied workers with much-needed dry goods and staple items. The plantation workers were often paid in store coins to be redeemed at the company store. Maryland Plantation was the childhood home of Gov. Mike Foster. (Courtesy Perry Lowery.)

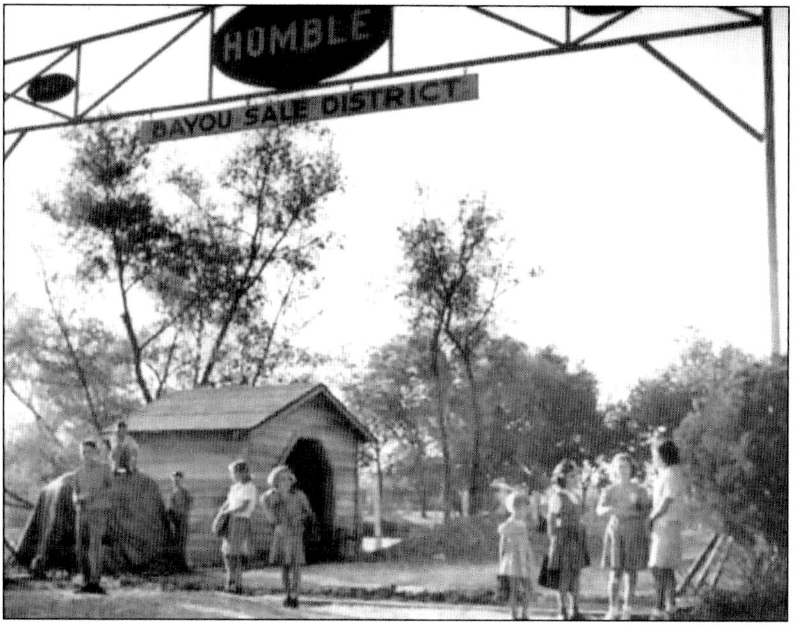

Much like the community built by the Hanson Lumber Company in Garden City, Humble Oil housed its workers in an area called the Humble. These children lived at the Humble and are waiting at the bus stop to be transported into Centerville for school. (Courtesy Perry Lowery.)

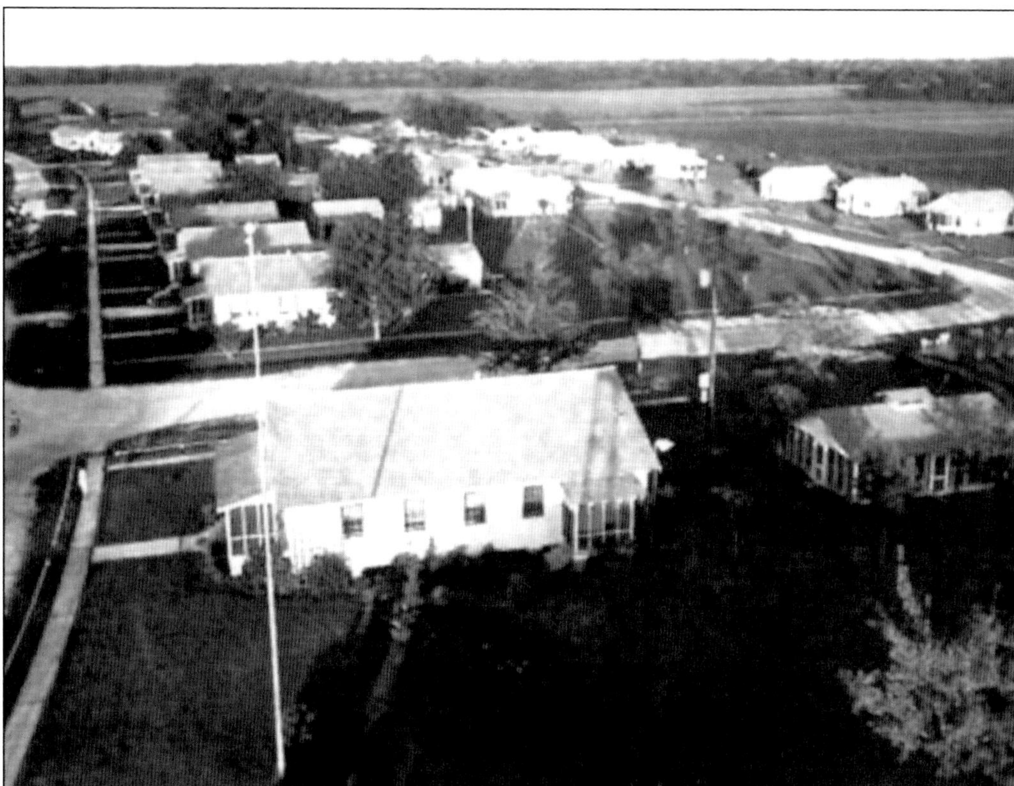

A community was developed for Humble employees who lived and worked in Bayou Sale, with quaint houses, wide streets, and massive lawns; a perfect family setting for children riding bikes and enjoying outdoor sports. Humble later became Exxon and this community ceased to exist. (Courtesy Perry Lowery.)

Six
Morgan City, Patterson, and Berwick

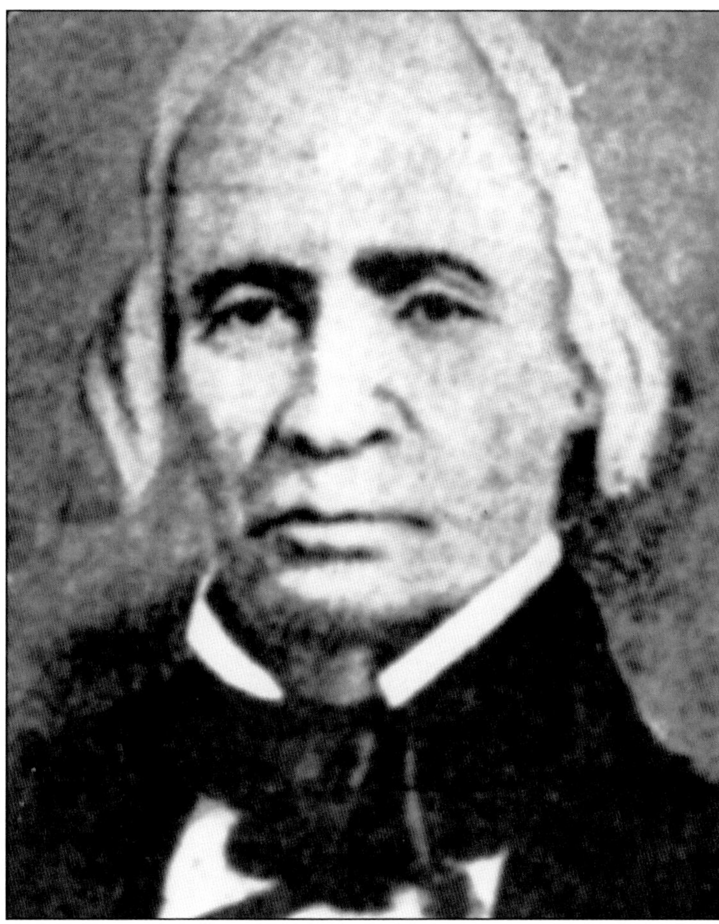

Dr. Walter Brashear (1776–1860) came from Kentucky and established the community of Brashear, which was first known as Tiger Island when it was inherited by the Brashear family in 1842 from a Spanish land grant to Joseph and Elinor Berwick in 1797. One of the oldest towns in the area, it sits on a broad prairie overlooking Berwick Bay, surrounded by rich-yielding sugar lands. (Courtesy Morgan City Archives.)

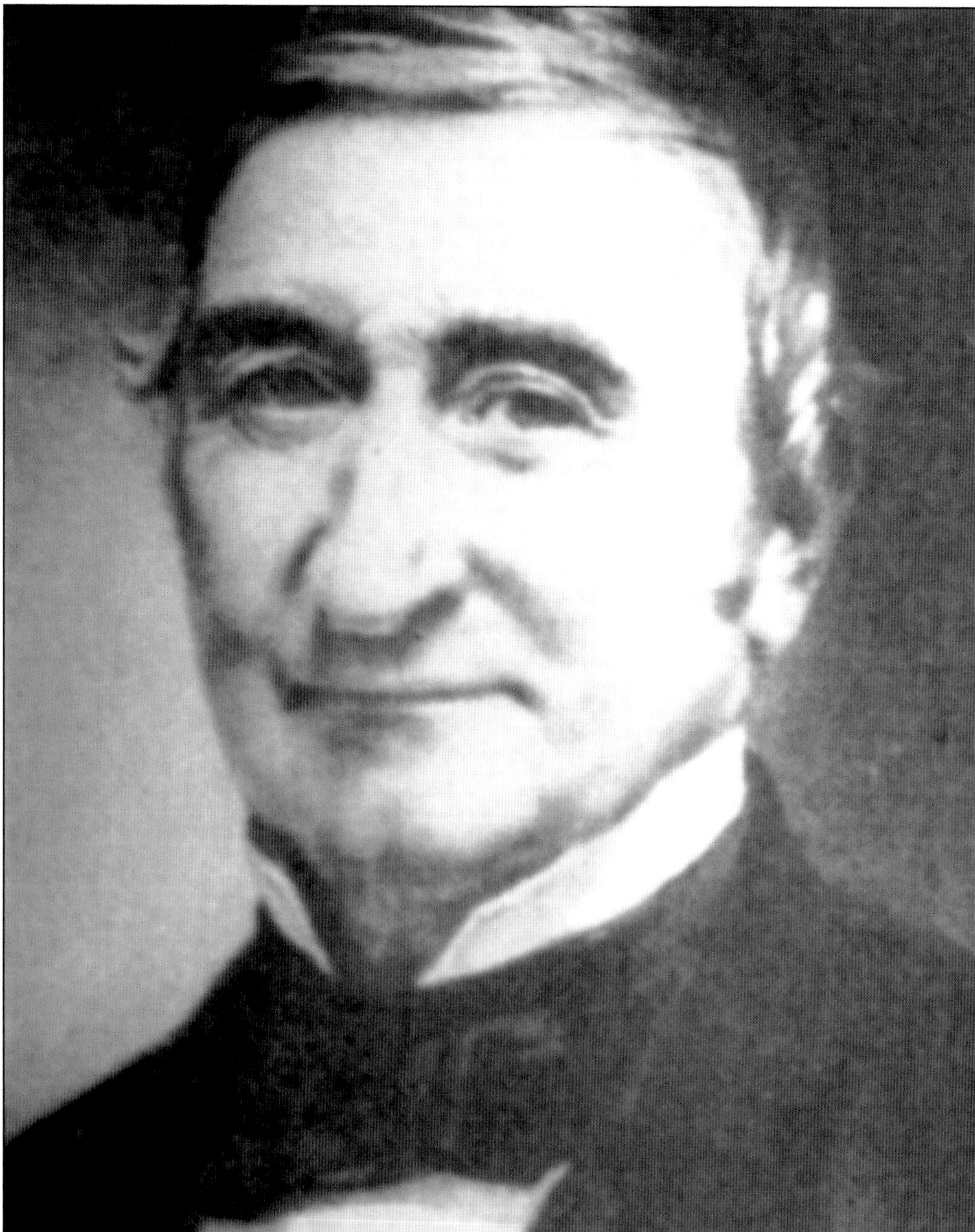

Brashear was renamed Morgan City in honor of Charles Morgan, who, after acquiring the New Orleans, Opelousas & Great Western Railroad, extended the rail to the settlement on Tiger Island in 1869. Immediately, Morgan began building 1,800 feet of wharves around town and operated a boat line from Brashear to ports in Texas. Morgan is also credited with dredging an outlet that helped the area evolve into a seaport. (Courtesy Morgan City Archives.)

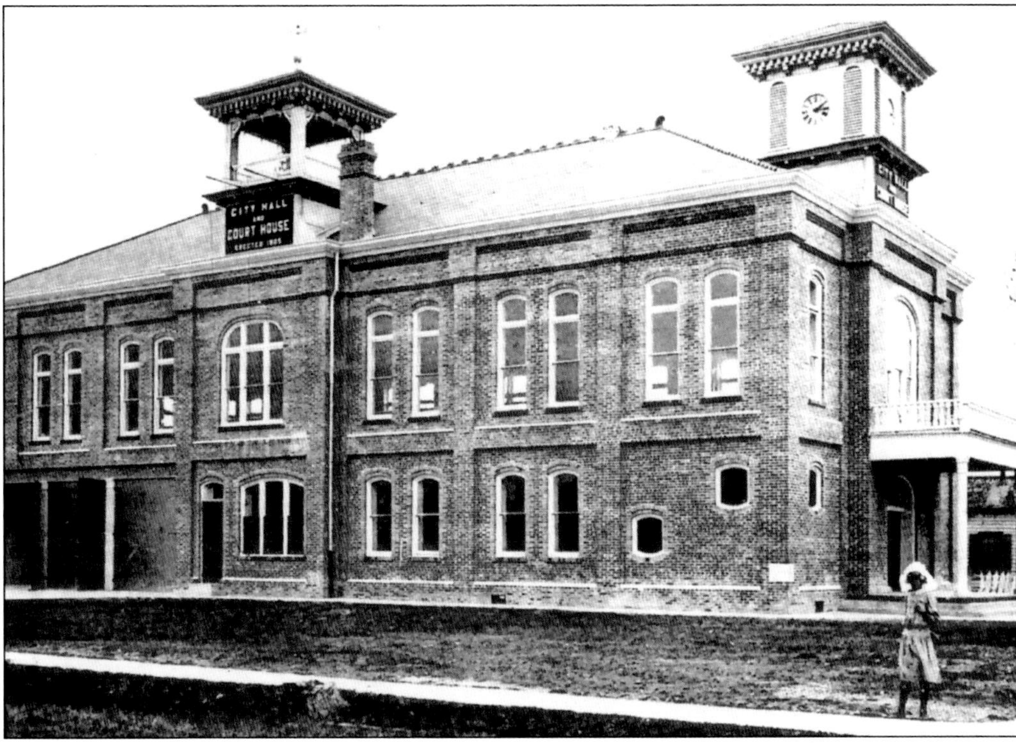

With a population of 2,500 in 1898, Morgan City supported a number of manufacturing and business establishments. Its public buildings included a customhouse, a courthouse, city hall, and a post office. In 1876, the name was officially changed from Brashear to Morgan City. (Courtesy Morgan City Archives.)

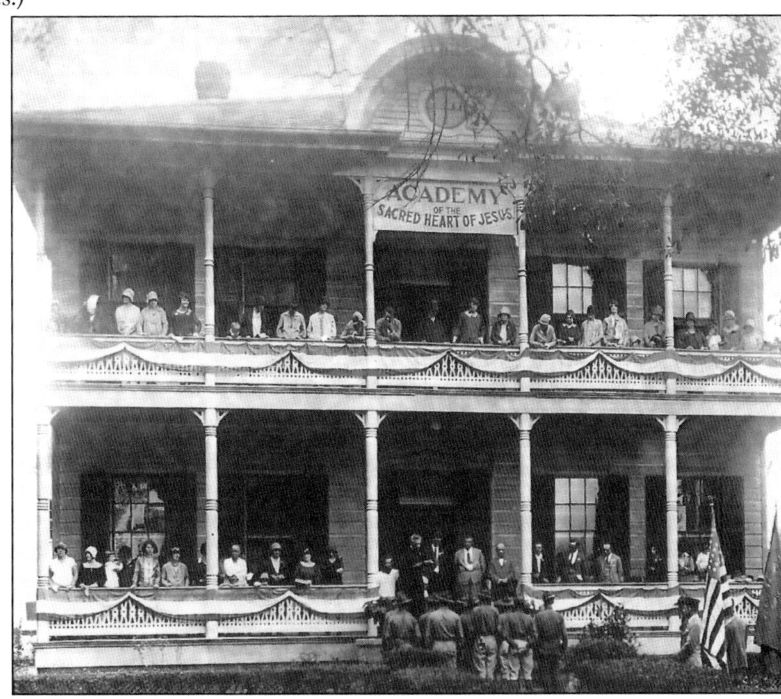

The first movement to open a public school in Morgan City was the Academy of the Sacred Heart of Jesus in 1861. By 1876, a new public school opened for only a portion of the year. Other schools included Morgan City Academy, Catholic Parochial School, Select Group for Girls, and Knitting School. (Courtesy Morgan City Archives.)

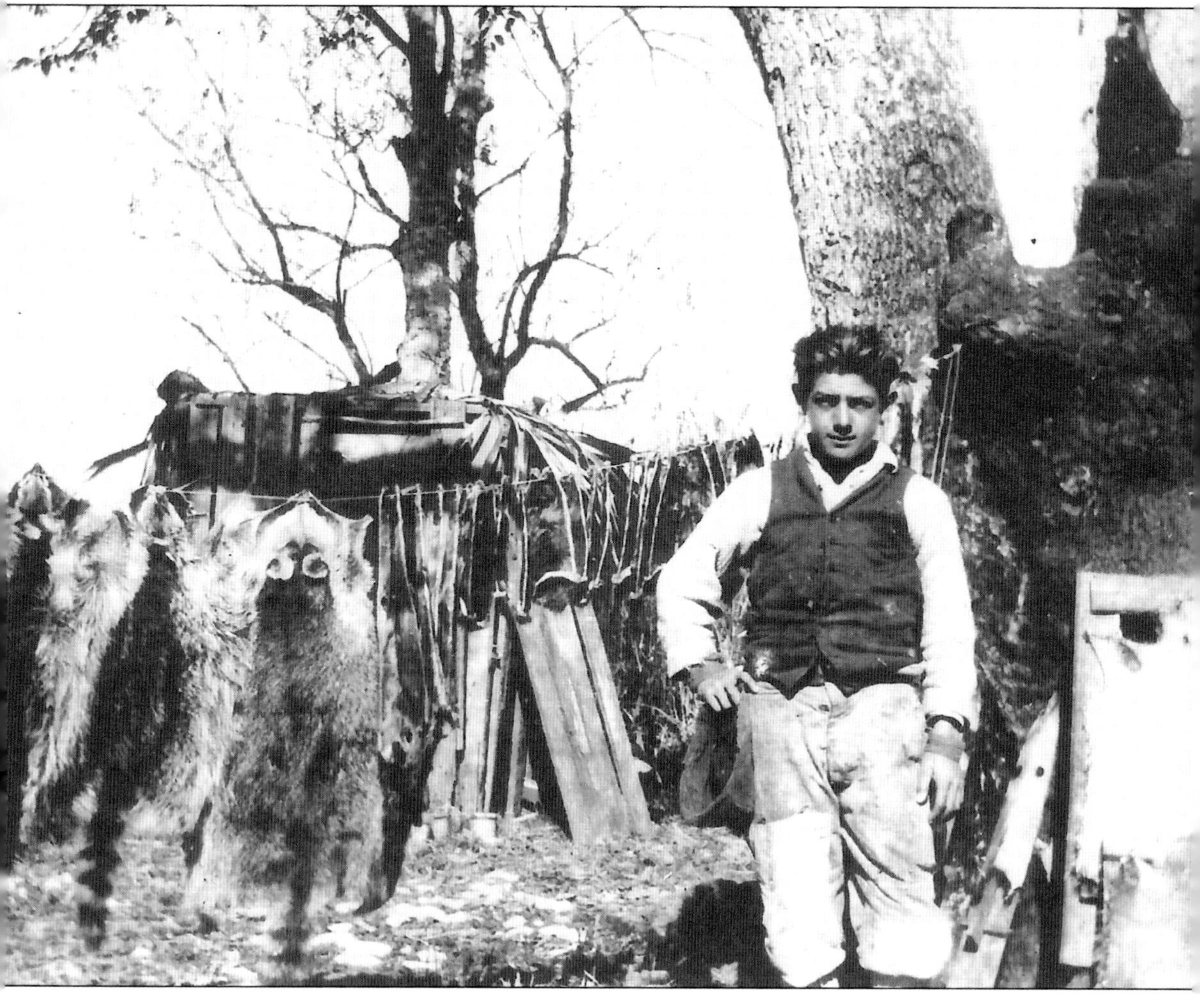

This young man on Avoca Island shows off the fur hides he has drying in preparation for being taken to market. At one time, Louisiana was the leading producer of mink and muskrat fur pelts in North America. The state's history of trapping furbearers and alligators has played an important role in its culture and economy. In the 1720s, New Orleans was a major trading center on the Mississippi River, making it a natural hub for the fur trade. (Courtesy Morgan City Archives.)

Cut timber was pushed down the rivers to the sawmills that dotted the bayou banks. The timber industry was the mainstay of Patterson, where up to 100,000 feet of lumber was cut daily. When the short side and long side were both in operation, Patterson's mill worked on 24-hour shifts. (Courtesy Morgan City Archives.)

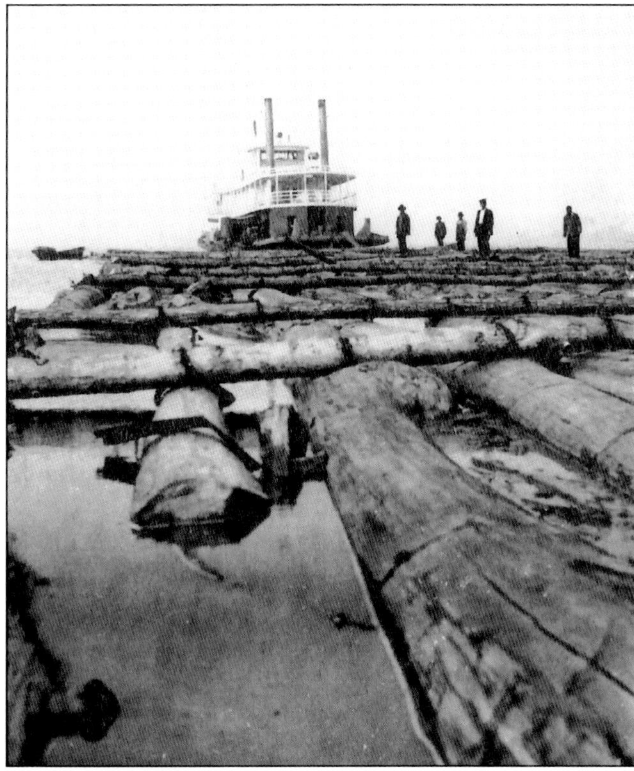

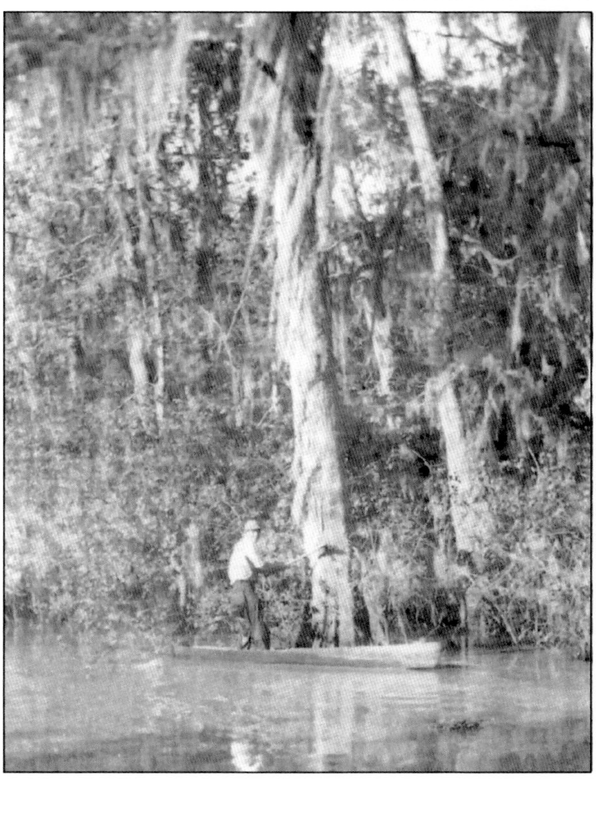

In the 1920s and 1930s in south Louisiana, work in the lumber industry enabled citizens to supplement their income from trapping and fishing. In fact, by 1912, trapping was so widespread in Louisiana that the legislature imposed trapping season dates and required trappers to be licensed. (Courtesy Morgan City Archives.)

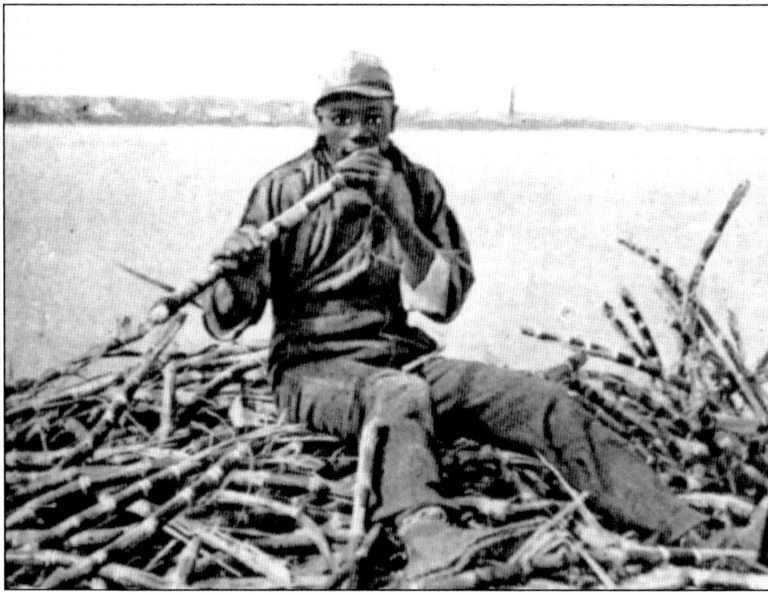

Sugar boats such as the *J.N. Pharr* docked at the Atchafalaya River in Berwick during the steamboat era in St. Mary Parish. Sternwheelers were the principal means of transportation before the advent of the railroad in the area. Loaded with cut cane, they would make their way down the bayous to the mills to be refined. (Courtesy Morgan City Archives.)

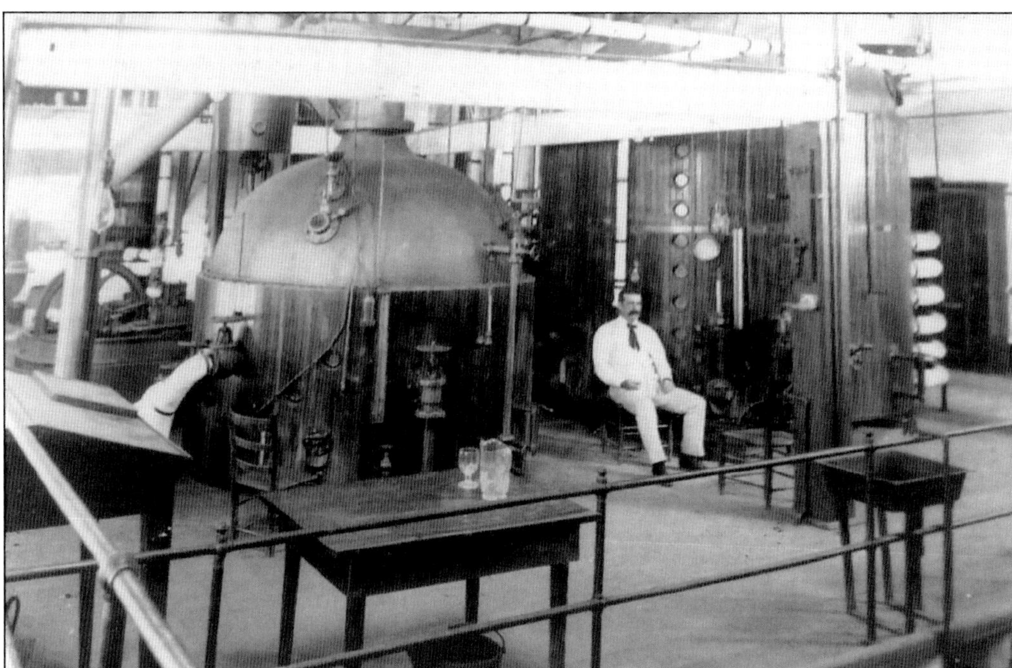

The sugar industry continued making great strides in the refining of raw cane into sugar and molasses. The Calumet Plantation was a new, up-to-date refinery that used the Deming system of clarification, which was in vogue at the time. Calumet also housed an experimental station, employing chemists year-round. (Courtesy Morgan City Archives.)

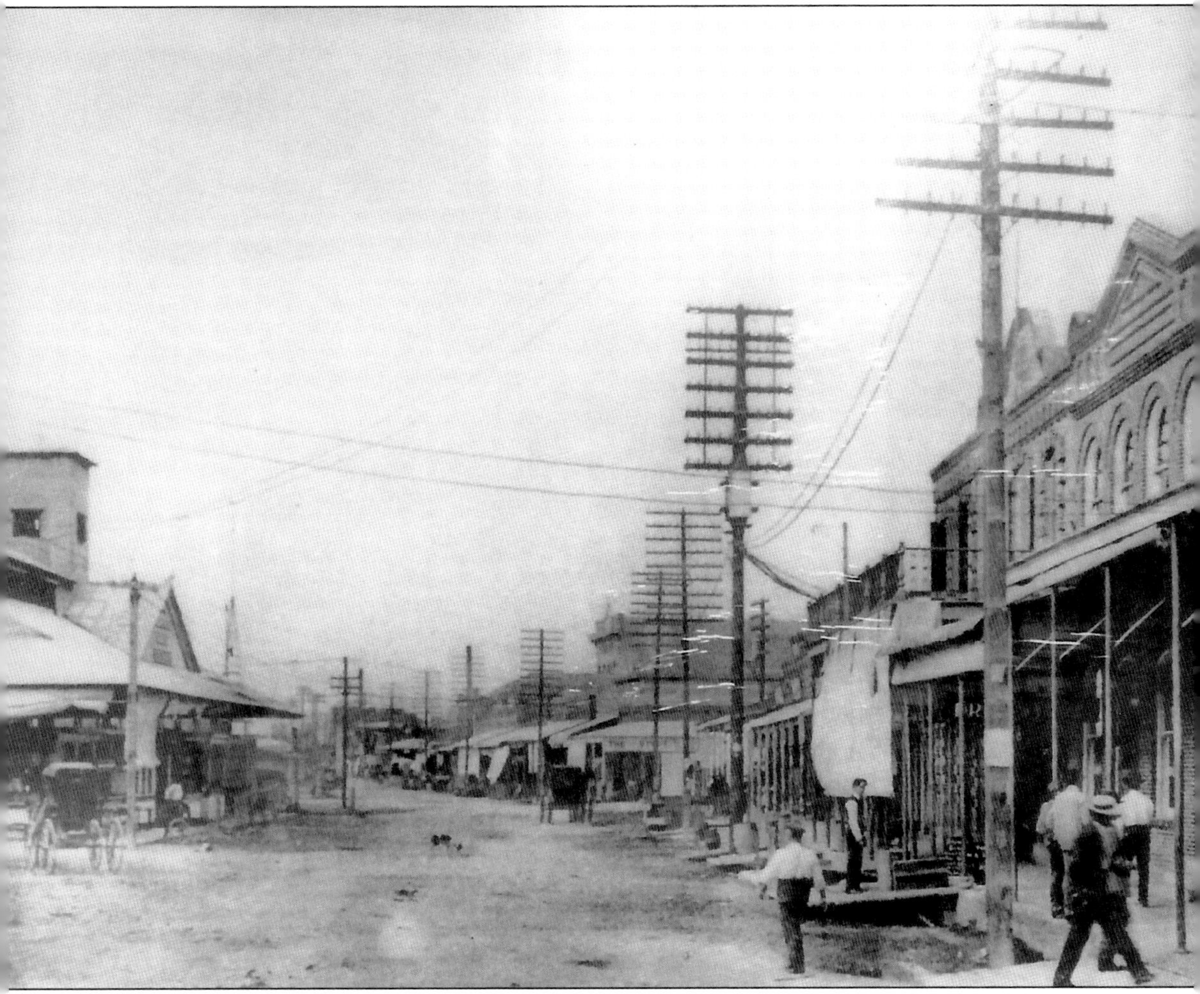

Morgan City is unique in that its waterfront docks are open to Front Street and Railroad Avenue businesses, making ship repairs and the purchasing of supplies like ice and other necessities easier. The fishing fleet would arrive dockside each day and load tupelo boxes full of iced-down fish, shrimp, oysters, and crabs onto the railroad dock for the 2:00 p.m. departure to markets along the railway. (Courtesy Morgan City Archives.)

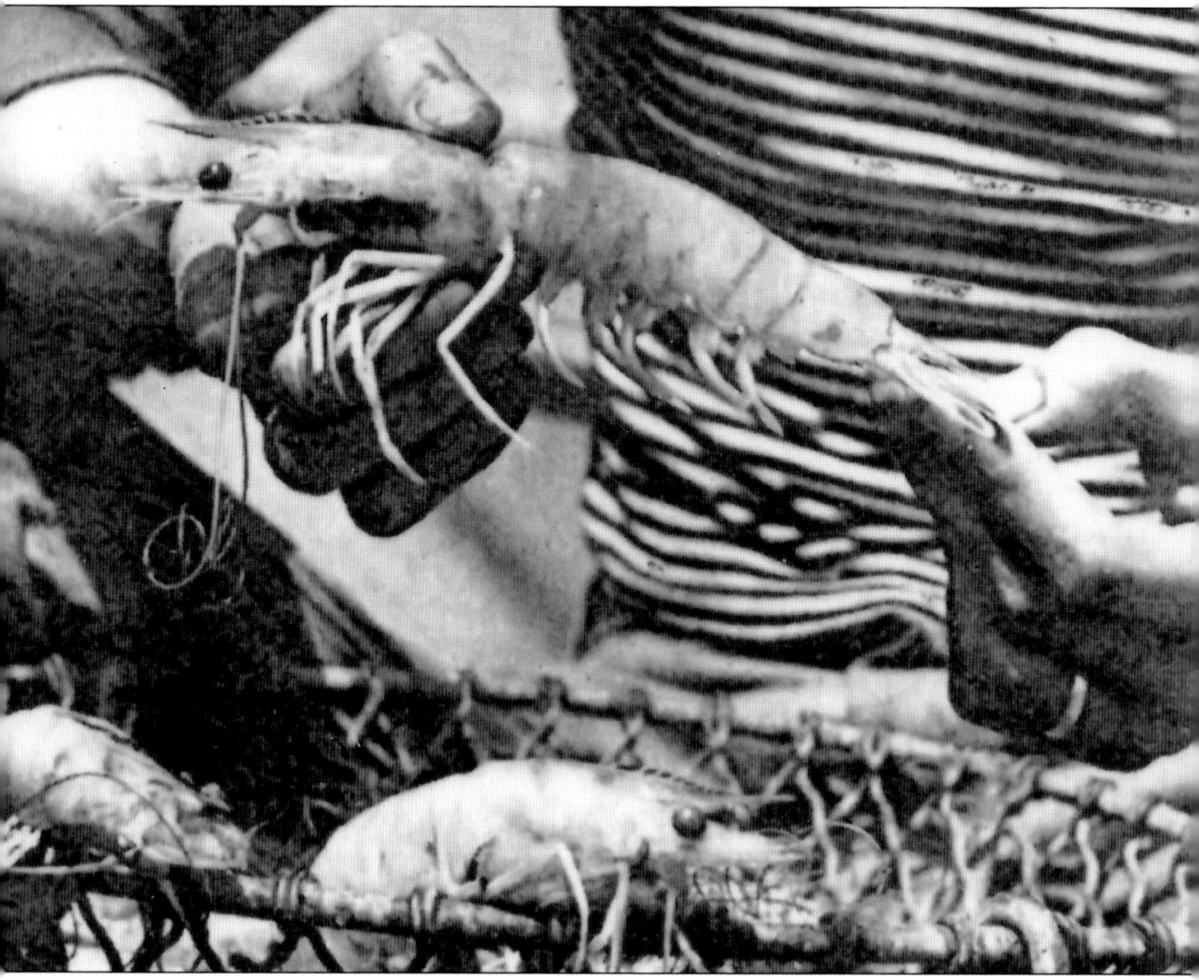

Shrimping has a long history in Louisiana. Waterfront legend tells of the first catch of 40 or 50 barrels of jumbo shrimp by a rugged Scandinavian captain, Ted Anderson, who found that dealers refused the huge shrimp, saying, "There has to be something wrong with shrimp swole up like that." That was the beginning of a revolution in the shrimp industry in Louisiana, a product of which is seen here around 1900. Fishermen have taken advantage of Louisiana's marshes and estuaries since the earliest settlement. Two types of fishermen shrimp in coastal Louisiana; those with smaller vessels in the inland bays and shallow water zones and those with larger vessels, who shrimp offshore in federal waters. In the early years, shrimp was largely sold fresh in local markets. (Courtesy Morgan City Archives.)

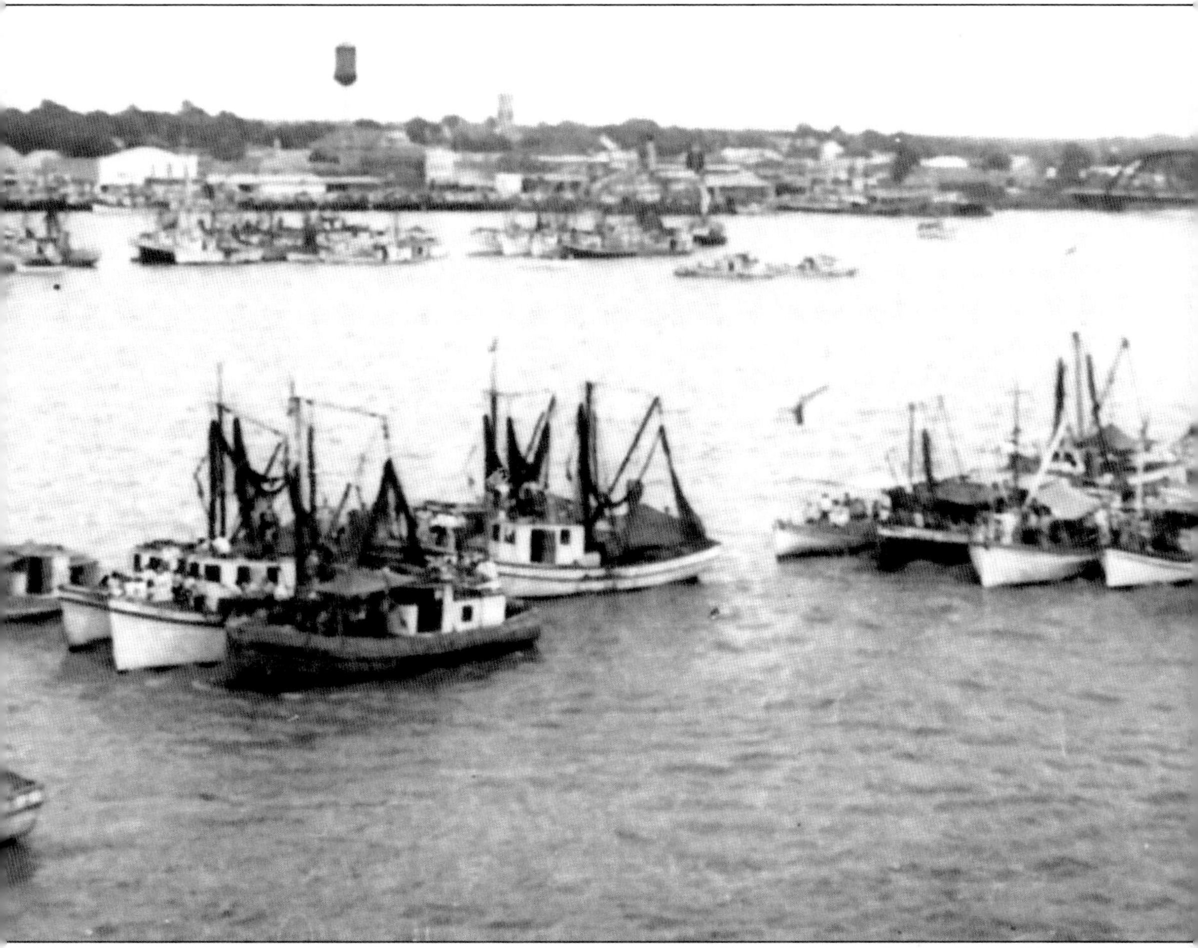

The Blessing of the Fleet and water parade on Berwick Bay is a tradition that began centuries ago in fishing communities. The practice is predominantly Catholic, with the priest's blessing meant to ensure a safe and bountiful season. In most ports, the event was brought by immigrants who held strongly to their Catholic beliefs. The events that make up the ritual vary by community and range from simple ceremonies to multi-day festivals involving a Catholic mass, parades, and pageantry. (Courtesy Morgan City Archives.)

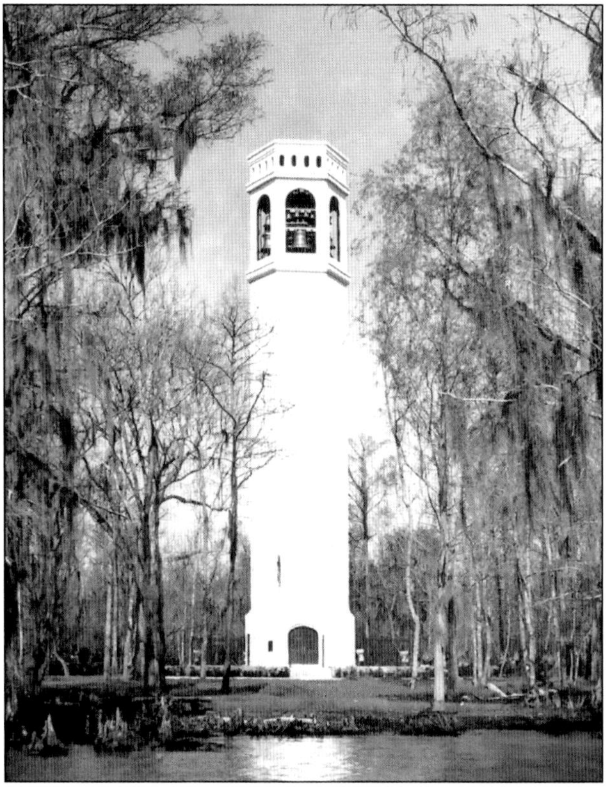

The Brownell Carillon tower on the shore of Lake Palourde was a gift of Claire Horatio Brownell, a member of one of Louisiana's pioneer families. She was always devoted to the land that contributed so much to her family's comfort and welfare. In order to show her gratefulness, she conceived the idea of perpetuating the serenity, beauty, and abundance of the swamp with the development of a quiet park, native to the area. It was her wish that the park be a nondenominational setting retaining its wild atmosphere, where a person could retreat to commune with God. (Courtesy Morgan City Archives.)

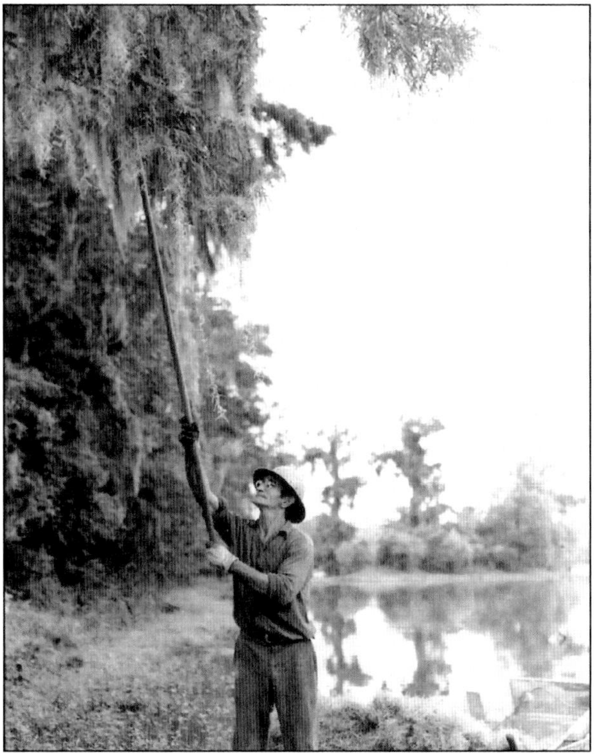

In this 1930s image, a man picks moss, a renewable resource that grows on many of the trees in south Louisiana and can be harvested and sold for use in mattresses, upholstery, and exterior plastering. It has a mysterious quality as it hangs from the low-growing branches of live oaks that can be both a scary or romantic reminder of yesteryear. (Courtesy Morgan City Archives.)

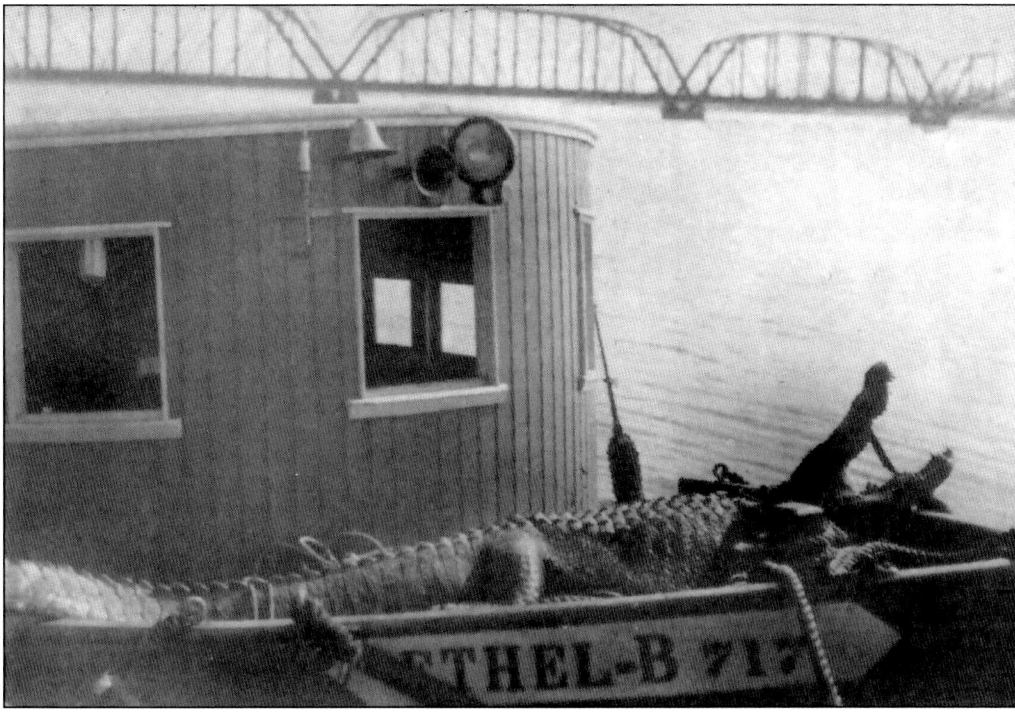

A 14-foot alligator lies on the deck of a boat docked on Front Street in Morgan City. The sensitive hearts of legendary naturalists would have been touched by the peaceful surroundings of the area. Thoreau would have likely taken long strolls through the wooded areas, while Monet would have been awestruck by the subtle contrasts of colors of plants, flowers, birds, and trees. But this is no Walden Pond; lurking beneath these seemingly peaceful waters are reptiles of monstrous proportions like this one. (Courtesy Morgan City Archives.)

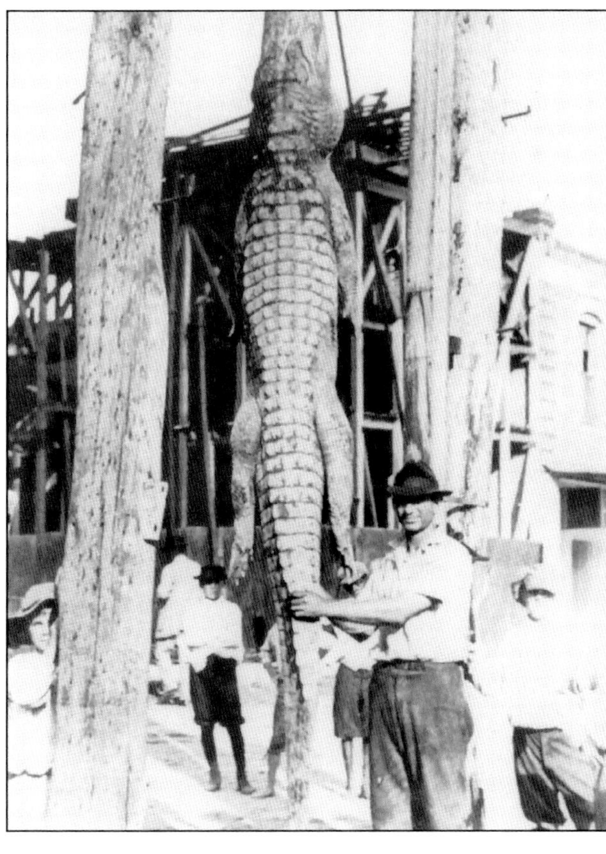

This large alligator is measured in preparation for a sale on Front Street. Alligators are often harvested for their valuable skin, which is sold for alligator-skin shoes, boots, purses, wallets, vests, and jackets. The skins of many of the alligators harvested each year in the United States are shipped overseas for tanning. (Courtesy Morgan City Archives.)

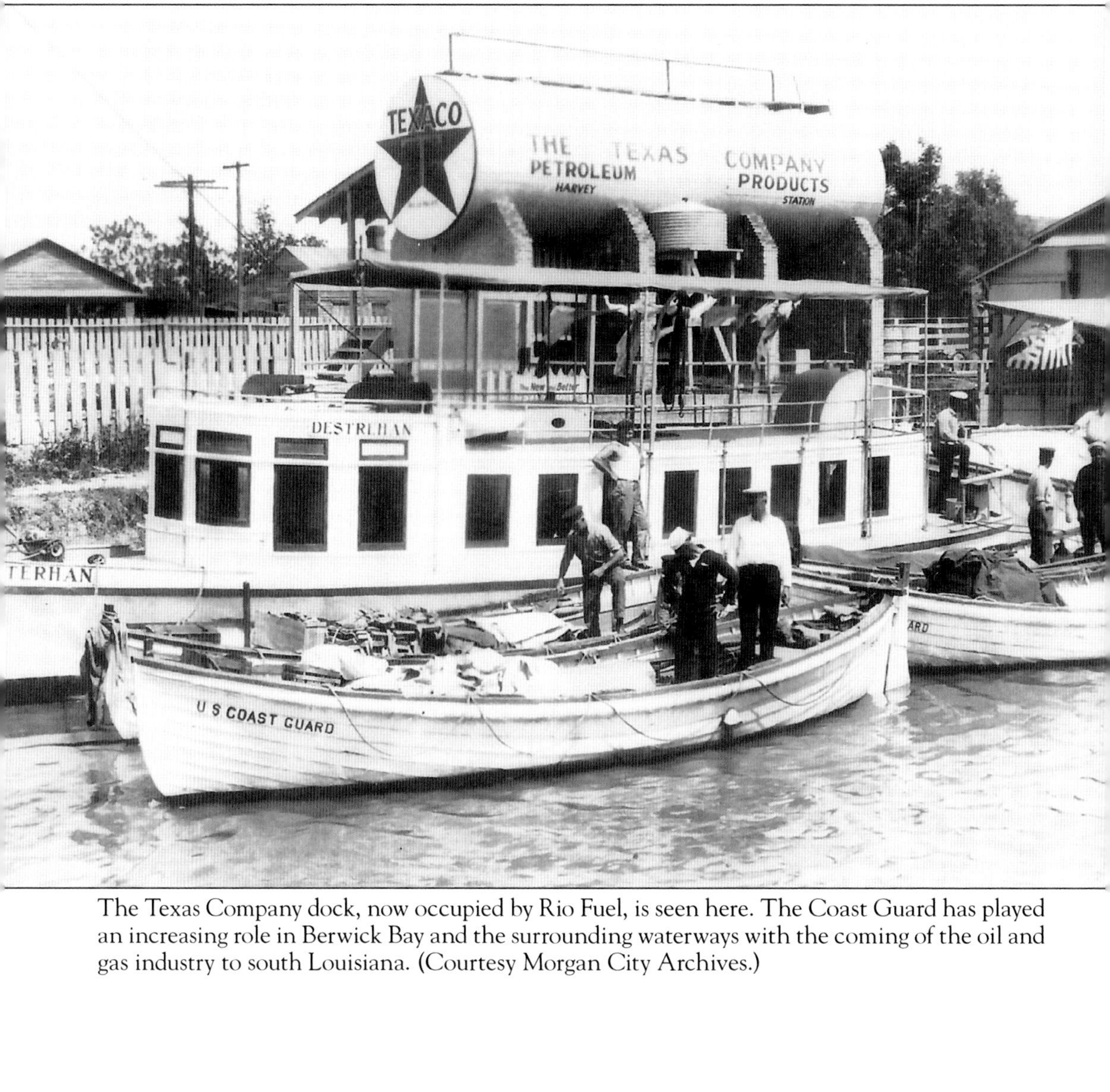

The Texas Company dock, now occupied by Rio Fuel, is seen here. The Coast Guard has played an increasing role in Berwick Bay and the surrounding waterways with the coming of the oil and gas industry to south Louisiana. (Courtesy Morgan City Archives.)

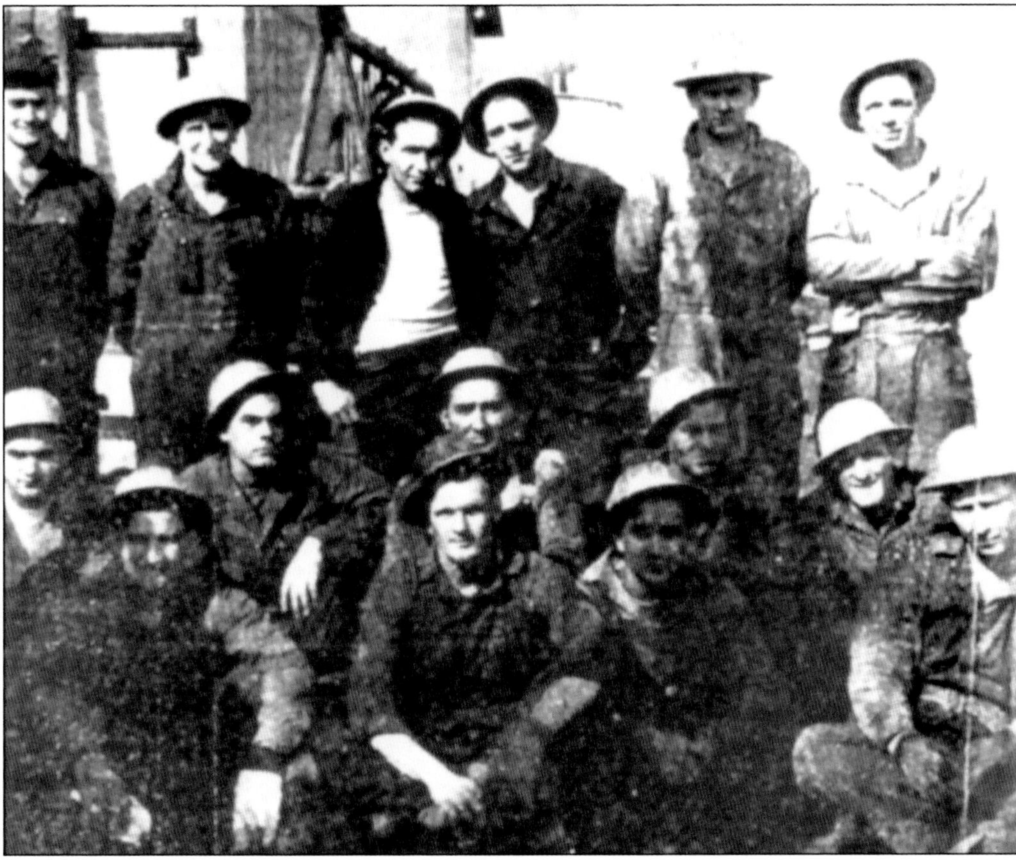

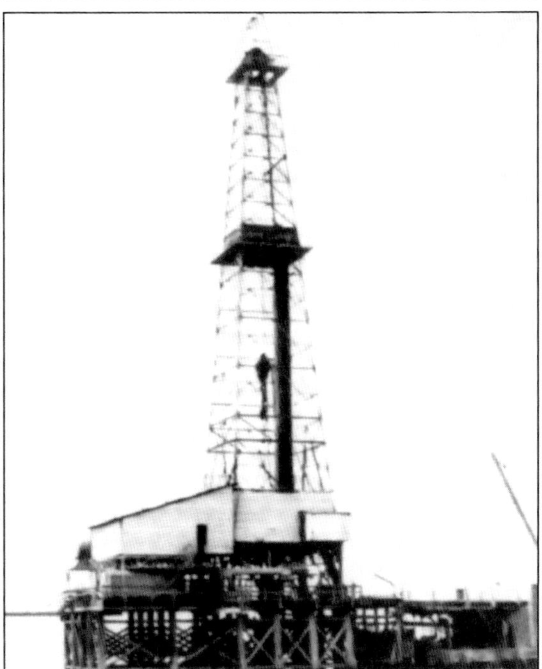

The crew of Kerr-McGee Rig No. 16 is seen here. Exploration activities continued to increase as Kerr-McGee expanded its drilling operations to the Gulf of Mexico. Seeking to capitalize on the increased need for refined oil products, the company also moved into "downstream" operations when it purchased its first refinery in 1945. (Courtesy Morgan City Archives.)

Kerr-McGee's Rig No. 16 was the first producing well out of sight of land. The well was brought in on November 14, 1947, as the energy needs of the postwar United States were rising dramatically. By then, the country was using as much oil in one year as the entire world used in 1938. Kerr-McGee responded to this trend with many firsts in oil exploration and production, including the completion of this well 11 miles off Louisiana's shore. (Courtesy Morgan City Archives.)

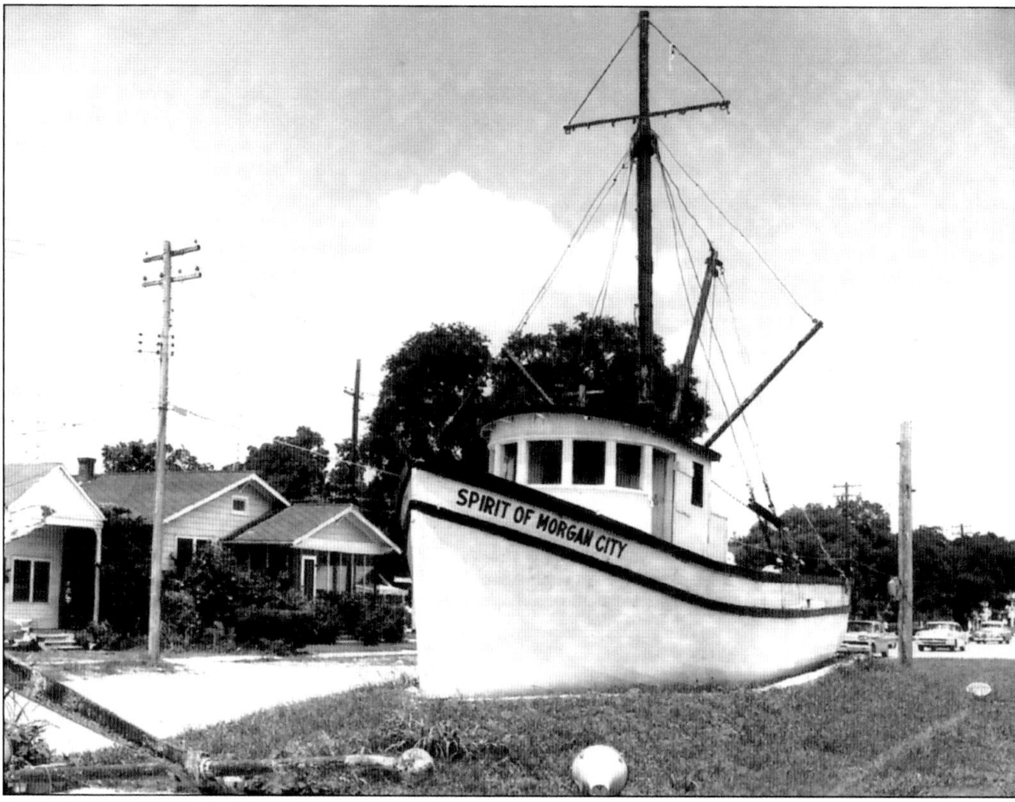

Spirit of Morgan City serves as homage to the discovery of jumbo shrimp off the coast of Morgan City and the fishing industries and welcomes visitors as they enter Morgan City. (Courtesy Morgan City Archives.)

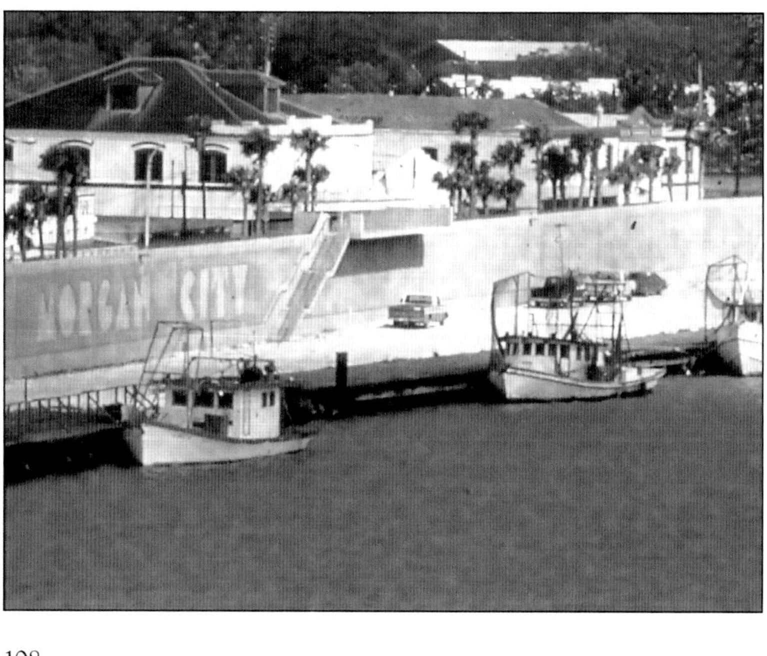

This waterfront view of Front Street in Morgan City during the 1973 flood proves once again that living and working along waterways has its disadvantages. After it was flooded numerous times, a wall was constructed to hold back floodwaters from the business and residential district of historic Morgan City. (Courtesy Morgan City Archives.)

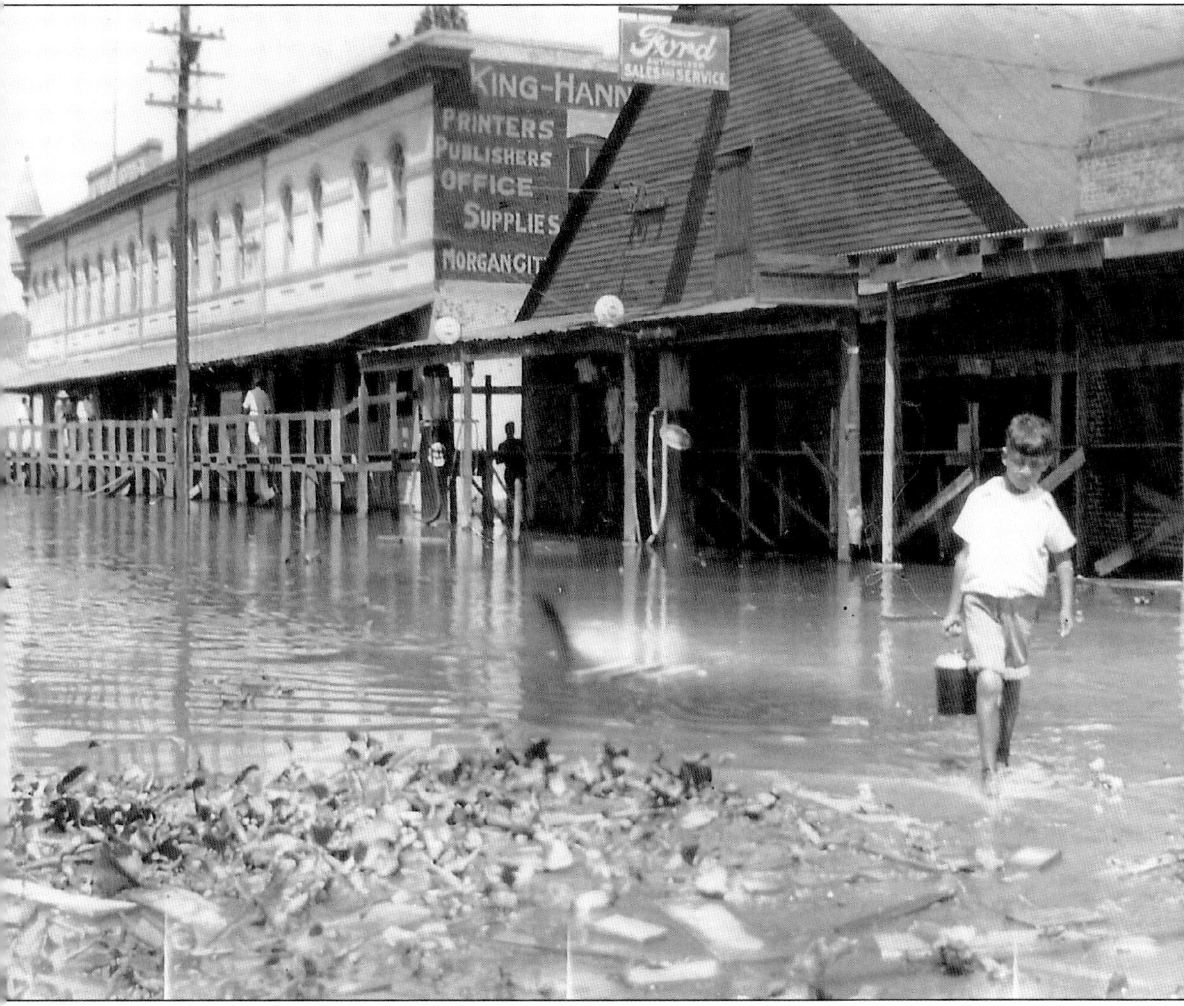

On the corner of Front Street and Railroad Avenue, the unique open dock area of Front Street did little to hold back the rising waters in 1912. (Courtesy Morgan City Archives.)

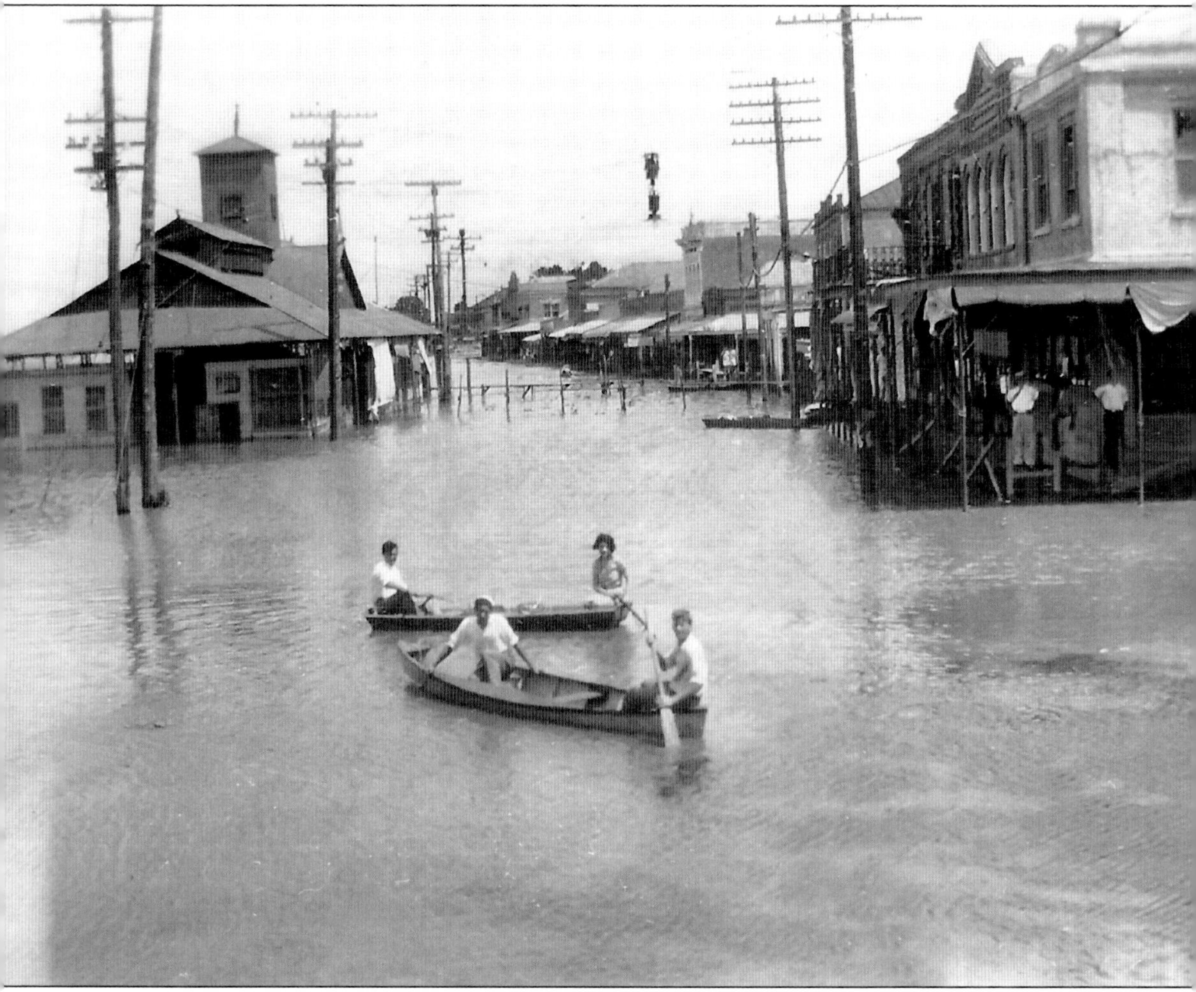

The corner of Everett and Second Streets is seen here during the 1927 flood along the 100-year floodplain. Once again, the floods caused damage to businesses and residences. (Courtesy Morgan City Archives.)

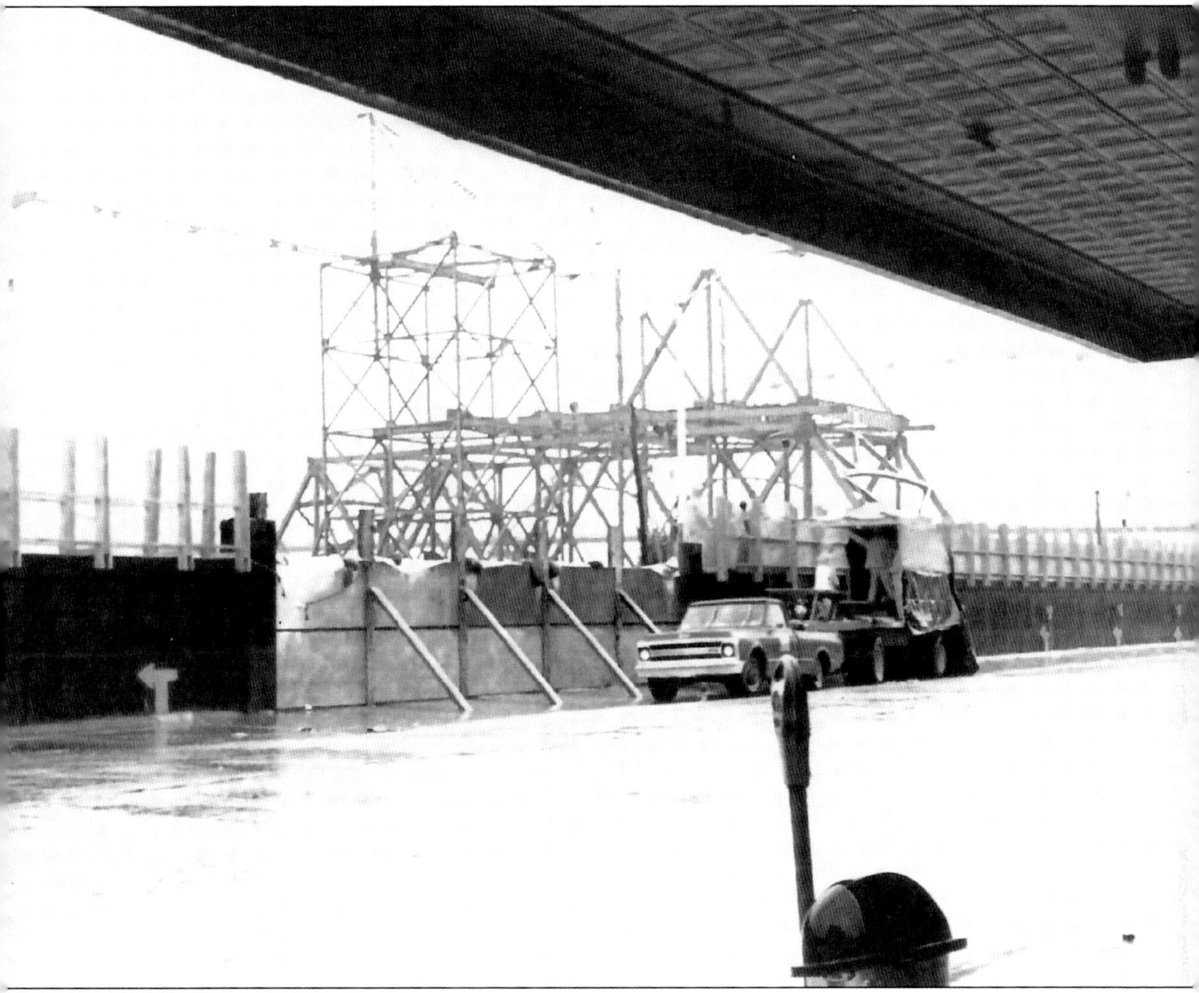

Wooden mud boxes were built atop the seawall in an effort to hold back the floodwaters in 1973. In the background is the ongoing construction of the Highway 90 Bridge across Berwick Bay. (Courtesy Morgan City Archives.)

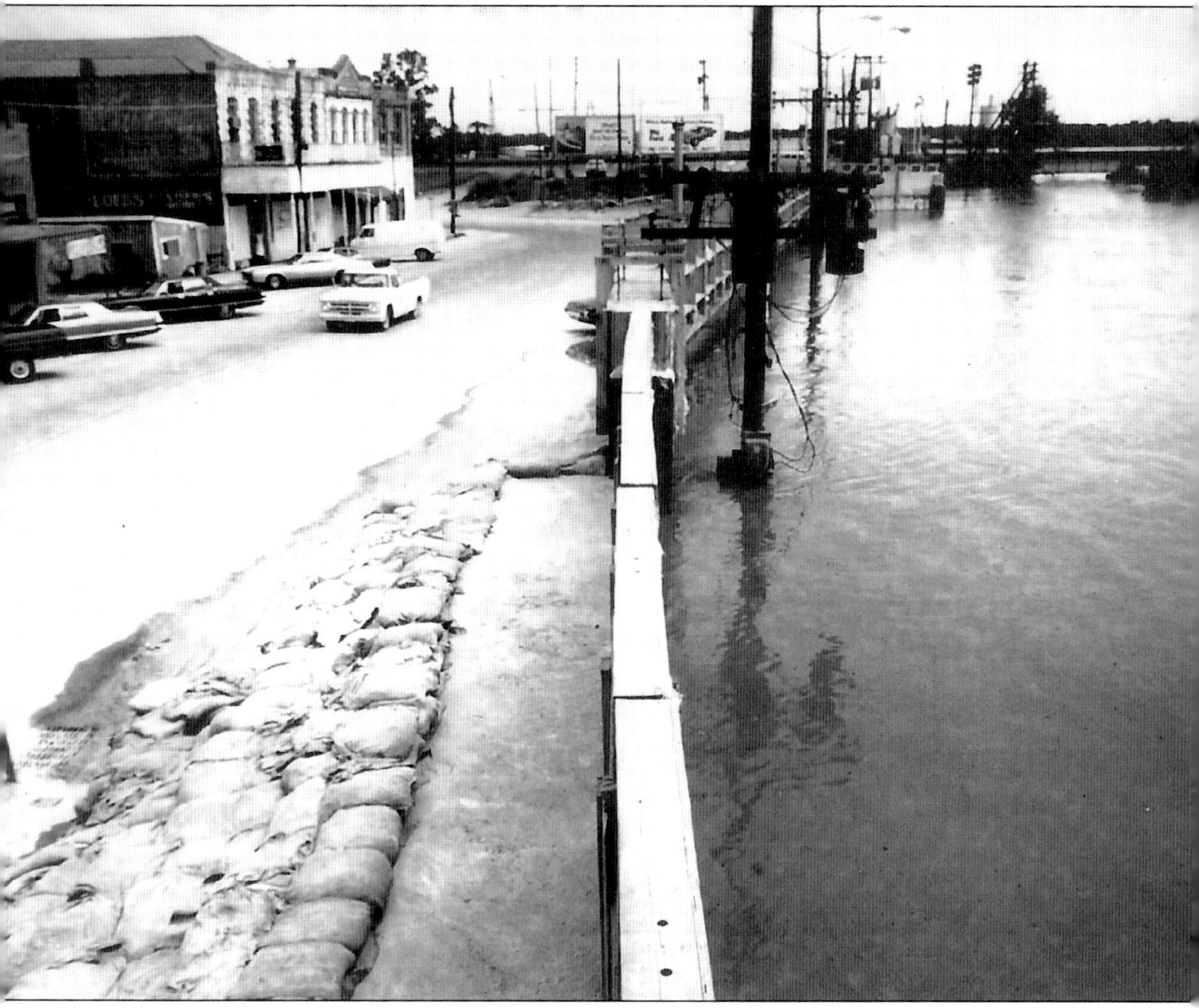

The seawall was reinforced with sandbags against the rising floodwaters in 1973. A new seawall has been constructed with thick concrete slabs that can be closed during flood events and opened to allow access to the businesses that service the maritime industry. (Courtesy Morgan City Archives.)

Seven

This, That, and Everything in Between

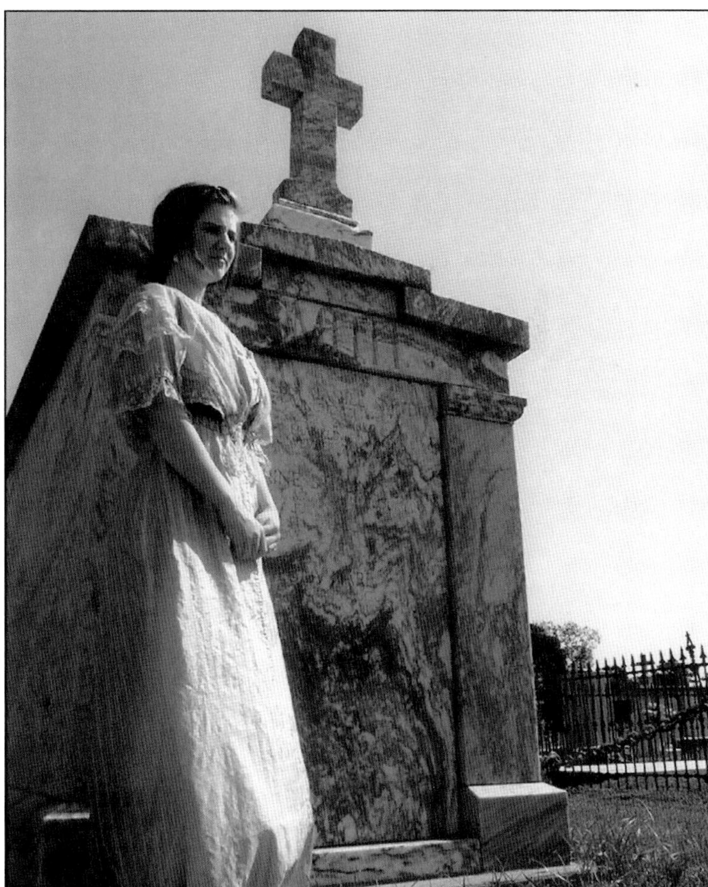

Sarah Stirling poses as a character from "Voices of the Past." Spend a weekend with us in beautiful Franklin, Louisiana, with over 400 properties listed in the National Register of Historic Places. Stroll down the oak arcade, drive along a boulevard of cast iron lampposts and early 19th century Main Street. Take the Sweet Remembrances cemetery tour in the Fall, visit historic homes, churches, and museums. Or take the walking or driving tour through the Cajun Coast's boulevards and byways. See for yourself the town Lyle Saxton called "one of the prettiest towns in Louisiana." (Courtesy Stephen Stirling.)

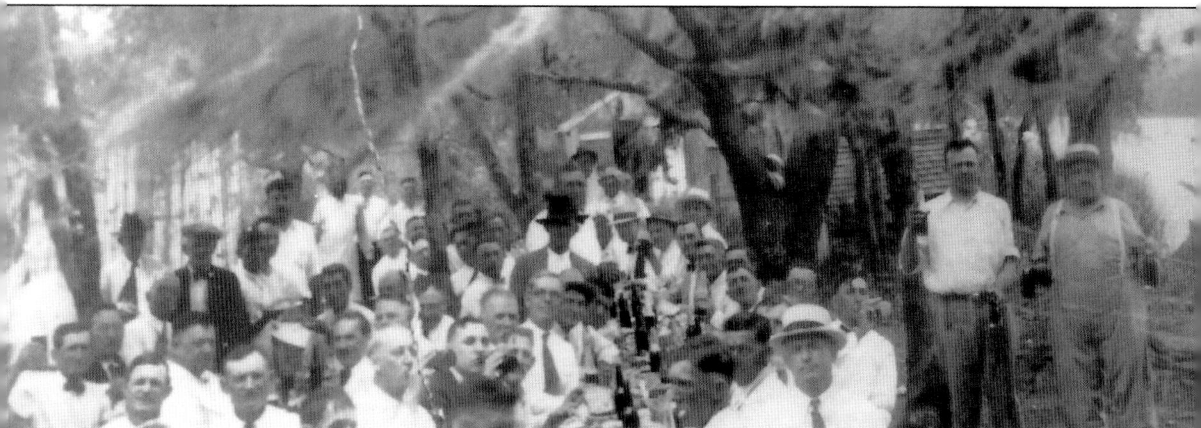

Shown here are the Druids, once a very active organization in Franklin, during a picnic at "Cozo" Naquin's camp at Onion Bayou along with the New Orleans Druids. Among those pictured are Louis Falterman, Sidney Guillotte, Pastor Chauvin, Archange Barrilleaux, R.E. Keenze, Mr. Guillotte, David LeBlanc, William Talbot, Joe Polito, Eugene O'Connor, Frank Clausen, Joe Jacobs, Duval Hebert, Eugene Larpenteur, Lee Charpentier, Arnold Barrilleaux, Numa Barrilleaux, Lloyd Kihnel, C.S. Brenn, William T. Durr, Charlie LeGas, Henry LeGas, Marion Lombardo, Easton Charpentier, Wilsie Chauvin, Joe Lombardo, Lyman Alpha, Wilfred Borel, Nelson Borel, and Oscar Borel.

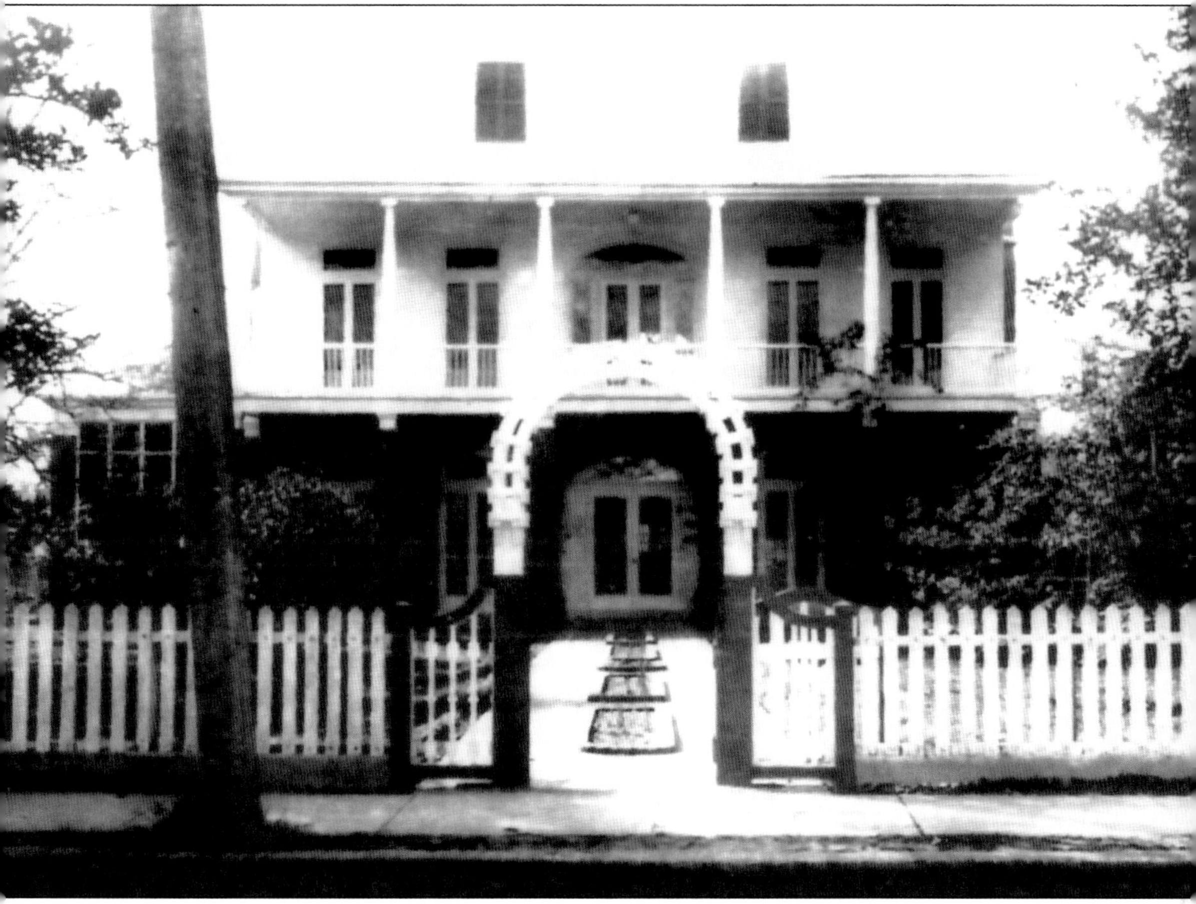

The Allain House at 909 Second Street in Franklin is a colonial home built in 1832 that housed the first bank in southern Louisiana outside New Orleans and west of the Mississippi River, from 1837 to 1847. It was occupied by Union forces during the Civil War, who were quartered on the second floor. Displaying their usual audacity while swarming over Southern homes, they stabled their horses on the first floor. But perhaps its most noteworthy guest was none other than Davy Crockett, who stayed in the home while on his way to the Alamo. Legend says that Crockett made a promise to his wife that he would free his slaves while in Franklin before heading to the Alamo. (Courtesy Perry Lowery.)

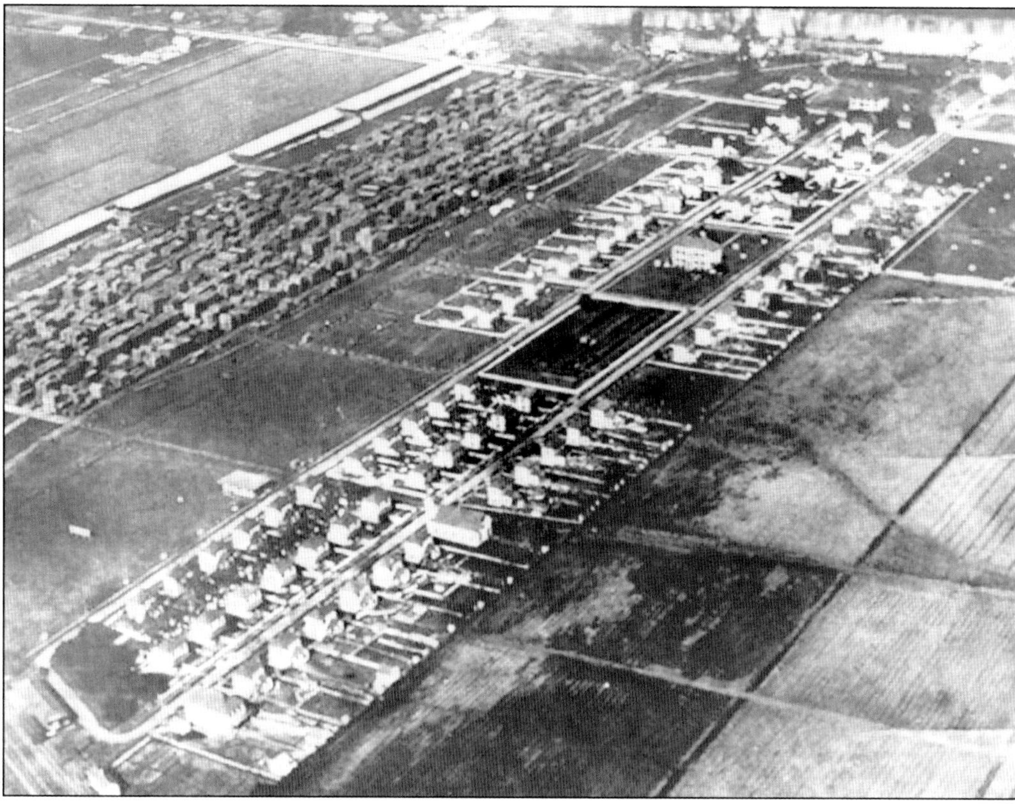

This aerial view shows May Brothers Lumber and the community built around lumber in Garden City. Today, a relatively small number of the cultural resources associated with the industrial production of lumber remain. The lumber company town seen here, including company commissaries, owners' and managers' houses, and company-built public buildings such as schools and churches are all gone, with much of the land returning to sugarcane production. There is almost no trace of the booming industry that encompassed this little town; only the main office and the manager's house remain, all others have been torn down except for one building that was moved into Franklin. This photograph shows all of the workers' housing, the lumber stacked and waiting to be shipped by rail, the rail line, and all the other necessary buildings the large working community needed. (Courtesy Perry Lowery.)

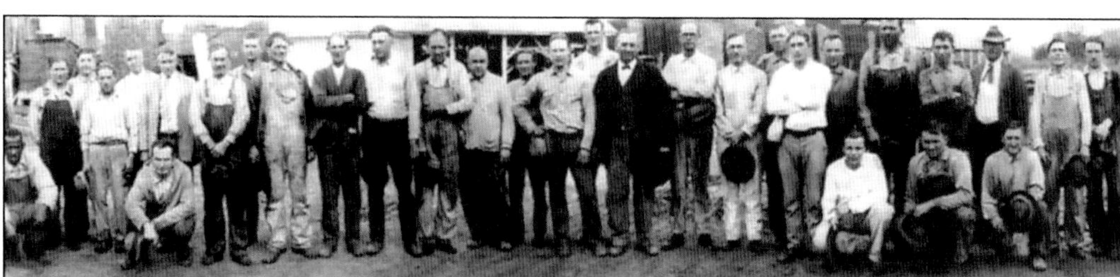

This photograph, a companion to the one on page 57, is a staff photograph of the supervisors of the Kyle-Taylor Lumber Company, which unfortunately burned in 1897 and was not covered by insurance. Because of generous lending from Edward Hanson and Frank Williams, credit was extended and the mill was rebuilt that year, later becoming the Blakesley–St. John Lumberyard. (Courtesy Perry Lowery.)

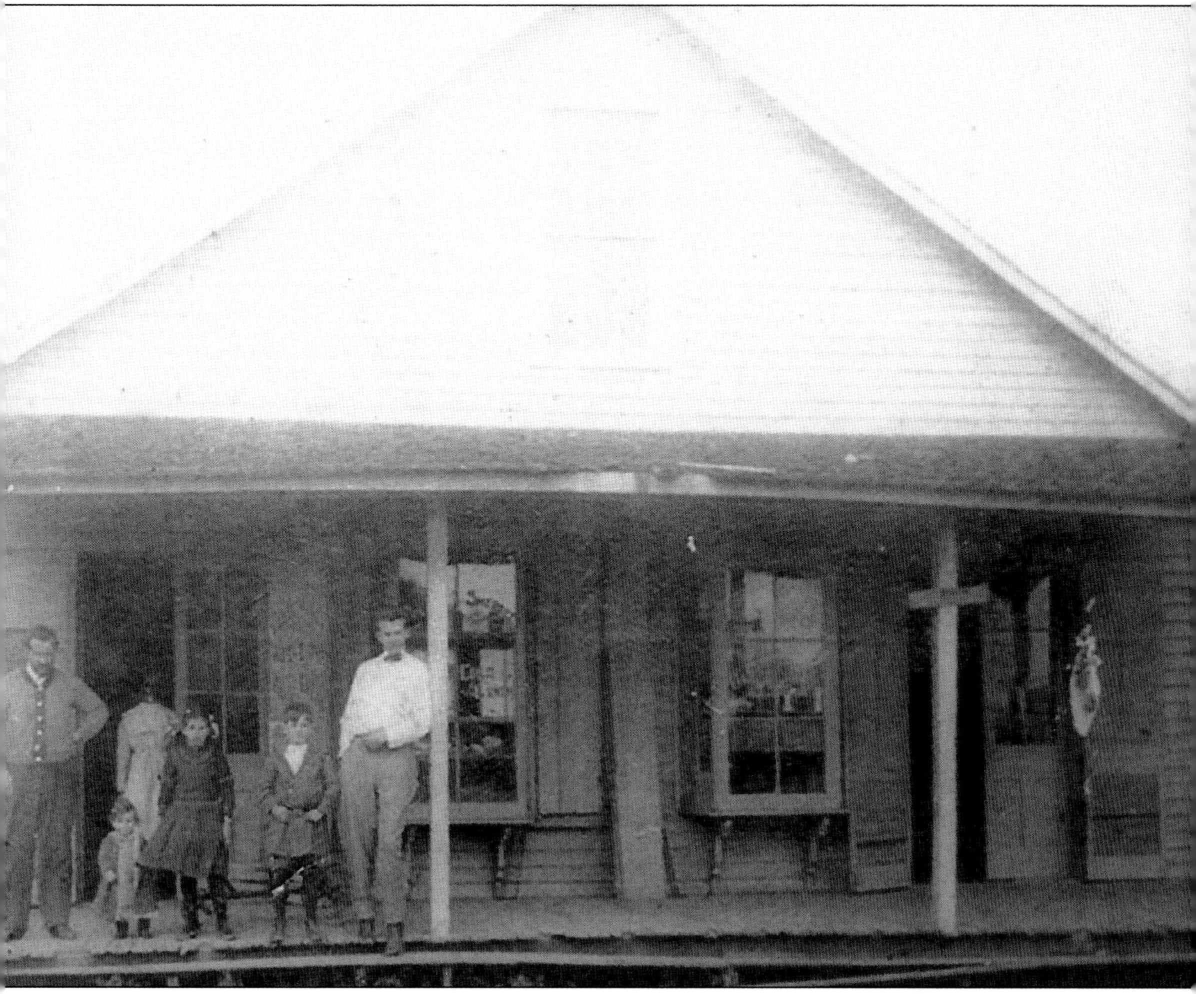

This is a companion photograph to the one on page 24, showing the Navarro Saloon in Baldwin after the renovations were complete. Even as late as the 1970s, many of these small grocery stores were still open and offered something unique and wonderful. For instance, Achee Grocery offered boiled hams; another stocked hard "stinky cheese," or Romano; yet another sold cokes in glass bottles. Each was a neighborhood fixture, but the special nature of the local stores was lost with the advent of supermarkets.

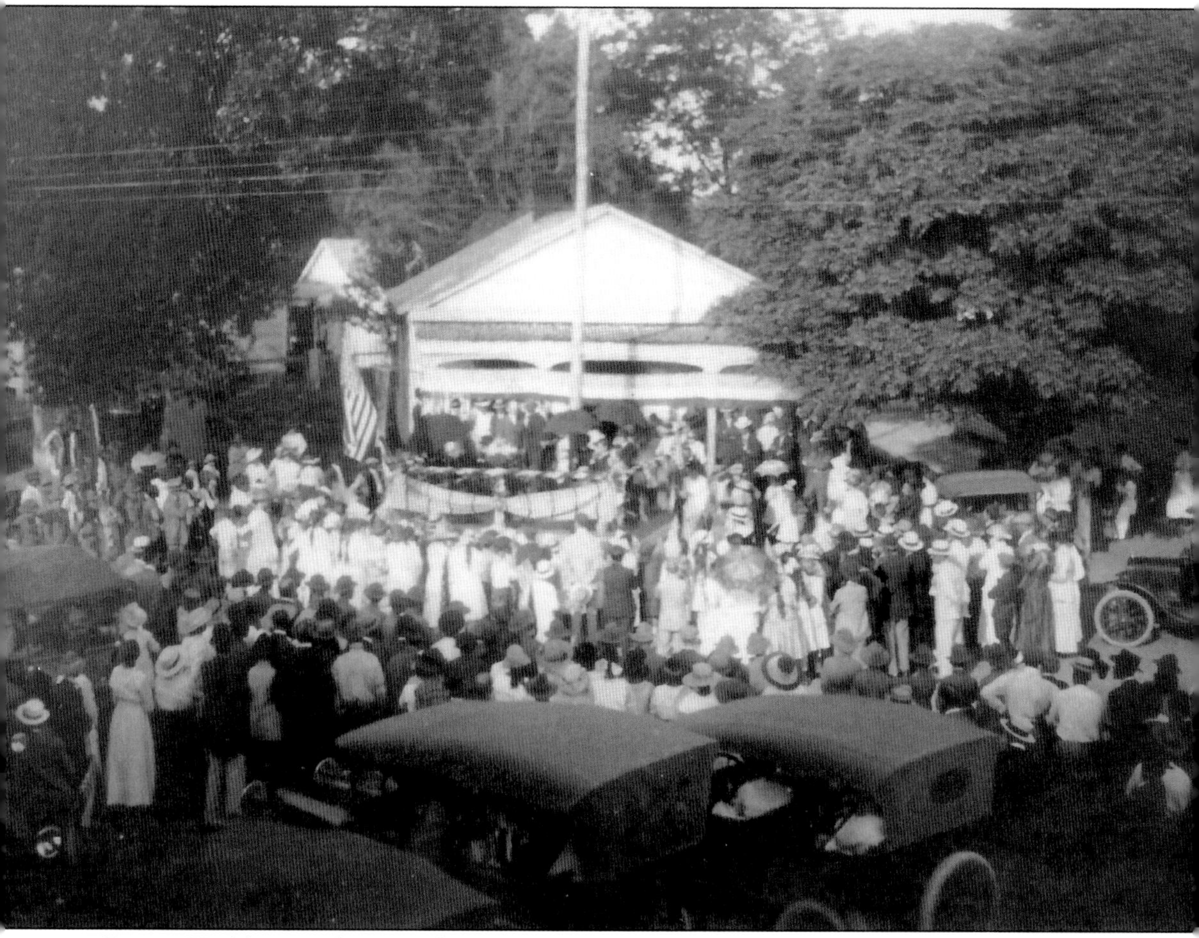

During World War I, the United States sold liberty bonds in an effort to raise funds for the Allied cause. Baldwin residents also showed their patriotic support for these efforts, selling war bonds at the Baldwin post office. (Courtesy Perry Lowery.)

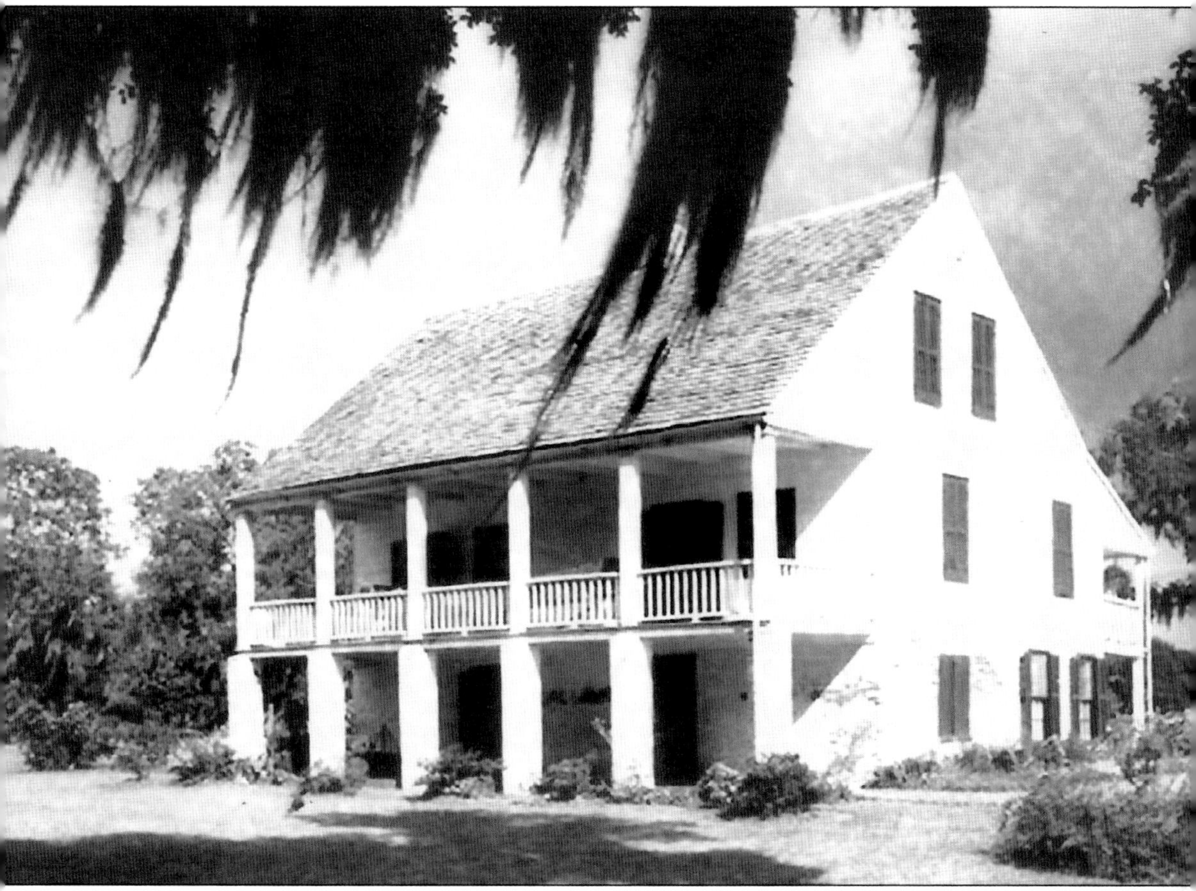

Francis Plantation, between Garden City and Centerville, operated a refinery and, along with its adjoining sister property, Susie Plantation, cultivated 1,050 acres of sugarcane on land near the Hanson Lumber Company. In the 1970s, Frances Plantation was an antique and gift shop owned by Fairfax Foster Bailey. Residents still remember lovely antiques from Europe, fine china, and the scent of Claire Burke lightly floating in the air. (Courtesy Perry Lowery.)

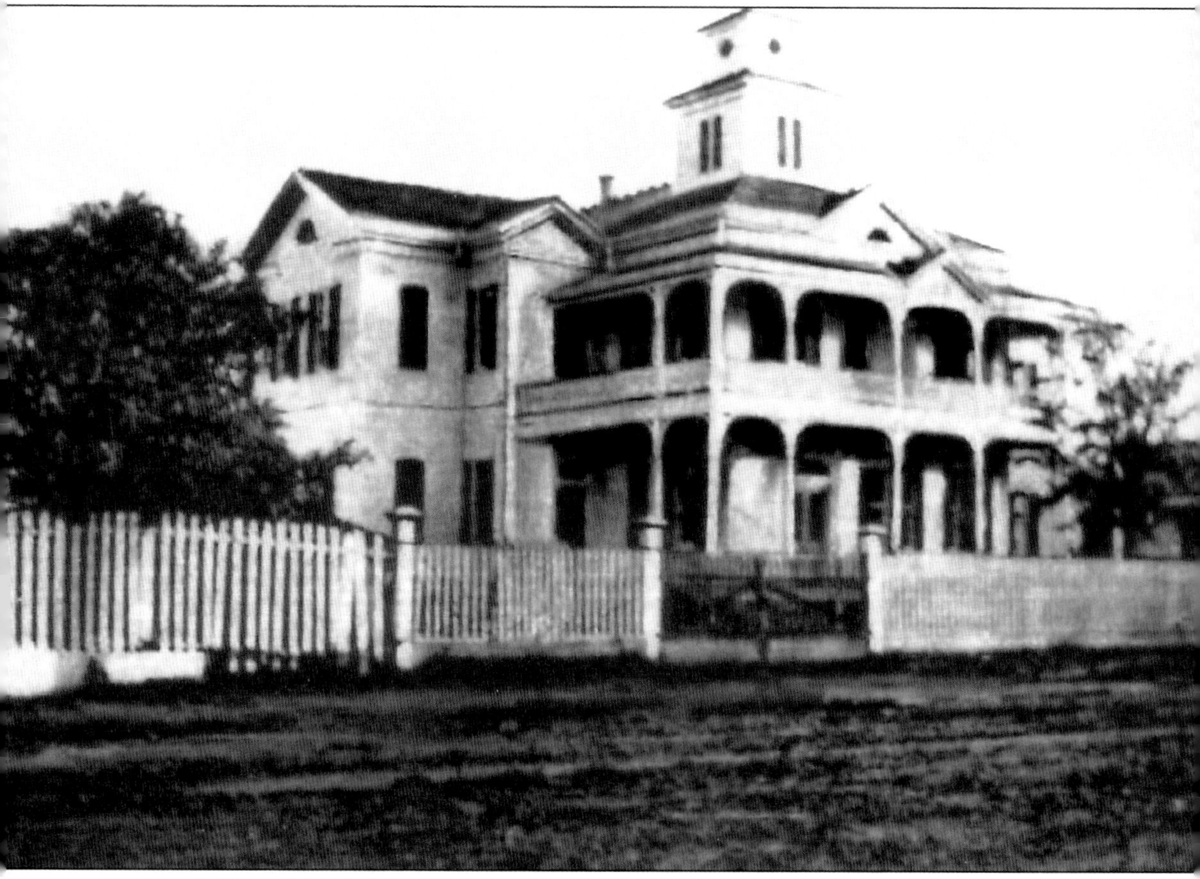

St. Mary's Central High School was built in 1893–1894 by architect Emile Cornay on the corner of Iberia and Perret Streets, one block off Main Street near the Church of the Assumption. The first session of St. Mary High School opened on November 4, 1894, under the direction of Prof. J.M. Ferguson. The quaint schoolhouse was quickly outgrown and it became necessary to build a new structure in 1932. A football and athletic field were also added behind the building. (Courtesy Perry Lowery.)

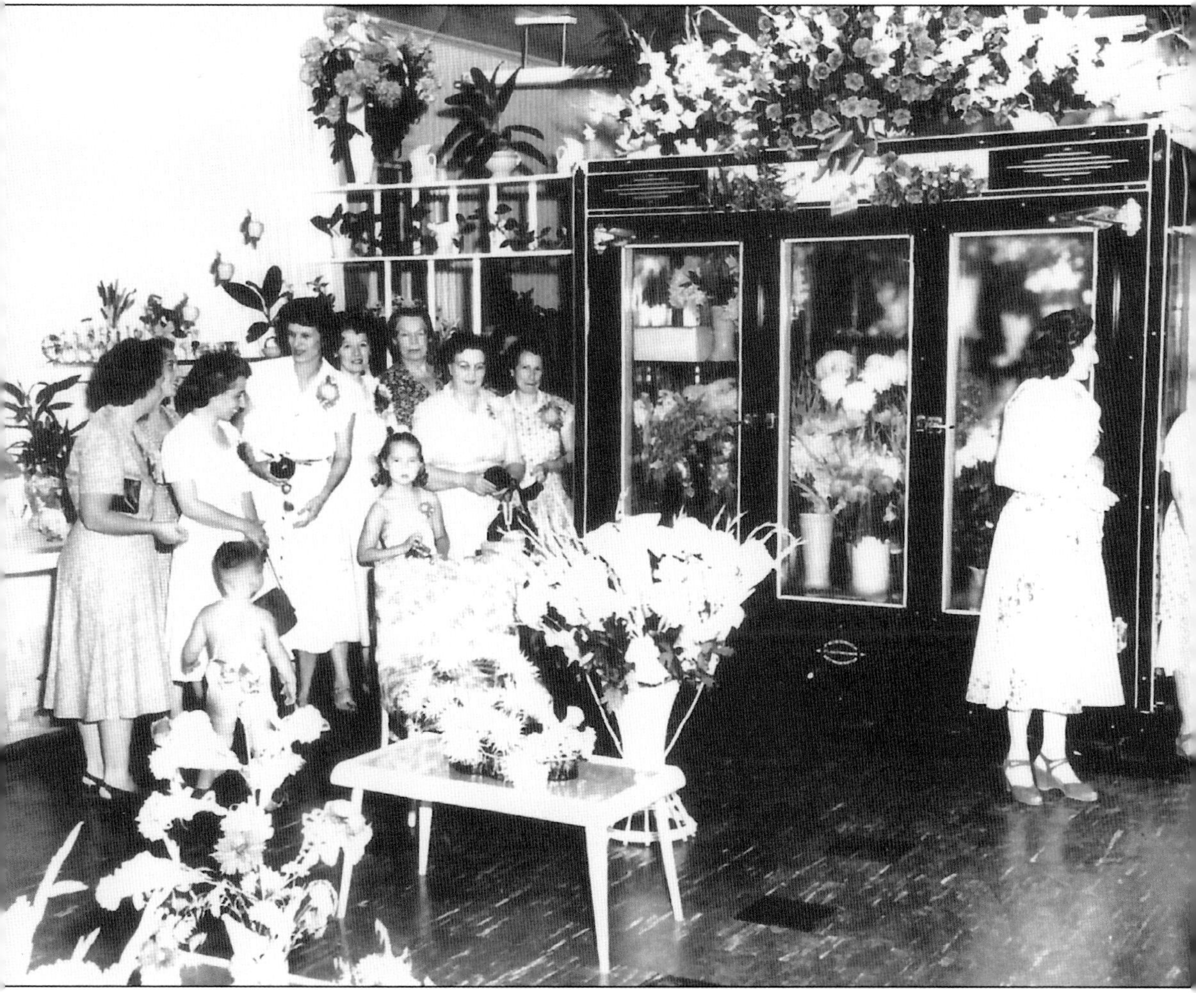

Hattie Martin's Franklin Flower Shop, previously on Mechanic Street, is now at 309 Main Street, offering flowers for all occasions. Beautiful displays in the windows offer stunning seasonal offerings to the eyes. The cooling unit seen here is still in use today. Sadly, Martin has passed on, but the long-standing traditions she started have continued under the current owners. (Courtesy Perry Lowery.)

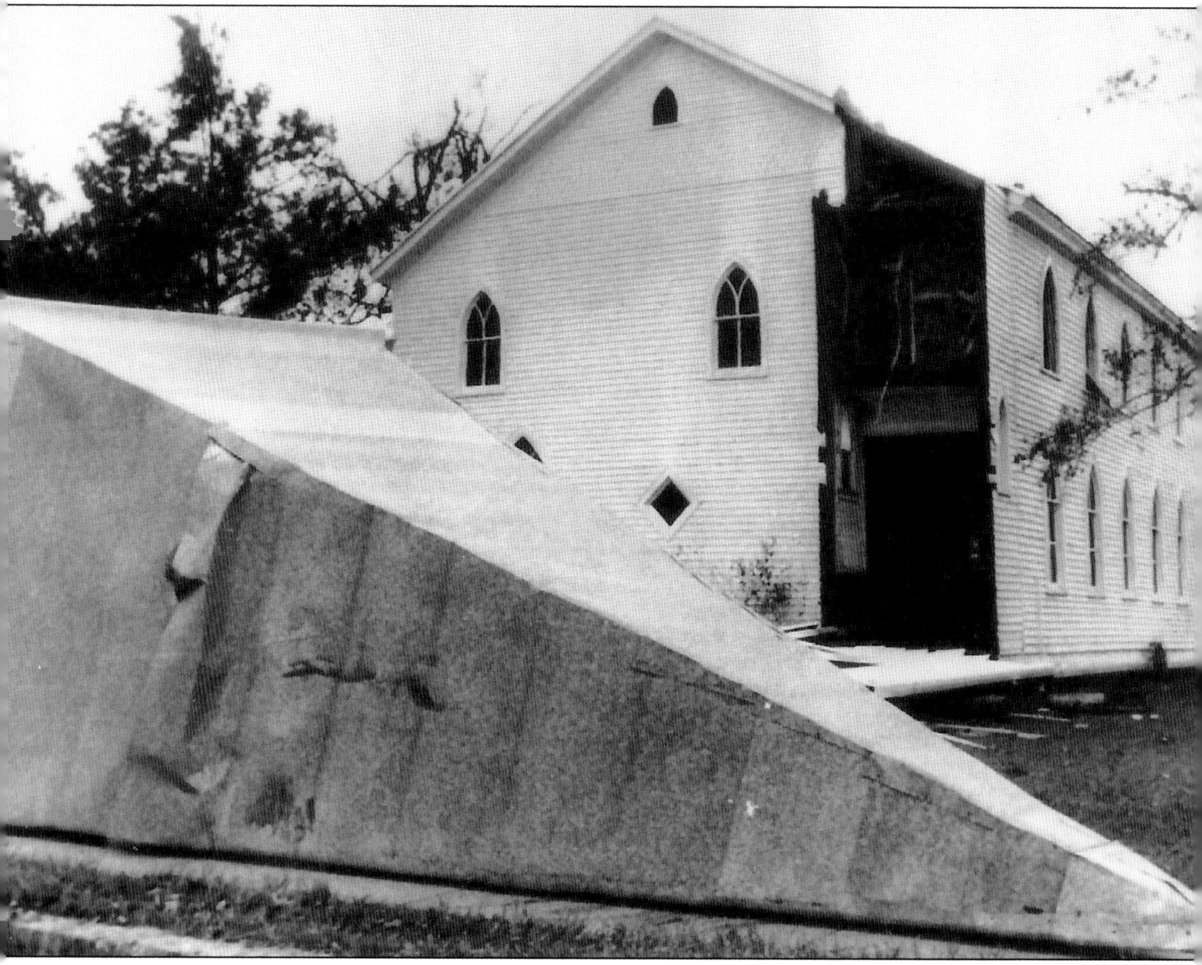

The Asbury United Methodist Church on Main Street in Franklin is seen here after damage from Hurricane Hilda in 1963. Hurricanes, floods, and the occasional snowstorm have disrupted lives and rearranged the landscape. After Hurricane Andrew in 1992, the Sager Brown School in Baldwin answered the call to serve the community by gathering thousands of volunteers from all walks of life to rebuild St. Mary Parish in the 10 years following the hurricane. The UMCOR facility in Baldwin is staffed weekly by volunteers who come to work on campus-outreach programs in and around the parish, and the UMCOR depot gathers disaster supplies used locally and around the world. (Courtesy Perry Lowery.)

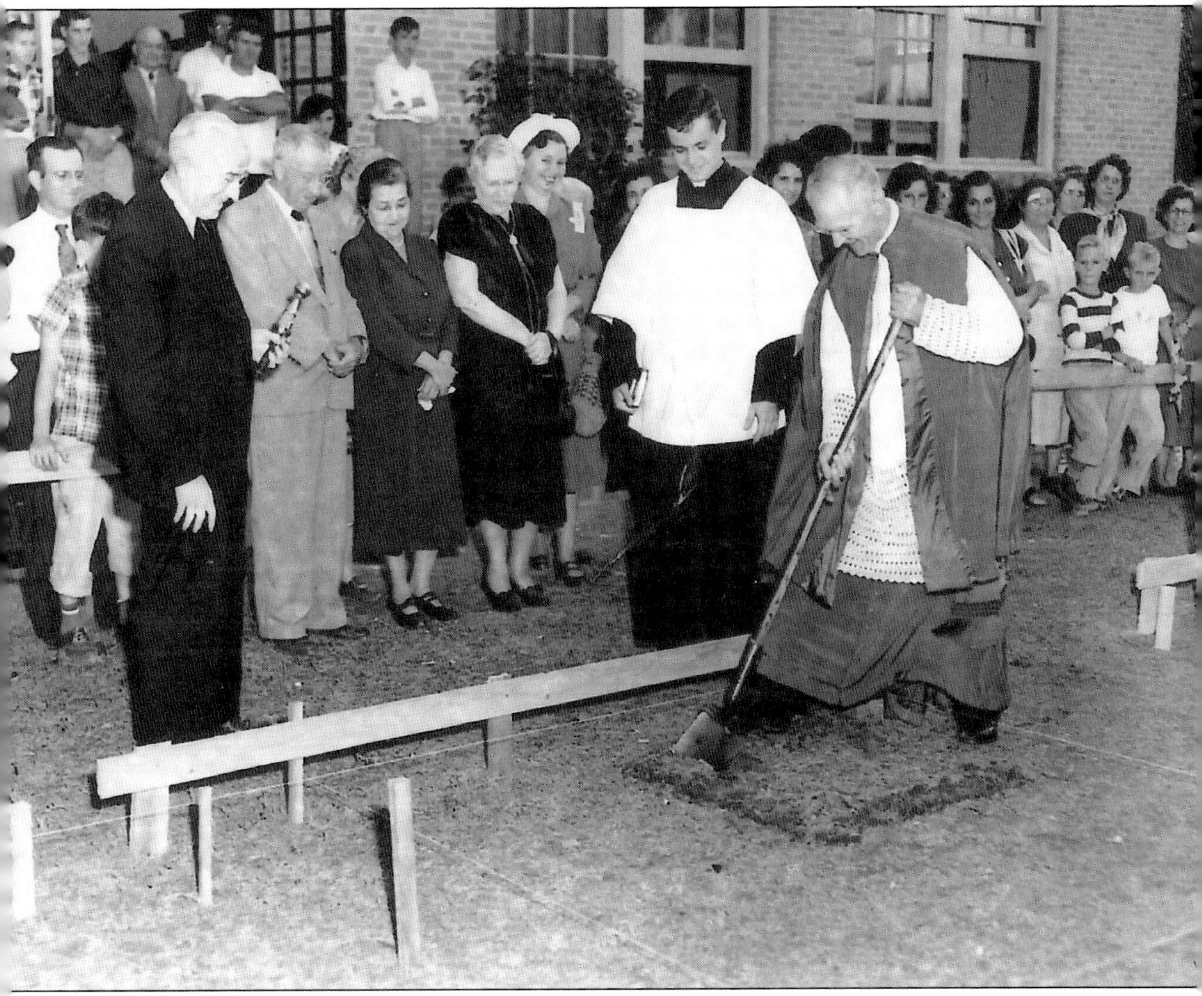

The 1950 ground-breaking ceremony for Hanson Cafeteria is seen here, with Msgr. J.J. Rousseau digging with the shovel. Hanson Memorial High School continues to grow and flourish and is now coeducational. Hanson recently completed construction of a new library facility on campus, continuing its tradition of positive educational opportunities for its students. (Courtesy Perry Lowery.)

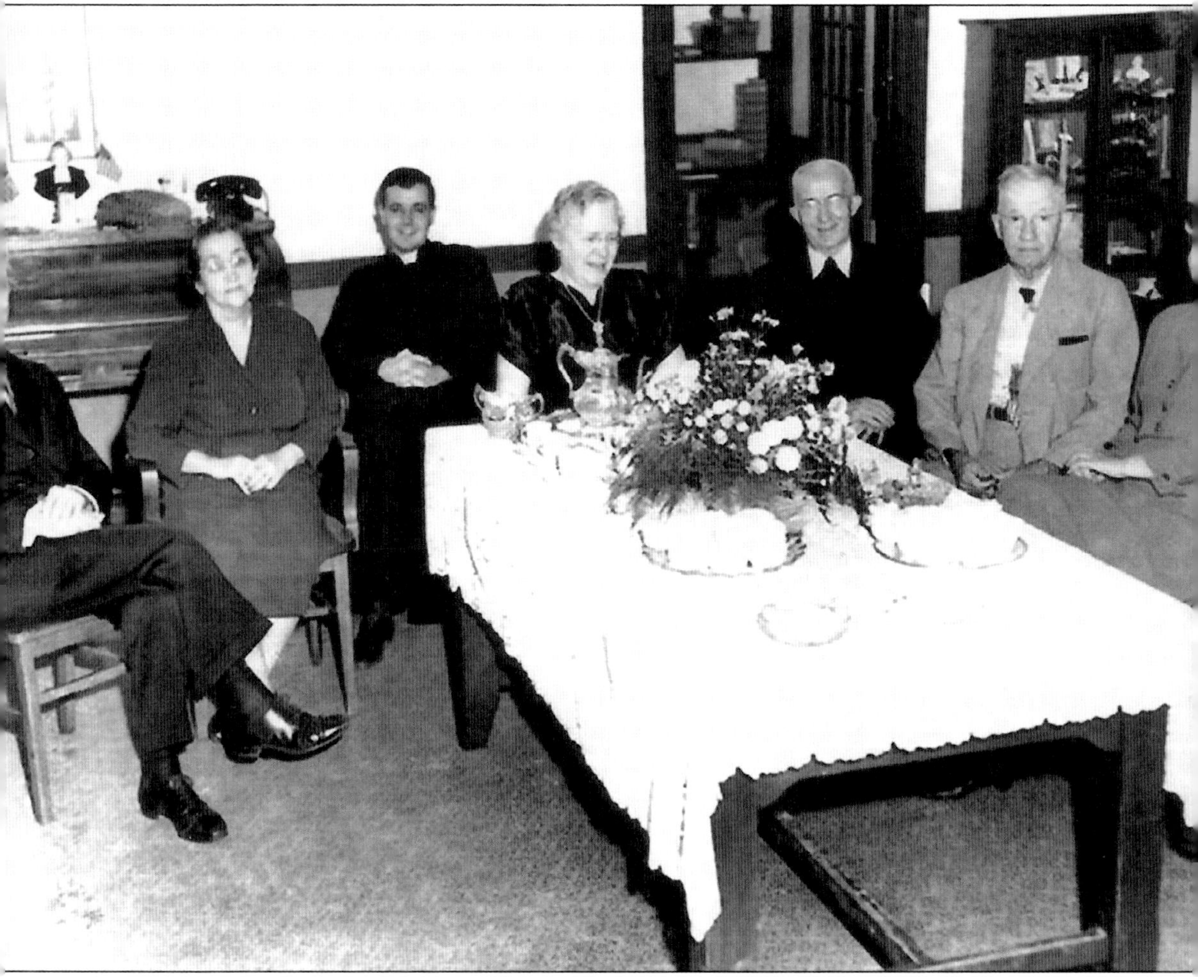

Attending the celebration after the ground-breaking for the new Hanson Cafeteria are, from left to right, Msgr. J.J. Rousseau, Mrs. Grillett, Father Oneal Landry, Alberta Blevins, Hanson principal Brother Anselm, E.A. Boudreaux, and Betty Shinn. (Courtesy Perry Lowery.)

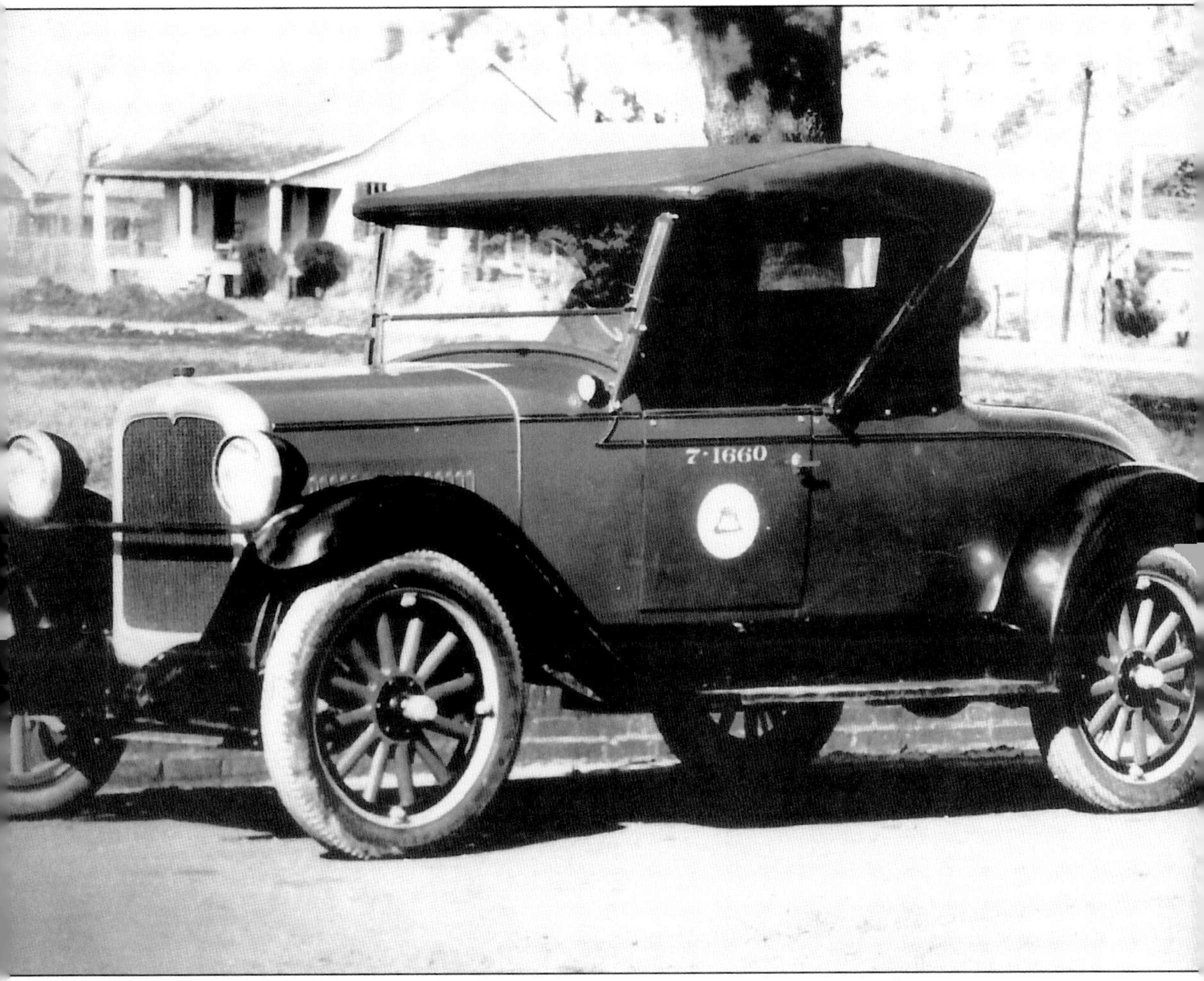

The transition from buggies to the Ford Model T did not happen overnight, as not everyone was convinced that the newfangled motor carriage was "the cat's meow." But by around 1912, the Model T was beginning to take over. However, the Patterson priest still used a horse and buggy to drive to Centerville Church for mass, which would have taken at least an hour or more. (Courtesy Perry Lowery.)

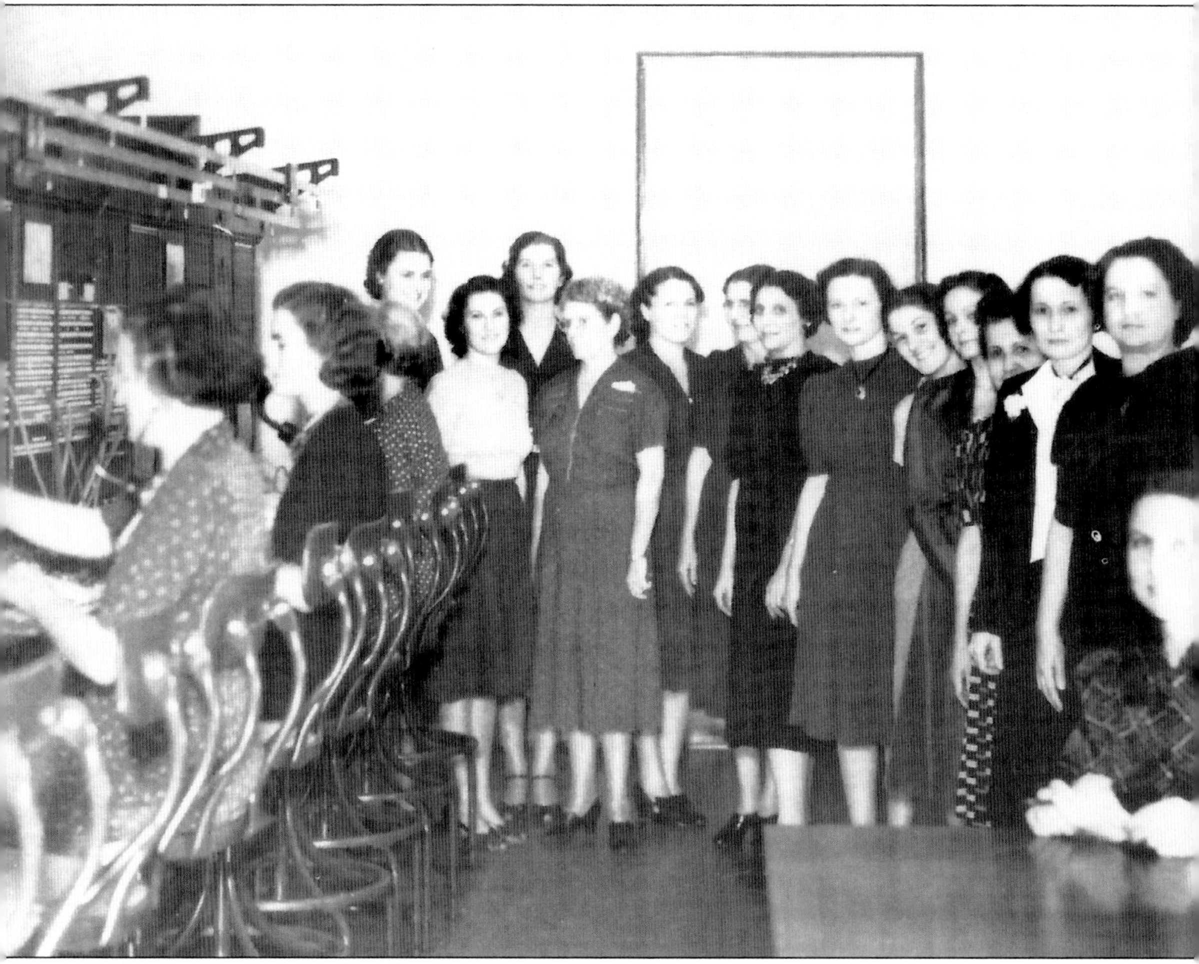

The South Central Bell Offices on Third Street in Franklin are seen here when operators were not recorded and telephone numbers had only three digits. A review of the history and growth of the telephone company in St. Mary Parish acts as a barometer of social and economic advances. In Franklin, the parish seat of St. Mary, old records refer to the Hodgsette Telephone Company operating around 1890, with only 100 subscribers. However, the Cumberland Telephone and Telegraph Company is officially credited with establishing the first citywide communications systems in 1895. Franklin's first telephone operator was Belle Thorpe, and although it is not known how long she served in this capacity, other records refer to a Miss Walker as the telephone company representative here in 1898. (Courtesy Perry Lowery.)

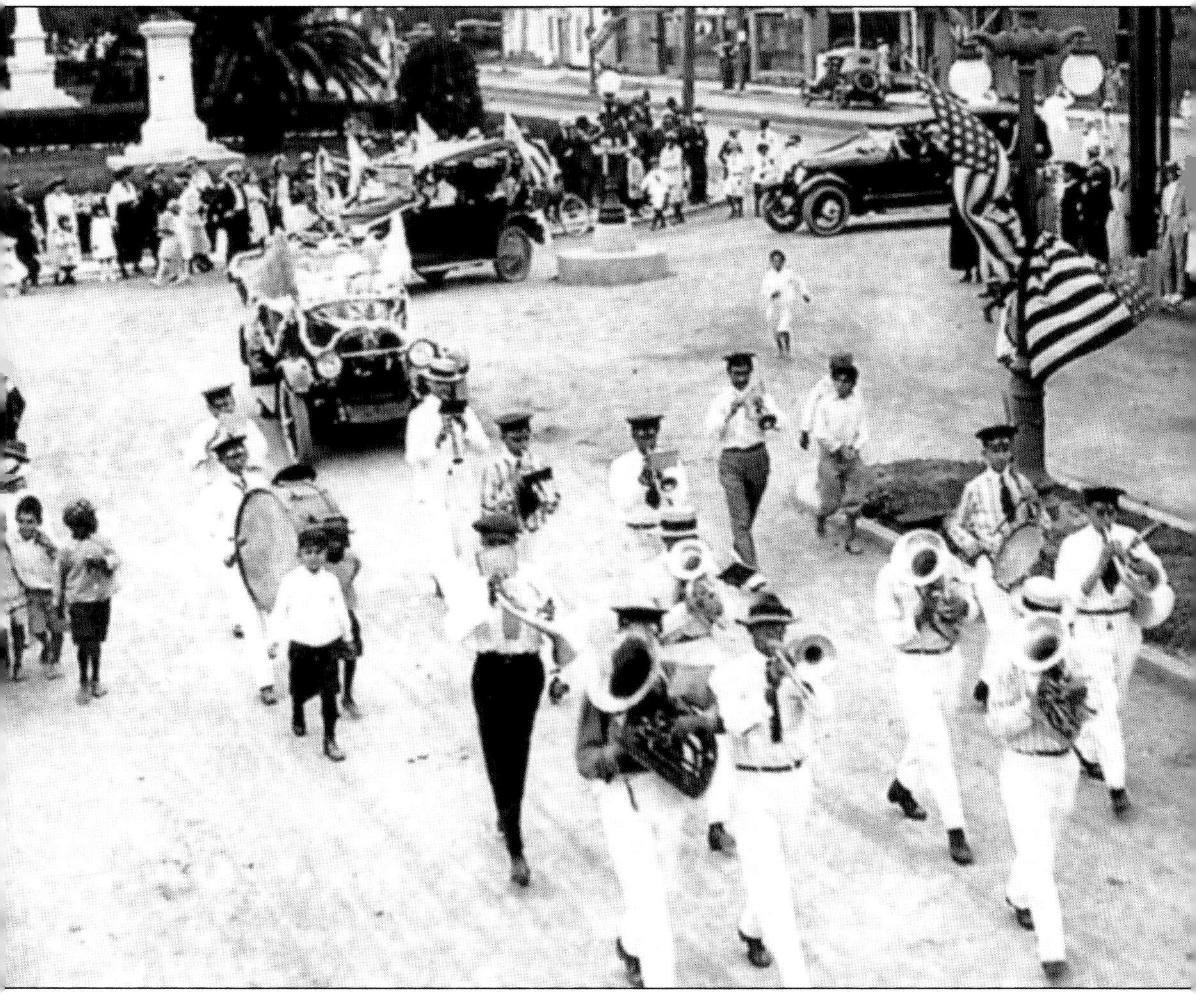

The 1925 Fourth of July parade in Franklin turns the corner of Willow Street onto Main Street.

Approaching this project, I had no preconceived notion of how it would come together. Living in a town with more than 400 properties listed in the National Register of Historic Places, you already realize that history surrounds you. You cry when an old property is ravaged by time and eventually torn down for lack of someone who cares. Your heart goes out to the loss of the old to be replaced by the new of less quality, less character, and you may not even realize why you have this sense of loss, but you do. How will the grandkids ever know what it was like to see a paddle wheeler floating lazily down Bayou Teche? When the call went out for photographs, a story began to unfold, the story of not only grand antebellum homes, but the life and times of everyday people. The culmination of this pictorial history of St. Mary Parish honors those shoe boxes full of old photographs that we all have on the top shelf of our closets. I encourage you to go to those boxes and embrace your personal history. It is quite amazing!

—Julana M. Senette

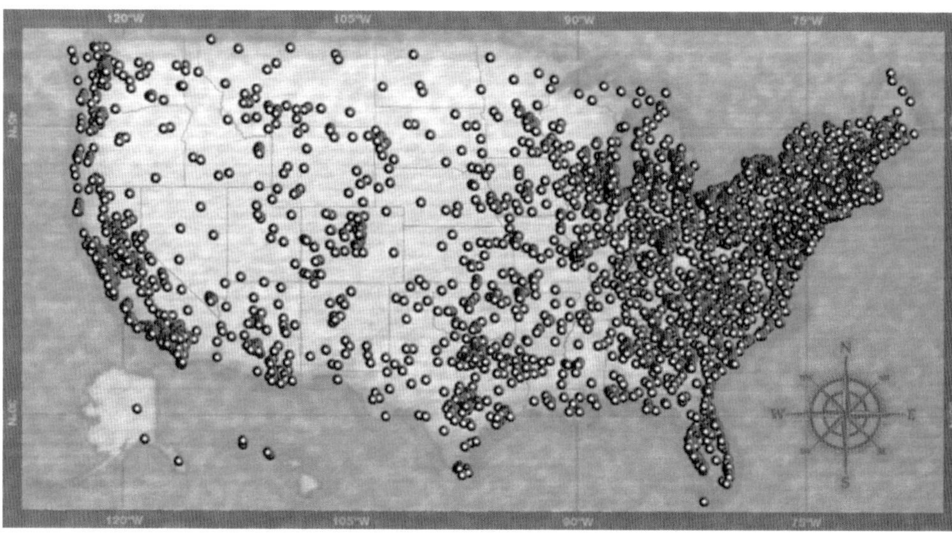